Language, Discourse, Society

General Editors: **Stephen Heath**, **Colin MacCabe** and **Denise Riley**

Selected published titles:

Peter Goodrich
THE LAWS OF LOVE
A Brief Historical and Practical Manual

Ashley Tauchert
ROMANCING JANE AUSTEN
Narrative, Realism, and the Possibility of a Happy Ending

Reena Dube
SATYAJIT RAY'S *THE CHESS PLAYERS* AND POSTCOLONIAL THEORY
Culture, Labour and the Value of Alterity

John Anthony Tercier
THE CONTEMPORARY DEATHBED
The Ultimate Rush

Erica Sheen and Lorna Hutson
LITERATURE, POLITICS AND LAW IN RENAISSANCE ENGLAND

Jean-Jacques Lecercle and Denise Riley
THE FORCE OF LANGUAGE

Geoff Gilbert
BEFORE MODERNISM WAS
Modern History and the Constituency of Writing

Stephen Heath, Colin MacCabe and Denise Riley (*editors*)
THE LANGUAGE, DISCOURSE, SOCIETY READER

Michael O'Pray
FILM, FORM AND PHANTASY
Adrian Stokes and Film Aesthetics

James A. Snead, edited by Kara Keeling, Colin MacCabe and Cornel West
RACIST TRACES AND OTHER WRITINGS
European Pedigrees/African Contagions

Patrizia Lombardo
CITIES, WORDS AND IMAGES

Colin MacCabe
JAMES JOYCE AND THE REVOLUTION OF THE WORD
Second edition

Moustapha Safouan
SPEECH OR DEATH?
Language as Social Order: A Psychoanalytic Study

Jean-Jacques Lecercle
DELEUZE AND LANGUAGE

Piers Gray, edited by Colin MacCabe and Victoria Rothschild
STALIN ON LINGUISTICS AND OTHER ESSAYS

Geoffrey Ward
STATUTES OF LIBERTY
The New York School of Poets

Moustapha Safouan
JACQUES LACAN AND THE QUESTION OF PSYCHOANALYTIC TRAINING
(*Translated and introduced by Jacqueline Rose*)

Stanley Shostak
THE DEATH OF LIFE
The Legacy of Molecular Biology

Elizabeth Cowie
REPRESENTING THE WOMAN
Cinema and Psychoanalysis

Raymond Tallis
NOT SAUSSURE
A Critique of Post-Saussurean Literary Theory

Laura Mulvey
VISUAL AND OTHER PLEASURES

Ian Hunter
CULTURE AND GOVERNMENT
The Emergence of Literary Education

Denise Riley
'AM I THAT NAME?'
Feminism and the Category of 'Women' in History

Mary Ann Doane
The DESIRE TO DESIRE
The Woman's Film of the 1940s

Language, Discourse, Society
Series Standing Order ISBN 0-333-71482-2
(*outside North America only*)

You can receive future titles in this series as they are published by placing a standing order. Please contact your bookseller or, in case of difficulty, write to us at the address below with your name and address, the title of the series and the ISBN quoted above.

Customer Services Department, Macmillan Distribution Ltd, Houndmills, Basingstoke, Hampshire RG21 6XS, England

---

The Laws of Love

A Brief Historical and Practical Manual

Peter Goodrich

palgrave
macmillan

First published 2007 by
PALGRAVE MACMILLAN
Houndmills, Basingstoke, Hampshire RG21 6XS and
175 Fifth Avenue, New York, N.Y. 10010
Companies and representatives throughout the world

PALGRAVE MACMILLAN is the global academic imprint of the Palgrave Macmillan division of St. Martin's Press, LLC and of Palgrave Macmillan Ltd. Macmillan® is a registered trademark in the United States, United Kingdom and other countries. Palgrave is a registered trademark in the European Union and other countries.

ISBN-13: 978–0–230–00718–5 hardback
ISBN-10: 0–230–00718–X hardback

This book is printed on paper suitable for recycling and made from fully managed and sustained forest sources.

A catalogue record for this book is available from the British Library.

A catalog record for this book is available from the Library of Congress.

10 9 8 7 6 5 4 3 2 1
16 15 14 13 12 11 10 09 08 07

Transferred to digital printing in 2007.

For Linda—maior lex amor est

Ubi Helena ibi Troia (Where Helen is, there too is Troy), from: Gabriel Rollenhagen, *Nucleus emblematorum* (1611).

Contents

List of Figures

Figure 1 *Carte d'inclination* (map of desires)—Seventeenth century, source unknown.

Preface

You are at a dinner with someone attractive. She suddenly kisses you. Or he unexpectedly leans across and caresses your thigh. Whatever. You know the kind of encounter and the range of possible responses. Consider the kiss. What does it mean, and how far can you go? Does kissing imply more, and if so, how much? Does the brush of lips signal that your hands can wander? Does the touch of the tongue intimate a right to bite? And similarly, is the unannounced hand on your thigh necessarily a transgression? If you feel sick, if you lash out, if you later insult the character and malign the reputation of this inarticulately inquisitive individual, do you make them suffer more than you? What if the lecherous male is your professor, your boss, your supervisor, and you have invited them to the dinner with designs on their networking skills, their influence, their friends? Such and similar questions of amorous ethics and erotic disquisition are central to our desiring practices, to our everyday intimate public lives and they are the lost objects of the laws of love.

The laws of love, the *lex amatoria*—and why not use its proper name, be a little polite in matters of discipline?—has long provided detailed rules for the expression of desire and for the conduct of love affairs. The body is detailed and divided into erotic and erogenous zones; there is a protocol depicting the lovers' proper progression from seeing to smelling, from touching to sleeping together. There are trials or tests of love that challenge the amorous to converse, to write, to wait or on occasion to sleep together naked but without touching. Then the same again, second night, but now with kissing and touching above the waist allowed. You get the picture. That way desire can grow, and love gain standing. By the same token, because the movements of desire are discussed, because there is a language and discursive space for addressing the issues that erotic practice or emotional charge can arouse, the disaffected lovers can air their grievances and lick their wounds eloquently in the courts of love. A secret space, a safe auditorium is created for discussion and debate of questions ranging from thwarted desire to stolen embraces, from erotic depression to intimate violence, from purloined love letters to acts of infidelity, from mourning to trysts in the night. The gay scientists, the orators of the amorous, the lawyers of love were experts in what history taught, in what precedent suggested, and in what justice dictated.

Put it like this, the lawyers of love produced meticulously drawn maps of the heart. Take these up again. They detail the affective routes from fantasy to attachment, from indifference to warmth, from distance to tender inclinations, from the erotic to the erogenous. They attend to the protocols of seduction, the diplomacy of relationship, as well as to the consequences of libertine behavior, both faith and infidelity. Above all, the laws of love offer insight into erotic technique and the occasions of its practice in our everyday intimate lives, in institutional interactions, in the political economy of public life. Desire drives action. Emotion suffuses mercantile activity, political and juridical affairs. It is however not much recognized, little understood, scarcely analyzed at all. Hence the importance of a historical knowledge, a brief manual such as this, that provides a guide, a chart of the libidinal economy, an account of the authentic spaces and expressions of desire, of its demise and of its rekindling.

We should also recognize that we live in exciting erotic times. But we are hardly alone in that. In fact some of the dates we will cover, 1150, 1343, 1460, 1650, just to give a range, were probably even wilder than our trans-gendered, trans-sexual, acceleratingly virtual times. The troubadours, the early amorous professionals, the doctors and lawyers of love forged their art against unenviable odds, against Church and State and all the other more local sovereigns of diurnal economic norms. The laws of love are drawn from a gay science that was born of a world turned upside down. They taught an art of love, drawn mainly from Ovid, in which love was intrinsic to public life and play drove the emotional margins of the social realm. It was an era in which pleasure, the theater of masks, the figures of verse, the song of songs gave a public space and rhetorical form to what later and agonistically got termed the *querelle des femmes* or as we now say, the war of the sexes. The laws of love provided an extraordinary site of public debate, of codes of conduct, of rules of justice which allowed parties to negotiate their amorous identities, their sexual preferences, their emotional orientations without falling into either the aphasia of ignorance or the belligerent babble of sex wars. The art of love was erudite, complex, mixed. It was hedonistic, heretical, inventive, and transgressive. Love was same sex and bi-sex, singular, plural, stable and changing in identity and role. In truth, as the greatest of the historians of troubadour erotics, René Nelli, has suggested, we have no idea what went on between the sheets but we do know it was often heretical, frequently perverse and without doubt as imaginative as the plurality of erogenous zones, the multiplicity of body parts, and the theater of their combination allows. Maybe they were more into armor than leather, but product differences aside, there was a lot of experimentation. Much like love today, sex @ the twenty first century.

Contemporary upheavals in sex roles, rapid changes in the theater of justice and love mark the necessity of returning to the early erudition of an intimate public life. The war of the sexes has taken numerous novel turns. It has proliferated into new forms of sexual orientation, diverse performances of desire, differently defined gender identities, subcultures and improvisations in the codes and practices of love. The domain of desire, the realm of love has never been more visible, seldom more plural. Everybody seems to be getting a makeover, experiencing "doubts," writing to the editor, calling their attorney, or joining a cause. But nobody really knows what is flying: there is no safe public space of discourse, no intimate language of mutual recognition, just high stakes, jobs threatened, and the ever accelerating virtual speed of market driven manifestos. The best that is offered are satirical warnings "against love," lucubrations on "gender troubles," or superficial meanderings about pick up artists and the new rules of "the game." And that is the positive side.

On the dark side, visibility drives competing political movements for censorship and repression. Sex gets criminalized. Public expressions of erotic desire—from breastfeeding in public to gay marriage—are treated as harbingers of an amorous apocalypse and what is not recognized is condemned. Puritanical symbols come thundering down in the form of codes of political correctness, dictionaries of proper terms of address and expression, rules of amorous distance and emotional closure in institutional spaces. As if during the day, we don't feel. Lack intimacy. Cannot love or hate. In which case, anxiety drives reaction. Denial reigns over the erotic. The knowledge gap grows.

The gay science and the laws of love have a role to play. I am not suggesting that lawyers "sans culottes," Rabelesian bare assed advocates, are the answer to the melancholy ignorance of contemporary law. Some have made that suggestion—the feminist Michèle le Doeuff, for example, just to get esoteric with you—but it was relegated to a footnote in a scholarly text so dense with technical terms and elongated expressions that it doesn't have any very broad audience or appeal. But that is not to say she is wrong. The gay science does offer a necessary element of humor, both play and erudition, a spirit and a language with which to address extant intimacies, amorous expressions, desiring practices as they impact our everyday lives. No harm either in knowing how to talk about the libidinal economics of institutional affairs. A positive boon to have access to a discursive space where the intimate intensities, the affect in conflict can be humored and addressed. And all this in a forum where eloquence is sovereign, where love matters, where we recognize that desire drives the day.

The laws and judgments of love provide a detailed and coherent cartography of intimate relationships, the map of the heart is traced and the appropriate forms of amorous conversation and interaction are spelled out. In the text that follows, I start with a broad historical account of the textual evidence for the laws of love, for women's courts and the long term of erotic jurisprudence or what I will term the "ethos and nomos," the ethical law of love. The remainder of the book translates, collects, and annotates the case law of love. I propose treating the cases as a systematic and coherent body of norms. A jurisdiction and case law much like any of the other local and minor bodies of law that preceded the imperialistic and limited rise of a singular system of common law.

Here then is a very different body of amorous law. A collection of judgments culled from amorous sources, from women's courts, from doctrinal treatises, from poetic, ethical, and rhetorical sources. I outline the sources and offer bibliographical details at the end of the book. No footnotes to the text. You will have to trust me. And as to the cases themselves, they are alternately playful and serious. Stolen kisses are disputed, lascivious acts are examined, intimate violence is adjudicated, broken promises are mended or defended, slights and other infidelities are debated and sometimes judged. It depends on the occasion and the court. The power of desire is directly depicted, and the variable rules of intimate interaction, from flirtation to consummation, are devised and promulgated. The laws are practical and poetic as all erotic erudition has to be. They address the anxiety of love, its disasters as well as the art of its pursuit and fulfillment. In the conclusion I show how this lost jurisdiction and law offers an invaluable resource for what is currently a troubled intimate public sphere. *Eros* and *nomos* need joining again. Love, to coin a phrase, deserves standing.

The book has been a long time in the making. I have worried about how to present medieval Latin and French literary and legal materials to a contemporary audience with an increasingly limited attention span for written resources. So I have tried to keep it brief and I have made every effort to retain the humor of the originals. And of course I know too that the prefatory genre of disclaiming difficulty is seldom authentic. Indeed the notion that whatever the particular scholarly book happens to be, it will delight a wide and general audience is itself usually formulated in so convoluted and complex a style, so laden with epistemological implications, so heavy with ontological gravity, that it is itself almost wholly cryptic and incomprehensible. I am doubtless at times guilty of that too. I have retained a few Latin maxims—though always scrupulously translated—to keep an occasional sense of the tone of the original, or just to please those few remaining semionauts who like a good *corpus vile* or abandoned body upon which to exercise their philological skills. But in the main, I have kept it simple and light, and this is in the hope that it may appeal to students and to scholars, to a general audience as well as a specialist one.

It is a book of law intended, as ideally all law should be, for general consumption. It is in that sense gnomic rather than legislative or strictly doctrinal. It treats of the principles and values, the examples and reasons, the casuistry and judgments of love that gave birth to the modern tradition, to love as passion, even though it is now an intensity most generally locked in the private sphere. The laws of love were better; more open and articulate than we tend to be on erotic questions as they impact our public lives. That is my motive for suggesting the recovery of this lost law. It should live on in our consciousness, it should advise our campaigning, and inform our debates. And this finally because the erotic erudition of the gay scientists often worked rather better, allowed for a greater degree of justice than current and more blinkered expressions of a merely positive law. I will borrow from Stendhal and with only a slight change of date can cite in edifying manner from his treatise *On Love*: "they seemed much more gay, more sophisticated, and happier in 1170 than in [2007]." Right enough. Love then, in the era of the gay science and the laws of love, was treated seriously, enjoyed, and most importantly acted out on the public stage of social life. No censorious lawsuits over kisses, no unwarranted legislation to prohibit amorous relations or the caress of a thigh. No bans upon breast feeding in public, nor puritanical calls for abstinence. The laws of love are lighter and more hedonistic. They are an eloquent blend of poetry and rhetorical rigor. They are, to borrow a long forgotten and probably unintended phrase, "rectorical" in their intent and impact. That is to say that they blend eloquence and judgment, *eros* and *nomos*, good humor and law. Now and to our considerable disadvantage they are forgotten. This book sets out to recollect and rethink the legal history of love so as to remedy our unhappy state of affairs.

Penultimate prefatory point, just ahead of the acknowledgements. There are in my experience two broad trajectories of scholarship. One genre consists of the scholar imparting what she knows. It is a project built upon the solid foundation of what is already known. It gives information, ideas, suggestions, policies. The other genre, one to which I feel much closer, is predicated upon a sense of ignorance. Scholarship here is directed toward what the writer does not know. He studies to fill a void, to unearth novelties, to understand what is missing, to find out and fill in. It is in such a spirit that honesty forces me to acknowledge that I have long been ignorant in love. This work is one of inquiry in the latter vein or genre. It expresses my own faltering stabs at loving, my failures in friendship, my fears of intimacy, just as much as it collates the case law and expounds the treatises that in the past made poetry into *nomos* and love into its own law. The work expresses a long-term quest. It puts my ignorance to work.

Many have helped and hindered in constructive ways. A while back, further back than I am comfortable in recollecting, Spring 1991, Anton Schütz in conversation on a hillside outside Fiesole first directed me toward the medieval sources. Many others have added little pieces of amity and knowledge. Daniela Carpi offered excellent editorial advice. Anne Bottomley, Marianne Constable, Simon Critchley, Marinos Diamantides, Tatiana Flessas, Adam Gearey, Hans Ulrich Gumbrecht, Anselm Haverkamp, Stephen Heath, Lorna Hutson, Eugene MacNamee, James Martel, Nathan Moore, Michael Purdue, David Rudenstine, Peter Rush, Barbara Vinken, have all in their way thrown insight at my blindness, and have contributed knowledge to my ignorance. But none more so than the "Queen of my friends," my wife, Linda Mills. She, more than any, has put flesh upon the antique bones of the medieval *lex amatoria* that I have uncouthly reported and interpreted. She, more than any, has suffered because of my ignorance; and she has experienced more deeply the wounds that blindness can inflict. So too, she has been the light in my amorous darkness and a fount of inspiration, of insights and ideas that have kept me moving forward, living on.

Peter Goodrich
New York
May 16, 2006

Figure 2 *Omnia vincit amo*r (Love conquers all)—*Emblemata amatoria* (1620).

1
Introduction: A Short History of the Laws of Love

Start with an example. A singular instance of the lost art of the laws of love. It comes from Plutarch and it is one of the earliest reported judgments of love. In his *Life of Demetrius*, Plutarch famously digresses into a case brought by the courtesan Theogonis against a young Egyptian whom she claims is in breach of a contract of love.

The facts were as follows. The defendant was a young man who shortly after arriving at the Athenian court fell in love with Theogonis. He courted her. He gave her gifts, showered her with his amorous attention: he flushed in her presence, doted on her image in her absence, and sought by all means to persuade her to return his affections. She remained cold hearted and ignored his pleas. Perhaps she wasn't that into him. We just don't know.

The young man was not well equipped to deal with rejection. The failure of his advances simply inflamed his desire and eventually he fell ill of unrequited love. The medicine of the time recognized erotic melancholy, the frenzy of love denied, as a serious condition. Lovesickness, as the poets have often reminded us, can kill. The medical wisdom of the time suggested that there were only a few remedies for this visceral an illness. The first recommendation was usually a cold enema with hemp seeds on it first thing in the morning. Failing that, other treatises suggested small doses of hemlock. If that did not work then the near universal opinion of the doctors of love, apparently first recommended by Diogenes, was enjoyment of the cause of the lovesickness. Even back then, long before Giacomo Casanova, Chevalier de Seingalt made it a primary principle of amatory philosophy, wisdom had it that desire was mainly prompted by lack. And erotic mania suggests a huge lack, a burning absence, a life-threatening lacuna.

On the advice of his doctor and his friends the lovesick youth was persuaded to seek out Theogonis and to offer to pay her a handsome sum if she would sleep with him once. After some bargaining, she agreed. A time and place was set for this curative tryst, for the remedy of physical consummation. The promises were exchanged, the agreement formed and the details settled, but before the time for performance arrived the young man's desire was requited in an unexpected way.

The night before the agreement was to be performed the feverish young man fell into a fitful sleep. He tossed and turned, woke up, lay down, and shortly before morning drifted into a curious dream. The sleeping lover was visited by a vision of his beloved. She came to him naked and passionate and together they enjoyed all of the pleasures of love. The dream was both vivid and eruptive. When morning came the young man found himself to be deeply rested, his fever had lifted and he was cured of his passion. He no longer needed to carry out the contract. The remedy now being otiose he decided to break his promise and never showed up to the agreed assignation. But he did talk about what had happened.

Theogonis heard the story. She was mightily displeased. She went immediately before a judge and made a claim against the young man pleading that he was in breach of their amorous agreement, their contract of love. Her argument was in its way ingenious. She claimed that she had performed her part of the bargain. It was after all her image that had cured the young man of his fever and for that he should pay as agreed. There had been what lawyers now call substantial performance and that is grounds for collecting what is due under an agreement. Put simply, she had conferred the promised benefit and he should pay the price.

The judge, one Bocchoris, was sympathetic to the plea. He ordered that the young Egyptian be brought before the Court and bring with him the money that he had promised to pay. When the bailiffs arrived with the defendant in tow he was informed that under the agreement he had made he must now pay Theogonis for curing him of his lovesickness. On the orders of the judge, the bailiffs took the purse of money, carried it to the center of the Court and there, in front of Theogonis, poured the coins into a brass bowl. Once this had been witnessed, the bailiffs then poured the money back into the purse and returned it to the young man. The judge pronounced his verdict as follows: just as the image of the plaintiff had cured the defendant of his erotic mania, so the sight and sound, the 'shadow' of the money due was sufficient payment for her services. The image of the gold was just payment for the image of the lover. An eloquent outcome.

The decision of the judge, this Venutian verdict, was well received by those present with the sole exception of Lamia, a friend of Theogonis. She disputed the decision on the basis that while the image of Theogonis had satisfied the young man, the sight and sound of the gold had simply whetted her appetite. There was, however, no appeal. Theogonis was left only with the memory of the money, the shadow of payment, and with it a lesson in the laws of love. Love being a spiritual thing is not sold but given, *animus gratia*, a spectral exchange and not a venal contract. Poetic justice if ever there was, and arguably a good illustration of Freud's later theory that dreams are all to do with wish fulfillment, with the satisfaction of unrequited diurnal desires.

Whatever the reason, the decision was a successful one. It was cited in numerous subsequent medical treatises on love and the passions. The law had here a positive contribution to make to medicine. Where herbs and hemlock fail, where potions are inadequate and the patient cannot be persuaded to flee from the face that inflames them then intercourse, either real or, more cheaply, imagined, is indicated as the proper remedy. The ancients and moderns agree at least on this point of doctrine or amatory law. Even the Reverend Robert Burton, admittedly writing under the ludic pseudonym of Democritus Junior, in his classic study *The Anatomy of Melancholy* acknowledges that "letting them have their desire" is dictated to be the last but most certain cure for the ravages of love.

The case became a precedent both by virtue no doubt of its subject matter, the lure of desire, and by dint of its resolution, the distinctly Lacanian ethical dictate that the lover should follow his lust. First things, however, first. The case provides an early and as yet rather indistinct instance of recourse to what was historically and jurisdictionally the higher or first law of Venus. This was a case concerning an amorous dispute and it required an amorous or affective determination. The judge resorted neither to positive law nor to common lawyers, but rather turned to a higher and natural norm, a *nomos* of the body that doctors and jurists together defined. While this reference to the unwritten laws of nature may now seem a touch extravagant or somewhat philosophical for a secular court of law this was certainly not always the case. The manuals on legal training, well into the modern period and some even today, have always insisted that the good lawyer also knows philosophy, ethics, geography, and the map of the heart.

From the judgments of Venus to Cupid's laws

The laws of Venus, to give them their proper name, have a venerable and lengthy history and there are ample if now somewhat understudied records of their courts and practices. To gain an initial sense of the scope of this history and the nature of these practices we have to return to the philosophical tradition, to Plato, and there trace the roots of a law that later spanned the courts of Europe and gave rise to the most enduring of forms of poetic justice.

The case of Theogonis made reference quite explicitly to the domain of images and to the "shadow" of the money that had been promised. It is a more or less direct reference to Plato and to the unseen, to the shadow realm of reflected ideas. The truth is visible only as a reflection, and it is properly apprehensible only through introspection. The laws of Venus, which gain their first expression in Plato's discussion of love in the *Symposium* belong precisely to this jurisdiction of images, of shadows and their representation of an invisible truth. In fact it is the female philosopher Diotima who in dialogue with Socrates links the beautiful and the good to Venus and her laws. These conjoined desiderata belong to nature, to the realm of ideas, and gain only a secondary or reflected representation in human judgments and positive laws. For Plato of course that order of descent from the realm of ideas to that of human norms suggests a gap between the laws of love and human judgment that the latter should tirelessly work to close.

Aristotle, to take the teachings of a second and perhaps in this context surprising philosopher, also acknowledges a prior and higher law of love that is closely tied to, if not coincident with, philosophy itself. Aristotle is very clear that human community, the constitution and its laws, belong to a second order of governance or are the consequence of a prior law of love. Consider the word philosophy, from the Greek *philein*, most usually meaning friend, attached to *sophia* or wisdom. Friendship was the driving force of knowledge, and friendship, defined by Aristotle as love of the similar, as love of oneself in others, was the bond that held civil society together long before there was any question of legislation, sovereign dictate, or secular law. As Aristotle himself puts it in the *Nicomachean Ethics*, it is exactly for this reason, because the laws of love precede and dictate the secular or secondary laws of social coexistence, that "the good legislator pays more attention to friendship than to justice." Love dictates friendship, and amity puts law into play.

The Christian tradition and the Renaissance reception of the classics picked up this Platonic and latterly scholastic reference to the laws of

Venus in multiple ways. I will focus on two. One legal in a more or less technical sense, the other more amatory and tied to the Ovidian tradition of gay science and courtly love. Both are essential but they are far from exhaustive. There is also a rich tradition of poetic tournaments, tensons or amorous disputes in lyric forms, disputed questions of love, amorous requests or *demandes d'amour,* and more. And beyond that there are early erotic fables, moral and didactic narratives, and later critical literatures that refer to and report cases of love. These later critical literatures must here take a secondary place as being what could be termed the lore of law, tributaries or indirect evidence of the more directly juridical sources that I will address.

We can start with thoroughly conventional legal concepts. Justice has always been tied to the jurisdiction of love. It is usually attributed to a divine source, but whatever the theological root the bond between love and judgment, between strict rule and the affect of mercy, between norm and indulgence is indisputable. Take an example, a treatise by the Renaissance legal historian John Selden. He wrote a book on the feminine dimensions of common law, entitled *Jani Anglorum facies altera* or, in the vernacular that lawyers have always been rather loathe to use, *The English Janus*. Back in 1610 when it was first published, the notion that law had two faces, that it could be masculine and feminine, was actually not that peculiar a topic, even if it seems so now. In any event, he reports that "the gravest writers do acknowledge" that in ancient times there wasn't any positive law as we would recognize it. There was "natural equity, like the Lesbian rule in Aristotle" which would determine all "quarrels and strifes." Lesbian rule refers to a pliable norm or flexible rule and it is traced by Selden to Homer who treats the King as the "Shepherd" of the people. His laws are best guided by virtue, "which the Platonics call the Laws of the second Venus."

One side of justice, perhaps the left hand of the sovereign, not *animus* but *anima,* was expressly to apply the laws of love. These were termed the laws of the second Venus only because those of the first Venus belonged to the Gods or existed in a primary and pristine form in nature. They required translation into human forms of application. What matters for the purposes of understanding and reconstructing these amatory laws is that they formed the source and ideal type of legal judgment. In early modern treatises on the constitution this finds expression in the notion that the sovereign and by extension the common law is "a nursing father" to its subjects. The ultimate function, the end of law is to watch over the soul. The legal delegates of the sovereign, the legislators and judges exist so as to tend to the inner welfare of the populace and wherever possible to promote amity, reconciliation, and love. Nor was this just some general principle or vague aspiration. It was enacted in legislation, reported in case law, and recorded in legal textbooks.

The source of the wording may have been the poet Virgil, but the laws of Henry II of England, 49 5a, expressly enact *pactum legem enim vincit et amor iudicum,* meaning that "agreement prevails over law, and love over judgment." This legislation codified an antique tradition within English common law that there was always a choice between love and law, between the norms of natural justice, an unwritten code inscribed on the heart, and secular legal proceedings. Love was preferable. The agreements of lovedays drew subjects together, while law merely separated them. The law of Venus was that of nature, it was the higher law, it promoted amity, it allowed for settlement, and it furthered the community in mending itself. To proceed by love was to remain friends and to forestall law in its coercive and punitive forms.

One dimension of proceeding in the laws of love and the one best evidenced in secular texts was that of appealing directly to the sovereign. There is a famous description of Louis IX, the mid-thirteenth-century French sovereign, hearing disputes in a very relaxed manner. He would sit at the foot of his bed, or in summer with his back against an oak tree in the woods, or on a carpet in the garden. In this clearly affective context, he would listen and encourage the disputants to compromise or to accept what was offered. Generally speaking there was no question of right or wrong, nor did pleading result in any mode of absolute judgment. The proceeding in love would rather and more simply address a question of equity and mercy, the attention of affect, the provision of a talking cure.

This was justice as eloquence, law as love. Another example, which can widen our sense of the scope of the jurisdiction of love, can be taken from a treatise on rhetoric more or less contemporary with Louis IX's lovedays or amicable mode of adjudication. So commonplace as to be used as an *exemplum* or standard, Raymond Llull's *New Rhetoric* illustrates the art of successfully pleading before the sovereign in the following manner. The plaintiff's husband had suffered mortal wounds while "fighting bravely" to defend the King. The plaintiff lost her husband and in subsequent skirmishes between the enemy and the King, she also lost her home and her wealth. She employed an advocate who went before the King and pleaded in the manner of lawyers that the plaintiff had a strict right, and the King an obligation to provide for the widow. The King ignored the plea. A woman friend of the widow then went before the King and tearfully and humbly, with "words full of love" begged him to provide for the unfortunate woman. Llull reports that "the force of the love in the lady's word was so great that her request was immediately successful." She achieved in a few tender words what the lawyer's lengthy and arid disquisition on the King's debt and duty had failed to effect.

The force of argument is affective as well as rational, particular as well as general. That much is common sense. Justice resides in the love of detail. It is law that is blind. It is a point that can be followed into the everyday practices, the customs and primary norms of local law across medieval Europe. Using the example of common law, it is reasonably obvious that the King, the font of positive law, could not sit, whether amorously or legalistically, all of the time. His jurisdiction of love had to be delegated to others in the court and to other courts. Thus we find one of the earliest of common law treatises, no less an authority in fact than Henry de Bracton in his foundational compilation of the laws of England, the *Treatise on the Laws and Customs of England*, referring to *dies amoris*—he was writing of the vernacular law in Latin, but that is how lawyers have tended to go about things—or lovedays when disputes would be settled by amity and accord. Here the parties would "wage love" and their quarrel would be settled according to the "spirit of law," meaning equity and affect, rather than by strict rule or the inflexible measure of positive norms.

The spirit of law, the amorous affects that make for virtue in relation to others found widespread application in local customs, in compacts and compromises, in agreements sealed with kisses, in food and wine. There is indeed an element of the festive to the concept of the loveday, a dimension of going beyond and above the ordinary law. Take a case from the records of Parliament in the early fifteenth century. Judge Tirwhytt, a justice of the King's Bench, was in dispute with Lord Roos. On the way to arbitration the Judge attempted to ambush Roos and in consequence the King devised the following remedy. Tirwhytt was to provide Roos with a feast: two barrels of claret, two fat oxen, a dozen fat sheep. At the feast, the judge was to apologize publicly—Tirwhytt to Roos, one might say—for the offence he had occasioned. And there is no reason to think that this remedy was anything other than highly effective. A better compromise, a more lasting outcome, a satisfactorily amicable result.

The rolls and records of early local law are full of reports of lovedays, of amorous compacts and other prudential applications of the laws of Venus used in compromising disputes. Although we are some considerable distance today from the explicit manipulation of an erotic jurisprudence derived from codes and norms of the laws of love we do inherit the spirit of amatory law in numerous indirect ways. Most obviously there is a jurisdiction of equity that is now inherent in law. It allows for flexible measures, for compromise, for settlement and arbitration according to more amicable norms and in a spirit of mercy or love. Not only is there equity in law, there are alternative forums of dispute settlement, there are women's courts, there are media events and televised trials that play to the court of public opinion and to the norms of unwritten law. That is not however my immediate subject here. You will have to wait, or maybe turn to the conclusion now, get abreast of history there invading the present. But I will stay of necessity with my chronology.

In recollecting the laws of Venus and the cases of love I am concerned to piece together and reconstruct a tradition of actual decisions, of codes and judgments of love that directly applied the amatory law. The technical legal sense of what Selden properly called "laws of the second Venus" are subordinate to a primary or greater order, that of the laws of the first Venus that gain expression more directly in Courts of Venus, in medieval women's courts (the *curia amoris*), in courtly love, in those lovers' laws that were also known as the flowers of gay science—*las flors del gay saber* to invoke momentarily the antique and "rectorical," appellation. Here we have to move from the recognizable if antique domain of mundane positive law, the "nursing norms" of the second Venus, toward what was in Plutarch's terms a more imaginative jurisdiction, the domain of conscience, the province of juristic fiction, the more speculative theater of justice and truth. The cases of love report decisions that pass, perhaps sometimes playfully, between the spheres of religious law, literary narrative or *annales galantes*, poetic devices, and dramatic representations. What needs recollection, because surprise and unfamiliarity are sometimes unsettling, is that these courts and decisions constitute socially significant symbolic rites, they enact judgments and norms upon the public stage, and differ only in terms of official location from the rituals of positive law. Again using Plutarch's example, these are trials that take place according to the spirit of a higher law, they exchange the shadowy tokens of a primary spiritual order, they pass on a natural *nomos*, they take their place within a Platonic order of truth that both encompasses and exceeds the dictates of merely human law.

The division between law and non-law is a very modern conception. For the earlier tradition the question was rather and more generously that of which law? *Quaestio quid iuris* as Kant summarized it. Which among numerous jurisdictions and codes of law was the appropriate one for the case at hand? Should it go before the Church courts, the King's courts, the Minstrel's Court of Tutbury, the Marshalsy, the court of a local landowner, the court of a specific locality or practice, of the forest, the sea, the mountains or even the carnival, the famous Court of Pipowders? The courts of love have to be understood within the plurality of jurisdictions that preceded the unitary agglomeration and methodological diminution of modern law. More than that, we need to recollect that the principal sources of record for courts of love were rhetoric, poetry, and history or what we would call fiction, *fictio iuris* to use the legal Latin. These sources were often the work of lawyers and they closely mirror legal forms not only because they were often texts written by jurists, but also because literature both secular and religious was a recognized source of custom and law.

For our purposes, which is to say to the end of reconstructing a case law of love, an erotic jurisprudence as it actually existed, the laws of Venus first emerge as a jurisdiction in their own right in the post-classical Western legal tradition in the poetry of the troubadours and the emergence of a concept of courtly love in the early twelfth century. The juxtaposition of love and court, of poetry and law is not accidental. A little touch of history is necessary. The court was a place, the household and following of the King. The court was the standard of manners, the arbiter of diction, and the place of judgment. It was a juridical and rhetorical site. When courts proliferated, when judges were sent out on the road or sat in the provinces, they took up the place of the sovereign. That was courtly that belonged to or came from the court. No less an authority than Dante can be cited to precisely that same effect: "the word courtliness was derived from the courts, and courtliness came to mean the same as custom of the courts." In that sense, courtly love was lawful love and just possibly, though this will have to be pursued later, love of law. The court was the law, and the law was to be found in court.

The play upon the word court in courtly love is important because it is unusual today to associate poetry with law. It is true that we retain the notion of poetic justice with its connotations of a poetry interior to law but that is something of an exception or limiting instance. It is not understood in its proper canonical sense as indulgence, as "giving time to" a plea or circumstance, occasion or person, foible or form. Poetic justice is almost never discussed as a poetic logic, a law of pretty rhymes and pleasing connections, but is rather thrown off as an emblematic witticism—a *mot juste* if you will—in the course of more secular and thoroughly prosaic philosophical maunderings on the justice of legality. It takes a leap of faith or a very long memory, historical record in fact, to recuperate the intimacy and importance of the link between the tradition of amatory poetry and the everyday work of *nomos* or what we now and more sadly term law.

Eros as law

We have seen that classical philosophy treated the laws of Venus as the essence of nature and the highest of all laws. Love conquers all, a sentiment that was also central to the texts of the Church fathers and a key element of Christian doctrine. The Anglo-Norman *Tretyse on Love*, for example, a fifteenth-century doctrinal work, begins with this principle and its opening sentence translates as: "The apostle Saint Paul says, 'The fulfilling of the law is love', and Saint Gregory says, 'All this that is commanded in the old law and in the new is only in love confirmed.'" The obvious point is that the *Tretyse* codifies established doctrine and founds community upon love in exactly the same manner as that in which Aristotle places amity before law.

The discourse of love is that of the poets and hence our earlier references to Virgil and Ovid who both volubly proclaimed the precedence of love and the laws of the heart. Poetry records law, just as much as law must have a rhetoric—a poetics—of its own expression. Theoretical digressions aside, however, the early tradition of troubadour poetry was concerned precisely with the development of a code for love. This can be taken at several different levels, and obviously there are vast variations over time and place. René Nelli, for example, cites the heretical trends within the troubadour tradition and argues endearingly that far from being either chaste or virtuous, the troubadours would regularly engage in sodomy as a medieval version of safe sex. There were many extremes, many hecatombs or caves, courtly and also discourteous, hetero, homo, and metrosexual. Progressive and regressive according to the norms of desire, sex @ 1174 CE or thereabouts.

Historians have argued in more complex forms that the courtly lyric was in fact not only discourteous but was strictly a homosexual affair. Love was a symbol that circulated between men. Women were tokens of status acquisition. The courts of love where women judged disputes between lovers were no more than cross dressing dramas in which men played the parts of female litigants and judges. The same argument holds that the women troubadours, the *trobairitz*, were also men using female pseudonyms made from anagrams of their own distinctively masculine names. And all of this may well be true but does not detract whatsoever from the fact that these social rites existed or from the fact that there are extensive records of judgments and other promulgations of laws of love. There are codes, edicts, precepts, rulebooks, statutes, and an extensive body of decisions. There is an erotic jurisprudence, a public map of intimacy that dictated the manner of love and the limits of desire. Put it like this, the constitution has two faces. Historically this was the Janus face of law, its dual jurisdictions being spiritual and secular, ecclesiastical and civil. The spiritual side faded over time. The jurisdiction of charity, of *caritas* and its laws of conscience was taken over by the common lawyers, suppressed, ousted even. The norms of municipal and administrative rule took over the other more intimate and emotional jurisdiction. The amicable and amatory face of justice was subordinated to a prosaic and bounded law of mercantile positivities. What is important to recognize now, looking back in an era of significant feminine political resurgence and witness to the return of affect in public life, is that both laws have a Janus face, that both jurisdictions exist and play a part in what we term law for us. While it may be possible to delineate conceptual divisions between the two, between law and love, legalism and interpretivism, they are in practice mixed. There is spirit in justice, pleasure in judgment, affect in law.

Courtly love was the product of, and was practiced within the court. It had what in cultural terms can only be described as a broadly legal origin. It developed an erotic jurisprudence or knowledge of lawful forms of loving and it is in that sense fitting that the bulk of systematic records of the courts and judgments of love are recounted by lawyers or come in a juridical format with strongly legal titles. No reason to treat the cases of love as anything other than law, provided some imagination or simply some historical sensibility is applied to the rituals and other symbolic practices that we term law. Erotic jurisprudence was the bedfellow and progeny of a "gay science," of a poetic and rhetorical tradition that shared the methods, techniques, and frequently the personnel of law. It formed a system, replete with codes, precedents, and precepts; it had courts and a parliament staffed with judges, procurators, advocates, and doctors of love; it heard pleas, decided cases, promulgated decisions and doctrines, published statutes and ordinances. The laws of love also, however, have another meaning. They form part of a poetic tradition, they establish the rules of a rhetorical form, and that is where an overview of the sources of the Ovidian tradition of judgments of love has to begin.

The poetic tradition of courtly love stems from philosophical and theological roots that treated love as the origin and fulfillment of law. Love was expressly the first bond of the social, it was the mark of belonging.

Amity was the avenue and affect that produced both citizenship and Christian brotherhood. Whatever its many variations, its gaiety, its inversions, its heretical tendencies, its moments of misogyny or misanthropy, the courtly lyric was predicated upon the highest of aspirations. It sought to codify an art of love that was spiritual and pure in its goals. It provided practical maps of the legitimate avenues of desire, as well as tabulated the ways in which love could be expanded, extended, and expunged. It governed the most intimate aspects of erotic manners, all the way down to prescribing the stages that lovers should follow in sleeping together. First they were to sleep together fully clothed. Then they were to sleep together half naked. Finally, if successful in the earlier stages, they were to sleep together naked but without touching. Thus was desire brought to a height and yet kept within the law. And what is the law if not for breaking? That however takes us into the domain of the cases of love, which is further than intended just here.

The troubadour tradition recited and sang poems that depicted both the perils and the proper path of pure love. Granted the degree to which the troubadour poets suffered and longed for the distant objects of their desire, granted how love wracked their souls, how they wept and waited, it is clear that pure love was the object of an extended quest rather than being a steady state or an easy acquisition. Many are the poems in which, even where the troubadour has promised discretion, lust has overtaken caution and the *faich* has been done, the love consummated. The trials and travails of desire, the *assag* or test of pure love, was frequently and admittedly failed, and such failure was generally not condemned provided that it remained within reasonable limits. To give way to sudden and sporadic lust was understandable. As is true of all law, doctrine met constantly with its exceptions. The laws of love explicitly recognize that physical desire will sometimes overpower the subject while also insisting that what matters is the honesty and devotion with which the primary goal of a purer love continues to be pursued. It is that mixture of pure love and carnal embrace, that slippage between the spiritual and the bodily, that is of the essence of amatory law and of the cases of love.

The courtly ideal is highly ambiguous. Like any law, it is primarily of symbolic value and it is met with failure as often as it is successfully embodied. It does however constitute a rigorous doctrine, a creed and quest. For the troubadour poet, the goal of courtly love was not simply a civility or courtesy of amorous expression but a greater obedience to a code of honesty, moral beauty, and unselfish rigor in the appreciation of desire. Dante can again come to our aid. The lover should believe that the end of life and love, the *fin' amor*, is ethically honesty, and this means that the lover "is rigorously, without any concern, to follow truth and justice." Honesty in this broad and ethically probative sense lies at the base of the justice of love and its laws of desire. It helps to explain the casuistry or intricate practical rules and rulings that courts of love devoted to the pragmatics of loving.

Courtly love is a doctrine that develops in parallel with law. This is important because it helps to explain the concern with justice and with the laws and other precepts that will govern the various promises, contracts, obligations, and pleadings of love. The justice of love mirrors the *nomos* or more loosely the rule of law. It is defined as *mezura* or the proper and proportionate measure of desire. As one troubadour, Folquet de Marselha puts it, "courtliness is nothing other than *mezura*." This means that civility, the citizenship constituted by amity and love, is ideally gentle, discreet, well mannered, well spoken, urbane, and tempered. The last term, temperance is indeed the key in that the moral of courtly love was concerned with the augmentation and accentuation of desire rather than with its fruition or expenditure and demise. What mattered was keeping love alive, keeping souls within the voluntary jurisdiction of the *lex amatoria*, keeping the couple writing their letters or expressing their love, nothing less, nothing more.

The essential feature of *mezura* was not simply continence but the suspension of lust, the elaborate theater of delay encapsulated most simply in the figure of *amour de loin* or distant love. The element of suspension is crucial to any thorough understanding of the case law of love. There are two facets to suspension. The first is philosophical. The troubadour is in love with an ideal. The path of lawful love is ever toward that ideal but it can never be captured or possessed by the lover. In Platonic terms it is an idea. The troubadour loves a shadow, an image, a reflection of another world. The lady whom the troubadour serves obediently is unapproachable, distant, and idealized because she represents the law of Venus, she is the shadow of a higher law. What is sought is literally impossible. For our purposes it is sufficient to note that pure love is a passion and movement toward a vision of the beloved, an image or imagination, a phantasy. Plutarch's case of Theogonis is thus well in point, what matters morally is our relation to the imagined, to the shadows or spectral forms that in dream or otherwise represent the climax of love toward which the lover's life is dedicated. The justice of love is as much as anything else a fidelity to an image, loyalty to a face that is but the shadow of the ideal. To do justice to the image is to recognize that love is the royal road to truth.

The other feature of the suspension of lust and the path of continence lies in a more pragmatic concept of discretion. The justice of love mirrors the practice of love. It too should suspend completion or judgment in favor of delay. The function of the Court of Venus is to facilitate the path of love and so too the journey of the lovers. If the lovers can be persuaded to compromise, to kiss or eat together, if judgment can be suspended in favor of keeping the space of love open, then that is what the court of love will determine. Put it like this. The troubadour lyric has no narrative. There is no plot. There is only the eulogy of a beloved in conventional terms or as Arnaut Daniel famously put it "I am Arnaut who hoards the wind, and hunts the hare with an ox, and swims against the stream."

What is important within this jurisprudence is not judgment but growth. The labor of love it might be said is concerned not with determination but rather with a suspension of determination, a justice that holds open amorous possibility, and facilitates the growth of desire. The unfinished should remain unfinished, the paradoxical should be indulged and the impossible savored. Those are the rules of amatory process and in the tradition of the *fin' amor* measure means reconciling morality and lust by keeping them open. Judgment is equally open and initially most usually took the form of dialogue over a question of love. Whatever was resolved in the dispute—the *tenson*—could always be opened again. What is most important is that it is the questions of love that gain attention, not their resolution.

Quaestiones disputatae or disputed questions of love

The *tenson* is the earliest form of expression of questions that will come before the courts of love or that otherwise require deliberation according to the laws of Venus. The questions are numerous and varied. Some are highly abstract, such as: "Why is it that someone who is truly in love cannot dream of physical pleasure with his beloved before he has had amorous contact with her, while he is easily capable of dreaming of such pleasure with another?" Some are legalistic: "Do lovers have equal rights as between each other?", or "Can a spouse also be a lover?" Others are highly practical: "You are offered the choice of sleeping once with your beloved and then never seeing her again, or of seeing her all the time without any possibility of physical consummation. Which should you choose?" Or again: "Who suffers more, a lover whose beloved dies, or one whose beloved is unfaithful?" Some are socially penetrative such as: "Do clerics or knights make better lovers?"; "Can age be a bar to love?"; "Can a lover be rejected because of illness or absence?" "If your lover loses an eye, does that allow love to vanish?"; or, "Can a King who loves a mere knight allow himself to believe that he is loved for who he is?" Or take an example from the women troubadours: "Under what circumstances is it justified for a woman knowingly to allow a rejected lover to waste away and die from unrequited love?"

The list of disputed questions of love is wonderfully long and covers all aspects of relationship, from falling in love to maintaining love, to ending relationships. The questions covered all details of manners and propriety. Should one choose youth over wisdom? Beauty over moral intelligence? Under what circumstances is infidelity permissible? What are the costs of loyalty? When can a lover be spurned? Why is it not enough to console oneself physically when the beloved is absent? Granted the casuistic nature of these questions and the moral and social connotations of their resolution, it is perhaps not entirely surprising that the first works that systematize the questions of love and report the decisions that either determined or suspended determination of pleas based upon them take a legal form.

The earliest substantial references to courts of love come in the religious poems collated in the *Carmina Burana* dating to the early twelfth century. These take up the themes of the tensons and determine issues such as the effect upon love of differences of social status as between the lovers. The cases of love gain their first and most famous systematization in the work of a cleric, Andreas Capellanus, *Treatise on Love*, composed in the 1180s. This work lists 12 *Precepts of Love*, a *Code of Love* consisting of 31 rules, and the report of 21 cases of love decided by women's courts. The themes are both standardized and inventive. The first rule of the *Code* is that marriage is not a valid excuse for not loving. That establishes the domain of love or jurisdiction of the laws in an era when marriage was a property relation. And the last rule of the *Code* is the expansive one that "there is nothing to stop a woman being loved by two men, or one man by two women." Other rules deal with sensuality, gifts, jealousy, infidelity, and the physiological symptoms of love. "Every lover", for example, "tends to grow pale when their partner looks at them." The heart beats faster, it becomes hard to eat or sleep, and so on. The cases illustrate and exemplify the themes: How should a lover be chosen? In what circumstances is infidelity permissible? When must one accept that love has waned? Is marriage a bar to love? What gifts and other communications are appropriate between lovers? As well as such time-honored questions as whether clerics or knights, young or old, virtuous or sensual, make the better enamorata.

The most striking feature of the various cases of love reported by Capellanus, at least to modern eyes, is that they were exclusively the judgments of women's courts. It may well be that Lacanian theorists and other dogmatic hermeneuts, latter-day Christian conservatives that they are, would like to claim that the women judges were the alter ego of the male author or anagrams of masculine names but weight of evidence suggests that whether humorous, flirtatious, or melodramatic these judgments were performed within the female domain of the noble courts of Southern France. The key figures were the Countess of Champagne, Queen Eleanor of Aquitaine, Isobel of Vermandois, Countess Marie of Flanders, Countess Ermengarde of Narbonne. A flush list. A lot of ladies courts. And I think it fair to opine that whether or not inclination leads one to view such courtly exercises as frivolous, the judgments were a rite within the female side of the court and they did preserve and promulgate an ethics of love, a map of the heart that later tradition has borrowed from, inculcated and codified. They listened to, indulged the pleas of lovers in secret sessions. They heard cases of stolen love, lost love, inappropriate desire, betrayal, deceit, and amorous decorum. They set out rules for coming together and for separating, they tabulated the proper forms of amorous gift, the limits of correspondence, the duties of go-betweens, the desideratum of generosity, and much more.

Enough to say that the *Treatise*, and particularly its report of women's judgments, is a work that has generated a great deal of controversy. Here is what the academics say: "It is an obstacle to understanding the medieval practices of love." "It flounders in a tedious no man's land between fiction and reality." "It is like a syringe." "It separates us from the past of love." And so on. They unwittingly make the work and the practice seem curious and intriguing—who among us doesn't live somewhere between fiction and reality? When has love not been improved by the occasional obstacle? Suffice to acknowledge that the book is in varying measures ironic, satirical, critical of the tradition of courtly love, and at times has been deemed duplicitous, or fantastical. That is not the point. The past is necessarily ambiguous. What is important for the purposes of compiling a corpus of amorous case law is the legal character of the work and the transmission of both a code and a case law or a casuistry of love. Custom and law, written and unwritten, promulgator and reporter, whatever its intention, its status or interest to literary historians, the work standardizes the questions of love and defines the terms within which the later tradition elaborates the laws of love. The judgments of love may seem to us to have been parlor games conducted in the noble court but that detracts not a whit from their status as social rituals nor denudes them of even an iota of symbolic significance. Here women made the law, the feminine was given a social space and place, voice and a moment of authority in the shadows of Christianity and its dulling social norms.

The next important text is the anonymous Occitan *Cort d'amor* or *Court of Love* composed soon after Capellanus's treatise and written in some measure as a response to it. The title betrays a legal intent and the text early on makes reference to the decisions of women's courts and provides a description of an allegorical court of love that is asked to determine the nature of true love according to love's laws. Capellanus is again the principal reference point of the later thirteenth-century Latin *Treatise on Perfect Love* that debates and resolves 23 disputed questions of love. We can also note that the same title occurs again in the fourteenth-century work of Mahieu le Poirier who authored a poem *The Court of Love*, which records 32 amorous causes heard before a Bailiff of love. There is an anonymous sequel, written slightly later that reports some further cases of love.

Legal authorship and the use of juridical titles for poetic accounts of the judgments of love were surprisingly common. Citing only the most striking examples, note should be taken of the late thirteenth-century *Breviari d'amor* by the lawyer Matfre Ermengaud. The technical term *breviarum* comes from Roman law and translates as the brief for love, meaning a legal pleading, which is precisely what the very lengthy poem contains. There is the poetic work of the troubadour Raimon Vidal de Besalu's *Iudici d'amor* as well as the related old French *Jugement d'amours*. Slightly later, to anticipate a bit, Christine de Pisan authored *A Book of Three Judgments*, addressing disputed questions of love, and Giovanni Boccaccio in his *Filocolo* presents 13 set-piece judgments of love determined by Queen Fiammetta according to the laws of Venus. Her judgments, we may also note, were intended to be light and to delight. They were proffered tentatively and, in the manner of Homeric trials, they were revised in accordance with the responses that they received from the audience. The judgments of love were here generated through dialogue and formed part of what, I will later argue, was an explicit concept of justice as eloquence.

Women were the archetype and figure of judgment in courts of love. They played a key rhetorical role, whatever the actual status of their judgments in those cases where women actually did preside. Again, however, and contrary to the prevailing tendencies in the discipline, it is important not to get distracted by the elements of fiction or by the satirical interludes that mark some of these lyrical references to law.

Neither the hedonism of a ritual nor the playfulness of a discourse should detract from the fact that what is involved is a social rite and that its function is to educate and to transmit tradition or what we now more usually term law.

The laws of love are structured as law, and the judgments of love are judicial decisions. That is how I will treat them. That is the ambiguity that I am interested in pursuing. The question is always the same. What is the law that this antique and eloquent justice determines? What manner of practice does this case law suggest? What theory of conflict resolution does erotic jurisprudence propose? Simple questions based upon well-established case law, but a case law that no lawyer has lately deemed worthy of their attention. That has to be corrected and the revival of the troubadour tradition in the Gay Consistory of Toulouse in the mid-fourteenth century provides many of the clues as to how and why.

The amorous Fiammetta, who had judged the questions of love posed by Boccaccio's Filocolo, had explicitly stated that her judgments were handed down in a spirit of levity. They were intended to be affectively persuasive and so to provide an eloquent form of governance of desire. They were joyful or gay and the purpose of that gaiety was explicitly to banish the sorrows or melancholy that life and love can often bring. Gay science became the name of the movement to revive both the poetry and the ethos of courtly love in fourteenth-century Toulouse. A school of poetry, the Gay Consistory, was established in 1323 to revive the troubadour tradition and to teach the rules of poetic form and its amorous lifestyle. The Consistory re-instituted the poetic carnival of flowers, presided over poetic *tournoi* or tournaments, and the various other forms of dispute and contest over questions of love.

It was so as properly to apprehend the rules for judging the best poems that the lawyer Guilhem Molinier was commissioned together with Master Berthemieu Marc, another lawyer, to collate and promulgate the *Laws of Love—Las Leys d'amors*—alternatively known as *The Flowers of Gay Science*. These laws of love were rules of poetic composition. They were broader than what we would term grammatical dictates, in that they encompassed rules governing the ethics and proper poetic form that were to be used in composition. What is important is that according to the charter letter of the Consistory the laws were for judicial use. They were the code by which judges of poetic tournaments were to determine the merit of the performances they heard. Justice and eloquence were one and the same for the gay scientists, the latter-day troubadours, determined proponents of the lightness of being.

The laws of love established the constitution or rules of conduct within the domain of desire. These laws were first of all an ethical code, they provide a guide to the manner of amatory approach, a dictionary of the correct forms of address, of amity and conversation. They govern the use of signs. At one level, of course, the laws of love are rules of grammar and of composition—great practices need great words—but they are also more than that. Quintilian in his *Institutes of Oratory* defined rhetoric as the art of speaking well. Translated in contemporary terms, that means the art of speaking justly, precisely in the sense that speech is most usually how we act in the world. In the language used by one of the later troubadours, the winner of the poetic games of 1468, Mathieu Artigeloube, the laws of love taught the art of *rectorica*, a neologism that combines *rectus* or rule, and *oratoria* or oratory, law and speech, right and rhetoric, normativity and equity, or, in a word, law and love.

Again, because this is the criterion of selection used in the compilation of cases of love that follows, it is the judicial principle that is here of greatest importance. The laws of love were commissioned and promulgated so that there could be a published code by reference to which lovers and their pleadings were to be judged. The rules were explicitly for the use of judges and the judges were to be sworn to their exclusive use. No fear or favor was to be expected or received from the judiciary of the Gay Consistory. What mattered were the virtue of the poet and the beauty of their argument. Their honesty and temperance, if recourse is made to the language of the earlier tradition. The judges had to play a judicial role, they were the court that would hear the courtly complaint and seek to promote the better poetry and the happier outcome. The Chancellor and members of the Gay Consistory held hearings, adjudicated disputes, listened to appeals and fulfilled the role of a judiciary devoted to the service of virtue, of joy and love.

The Gay Consistory survived into the early sixteenth century when it became the College of the Art and Science of French Rhetoric, the forerunner of the French Academy, which still plays an enormous role in the promulgation of French culture and in particular the judicious preservation of the language and literature of France. Less well-known but vital here was the shorter-term success of the Gay Consistory in perpetuating the justice of love and specifically the judicial tradition of courts and judgments of love. In that respect the next milestone was the promulgation of a statute on February 14, 1400, establishing a High Court of Love in Paris. The legislation was in many respects a high point in the revival of the courtly spirit and even if one views it as a species of theater or burlesque entertainment that in no way lessens its didactic role or its symbolic functions.

The charter that established the High Court expressly founds the Court upon the principles of defending and honoring of women. Its doctrinal purpose was to define and expand the domain of letters and of love. To this end the Ministers, judges and other officials of the court, male and female, were to be selected on the strength of their rhetorical skills. They were poets who were to come together as equals and in the manner of the Inns of Court in London they were to dine together and converse before sitting in the High Court to hear appeals in cases of love. Cases were heard *in camera* or anonymously and judgments were enforced through the diplomatic channels of the domain of love. This meant praise and blame, the publication and disgracing of the names of recalcitrant offenders and at worst "the erasure of their arms and name from the register of love."

The surviving evidence suggests that the High Court of Love in Paris did not long abide by its original and lofty principles of equality as between all participants in the causes and judgments of love. The Court became a largely male preserve although as late as 1460 there is still reference to women counselors participating in the adjudication of the laws of love. What is clear is that the Court held session for some considerable time and the most important record of judgments of love, after that of Capellanus, takes the form of reports of appeals heard before the High Court in Paris. Around 1460, the poet lawyer Martial d'Auvergne, sometimes called Martial de Paris, authored *The Judgments of Love* (*Arresta amorum*), a record of 51 cases reported in considerable detail. In the tradition of gay science the cases heard were appeals from judgments of love and covered all facets of dispute between lovers. Poetic in character, the appeals came from the Court of Flowers, from the Provost of Mourning, from the Bailiff of Joy, the Court of the Forest and Waters, and similar primary jurisdictions of mood and place.

The cases heard by the High Court ranged from claims that a lover had been violent to matters of manners, such as that a chambermaid had been indiscreet and betrayed her mistress. Issues of amatory protocol and erotic manners occupied many other decisions. How was a contract of love, an amorous agreement, to be interpreted and enforced? What gifts were appropriate between lovers? What risks of exposure were worth taking in arranging amorous trysts? Could lovesickness be grounds for ending a relationship? All the way to a complaint by a young woman who had separated from her husband on the basis that he refused to let her wear clothes in the latest fashion. Her complaint was that he tried to dictate what she wore and that when she returned home wearing new clothes he would prevent her from wearing them on the basis that they were immodest, and exposed her breasts or legs. He fumed that these garments made her too alluring to other men, and then threw them away. The Court heard her plea and then ordered four dressmakers to review the plaintiff's wardrobe. Sartorial justice was achieved by allowing experts in fashion to determine whether her clothes were indeed in the latest style, and whether her most recent acquisitions were acceptable.

The Judgments of Love was an enormously successful work. It went through 35 editions between 1500 and 1735 and also spawned imitators and commentators. The most famous is probably the work of the jurist Guillaume Coquillart who in his *New Laws*, and in a dramatic work *The Pleading*, revived the gay science and devised numerous judicious and humorous determinations on questions and cases of love. Under the rubric of a legal treatise in verse, the *New Laws* pose and resolve many of the standard disputed questions in erudite and novel forms. The novel law replaces the antique law of love, so to speak. As to Martial d'Auvergne's work itself, the 1530 edition features a further case added by Gilles d'Aurigny, and in 1533 the lawyer Benedictus Curtius Symphorianus, writing as Benoit de Court, added a lengthy and detailed commentary on the Roman sources of the judgments handed down. Symphoranius' Latin treatise is titled *Commentary on the reason of both laws, and an exact account of the proper legal forms of action*, while the French title is a touch more amorous if a little surprising: *A Joyful and Juridical Commentary* and under either rubric the work is written in the manner of a glossatorial addition to the text. A comparable work, collating all the Roman rules relating to lovers was also compiled by the constitutional lawyer Etienne Forcadel under the title *Cupido jurisperitus*, let's modernize the title as *Erotic Jurisprudence*, published in 1553. The latter two works are both by well-established legal scholars and written with a degree of juristic detail that frequently betrays any humorous intent. They signal again—and in a manner that has been wholly neglected by literary theorists who remain oblivious to the legal dimensions of the judgments of love—a close link between the laws of Venus and secular governance.

The most obvious link between women's courts, their judgments and laws of love, and other legal jurisdictions is antipathetic. In the antique argot that one might use to label such things, these were the works and laws of the hecatombists—heretics according to the *Black Book of Heresies*—who abandoned Church worship on Sundays for play and leisure, for their own rules dispensed in the hecatombs. Most specifically, the Church banned Capellanus's *Treatise on Love* by a decree of 1277. Then again, invoking a much older Roman law banning citizens from acting or reciting on stage, the theatrical causes associated with Martial d'Auvergne and with the Basoche, French law clerks who performed satirical trials and heard a small number of cases in their own right, were also banned from time to time. The reasons are relatively obvious. The cases of love were often interpreted as being libertine in sentiment and frequently expressed a thinly veiled hostility toward canon and civil lawyers. They made fun of the unpopularity of the legal profession, they built imaginative alternatives to the venality of lawyering. They mercilessly exposed what contemporaries saw as the darkness, the chaos and foul smell of regular law.

That said, there were many jurisdictions and a plurality of laws during the long time span of the courts of love. Local, national, and international legal rules all had their own forums and professions. Religious and secular, mercantile and administrative, public and intimate governance had separate and sometimes competing procedures and courts. It is mainly contemporary prejudice in favor of a unitary profession and a singular rulebook or *Corpus iuris* that precludes understanding the Laws of Venus and the judgments of love as an established tradition and body of precedent, as an erotic jurisdiction and case law that offers intimate insight onto highly important questions of love, its protocols, ethics, and manners.

The work of Benoit de Court and Etienne Forcadel remains esoteric and encoded in the Latin tongue, a little comprehended antiquity, and part of the purpose of the present endeavor is simply to translate and make this work and the related case law available and accessible to contemporary study. More than that, however, gay science and the laws of love, the flowers of an affective knowledge, not only form an important part of the history of legal thought, of what can be termed an early mode of governmentality, but also provide important elements of critique and an alternative to the tired norms of juridical self-love. As Stendhal put it in his treatise *On Love*: "Weren't they a lot more gay, considerably wittier, and much happier in 1174 than in 1822?" Change the dates and the same holds true. Good question. Nice point. Take it up.

The theme of human well-being, of poetic justice and of love's knowledge, becomes a key to understanding why it is so important that there be a forum, a site of judgment for the disputes, the pangs and misprisions of affection, the tributaries of suffering, the breakdowns of relationship that afflict us all. Erotic diplomacy, the cartography of affect, and the limits of the libidinal are the key themes taken up in the later and more literary traditions of laws and courts of love. The later sources don't need extensive detailing here but some of the case law will be taken from later poetic, literary, and theatrical trials and judgments. As observed earlier, rhetoric—*rectorica*—became the discipline that preserved the rules of humor and the laws of love. That is just how it is in terms of the scholarly order of things or the hierarchy of disciplines and here is a good enough place to say that I am all in favor of rhetoric and positively tireless when it comes to reconstructing the esoteric subdivisions of the laws of love.

If the tradition of courts of love starts with the reception of the poet Ovid and the various translations of his *Ars amatoria* or rulebook for lovers, then it is appropriate enough that the later tradition of judgments of love is distinctively literary. A few later works deserve a momentary mention. There is the Chaucerian poem *The Court of Love* which lists the Statutes of Love and decides at least one case, that of a man charged with dereliction of amorous duty for having failed to have a lover for over five years. As you might imagine, he was guilty as charged and made to swear on the Statutes that he would mend his ways. That is just one illustration of a rich poetic tradition which includes Gower's *Confessio amantis* and numerous theatrical courts of love. There is Esther Sowernam's play *Swetnam the woman hater arraigned by women*, which tries and pillories a male misogynist and author of a play attacking women. The "Ladie Chiefe Justice" sentences him to be muzzled "to express his barking humor against women kind." There are numerous other poems and plays that feature courts of love and the Laws of Venus but I will not list them just now. There is one other development that requires at least a brief allusion. It is the French seventeenth-century tradition of gallant and precious love.

Courts, parliaments, and judgments of love returned in profusion in the literary traditions of what has been termed *mondaine* or worldly love. The seventeenth century was the era of the libertine and new codes and cartographies of amorous desire. There were codes of love for the gallant, the coquettish, the precious or *précieuses*, for men and women, for the married and the single, for the gay and for the nay-sayers. Leave the making of lists for lawyers. They are obsessed with that, with tabulations, itemizations, imbrication, and intrication. From the point of view of the laws and professions of love we have entered the era of the epistolary missive and of amorous fiction based around love letters. The love letter becomes a key figure of the law of love and the resurgent courts of love. Honoré d'Urfé, in the early seventeenth century, in his interminable novel *Astrée* revives the tradition and reinstitutes a Parliament of Love as well as the profession of procurators or advocates in causes of love. The Statutes of Love are republished and the old case law is reworked by numerous inventive minds, Rabelesian gay scientists, beardless lovers, lawyers *sans culottes*, one and all.

Among the amatory marvels of the age pride of place goes to the *précieuses*, to the women's courts that were associated with the revival of the doctrine of pure love as a criterion of taste and cultural sensibility in the 1650s. The *précieuses*, a radical group of women centered in Paris, formed what Madame de Montpensier called "a kind of Republic" within the French state. They were central to the founding of the republic of letters, they were advocates of women's causes and proponents of a reversal of the *querelle des femmes*, or literary war of the sexes. They sought most famously to ban all words of the masculine gender from the French language. They wanted, in less antinomic terms, to change the discourse, to bring about a revolution in the relation between the sexes, and no doubt for that reason their movement didn't last long. They were ahead of their time.

What I meant to say was that the *précieuses*—there is no adequate translation—reinstituted the questions, the statutes and cases of love. Centered around literary activities, 'bel esprit' and engaged conversation, they met in alcoves, corridors, dressing rooms, and similar spaces of passage. And they held courts of love where they judged the antique questions and cases as well as applying their statutes by way of criticism of works of literature. They developed new case law, they issued the new *Edicts of Love*, tabulated new Statutes, and generally expanded the rules of the art of amorous interaction. They focused most on the art of aesthetic intercourse, the subtleties of taste and conversation. They delayed physical consummation and no doubt for that reason were known as the Jansenists of love, adherents of a strictly spiritual model of relationship.

The aspersion of Jansenism was an extreme and negative description but it was popularized in a number of plays and other narratives, most famously by Molière, but also by the Abbé de Pure, by Charles Sorel in his *Laws of Galantry* from the 1660s, and best of all perhaps in Aubignac's *History of the Times: An Account of the Kingdom of Coquetry*, which includes a lascivious list of the laws of Kingdom of the Coquettes. We have encountered such criticisms or dismissals before. There is no doubt that these women, some of whom had fought in the Fronde, the civil war of the 1640s, were both powerful and threatening. Mostly, however, the furor unleashed by the work of Madeleine de Scudéry, Madame de Suze, as well as their contemporaries and followers reflects the importance of their discussion of amorous morals and particularly the transgressive move of treating intimacy as a matter of law and doctrine and so also as a fit subject for public debate.

The *précieuses* turned the alcove into a court of judgment, the *ruelle* into a tribunal, the salon into a legislature and there they promulgated the new and feministic laws of love. The justice of the alcove knowingly conflated the public and private, the social and intimate, so as to render the poetry and literature of love accountable, so as to subject amorous practices to criteria of justice. Women were judges and again it should come as no surprise if future grave and learned historians decree that the *précieuses* did not exist but were simply a literary phenomenon. That is a judgment, I suspect, that reflects more upon the latter day historians than upon the subjects whose existence they deny. Myriam Maître has argued at length in her meticulous and admirable treatise on all aspects of preciosity, that the feminine, the aesthetic, and the intimate are historically invisible and often subversive sites. The question is not whether they existed but rather do they exist for us, or we for them? Painful to admit, I know, but often there is just too great a divide. But don't give up. Let's try to budge it. Build a link. Reason a little. Know a bit more.

What is indisputable is that the political and literary movement generated by the *précieuses* soon faded from view. The laws of love became known, as they are known now, through their dismissal or marginalization rather than through their positive enactments. Their trajectory in the latter part of the seventeenth century was from law to literature, from courtroom to theater, from the serious to the satirical. The final reports of cases of love come from the second half of the seventeenth-century and are to be found either in novels or in literary periodicals. The prolific Jean Donneau de Visé, in *Love Let Loose or the Many Modes of Loving*, a work first published in 1669, for example, reports a Parliament of Love established by the women of Paphos in Cyprus where the laws of Venus were applied to "all of the differences" that arise between lovers. The charter that establishes this Court empowers it to decide and give judgment in "all cases of infidelity, negligence, unresponsiveness, distrust, cruelty, jealousy, injustice, indiscreet talk, contempt, false rumor, hurtful behavior and betrayal of secrets". Reports are provided of several cases argued before the Court by advocates of love and determined by the female President and judges of the Court who expressly take up the position of "Cupid, the avenger of all injustices of love." Take an example, the last case, a triangle of love. It is emblematic of the fate of the courts of love, of their wisdom, of their distance from what is law for us.

Like the first case, that of Theogonis, the last case also begins with an unrequited love. Zemon had fallen in love with Caldirée. He sighed and longed and wept for her. Whenever he encountered her he proclaimed his love and protested the sincerity and depth of his passion for her. She never returned his affections and so in time he decided to cut his losses and leave town for a life abroad. Before leaving, he was visited by a friend, Thirsamene, who confessed that he also loved Caldirée. Zemon comforted Thirsamene and explained to him that he had given up on his love for Caldirée, that he was no longer Thirsamene's rival. Zemon solemnly promised that he would make no further effort to seduce Caldirée. He promised to cast aside all further thought of loving her.

Before leaving Paphos, however, Zemon by chance encountered Caldirée again. Out of habit, without thinking, and influenced no doubt by her beauty, Zemon proferred her his love and declared his undying affection. This time, and much to Zemon's surprise, Caldirée returned his affections and indicated in no uncertain terms that she was willing to become his lover. Zemon instantly forgot his promise to Thirsamene and promised Caldirée his undying love. When Zemon encountered Thirsamene the next day, he recounted what had happened and declared that he was helplessly in love, that he would desire Caldirée until his dieing day. Thirsamene was unimpressed and insisted that Zemon keep his promise and end his relationship with Caldirée. Unable to resolve the dispute themselves, the friends took it to the judges of the Court of Love.

Thirsamene argued that although Zemon could not give him Caldirée's heart, he could keep his promise and abandon his love for her. He even conceded that Zemon might well not be able to cease loving Caldirée but he could cease to talk of that love and desist from seeing her. That, he concluded, was the honest path for Zemon to take and he prayed that the Court enforce the promise.

Following Thirsamene, the Advocate General of Love also argued that Zemon should keep his promise to Thirsamene. The Advocate's argument was that according to the precepts of love, Zemon's promise to Thirsamene was a crime against Caldirée. His promise to abandon his love showed a complete lack of commitment, a fickleness of desire and a lack of seriousness in his pursuit of his beloved. His discourteous behavior betrayed his superficiality and betokened that he was incapable of loving over the long term (*longue durée*).

Zemon pleaded that he could not help himself, the *force majeure* of love had overwhelmed him and that should be adequate defense against enforcement of the promise. A curious case of frustration of contract, or *contractus interruptum*, one might say in the proper parlance.

The judges heard the pleas and following the time-honored procedure of the laws of love, suspended judgment. The order issued was that Caldirée be attached to the case, brought before the Court and made to publicly declare which of the two men she loved the best. It was her choice, but choose she must because choice alone would both augment love and promote reconciliation of the friends. Call it truth and reconciliation, before its time. A restorative justice of the intimate public sphere.

Zemon's case is hardly the last of the judgments of love, but it does mark the end of a lengthy history of specifically judicial procedures. After 1669 the cases of love are transformed into narratives—*nouvelles galantes*—and into more or less exclusively theatrical and literary forms. The logic and laws of love continued to be the subject of innumerable works of fiction and dramas, those for example of François de Callières, of Donneau de Visé, Monsieur Cotin, or the *Amorous Annals* of the incomparable Madame Villedieu. The cases and causes become what lawyers term fictions: analogies and examples, stories from which reasons can be drawn, a logic and justice of love defined and applied. Madame Villedieu—the nom de plume of Marie Catherine Desjardins—put it best and deserves full citation: "Great decisions and events do not take place instantaneously, they must be talked about and seen for their excess to be appreciated and their extremity loved. I, therefore, augment history with secret meetings and amorous discourses. If these are not those actually pronounced, they are those that ought to have been uttered. I have no more faithful memories than my judgment."

To the precious corrective offered by Desjardins, we can add the methodological caution that satire has always been a radical and significant genre of political and legal reform in eras of social change. Satire had its own law, its *lex operis*, and was one of the most effective modes of altering opinions, reforming practices, and rewriting doctrine. That, however, will remain another story for discussion at a later point. Suffice here to say that the change in form is not a reason to abandon the study of the later illustrations of love's laws but it does signal the end of the era of judicially formulated decisions in cases of amorous dispute. That change allows us to limit the case law that properly pertains to the jurisdiction of love. Or at least the plan is to focus on cases reported and judicially determined between 1150 and 1669.

* * *

In the ensuing collection of cases of love, I have avoided any chronological tabulation and have sought rather to classify the case law according to the general principles of the laws of love. The substance of the protocols and norms of love applied in the judgments varies over time. There is a discernible trajectory from the spiritual to the secular and from the amorous to the lawful. The laws of love also shift historically in terms of genre and tone. The general tendency is a move from the ponderous to the playful, from the serious to the satirical, from court to stage. That said, the questions of love addressed and the judgments delivered are remarkably constant with respect to subject matter and logic of analysis. As the indomitable François de Callières puts it in a work entitled *The Lovers' Logic or Love the Logician*, published in 1668, a whisker within our period: "the lovers' logic is the art of discerning true love from false, and of reasoning justly as to all that happens between them."

It is the admirable sense of seeking to reason justly in disputes between lovers that coheres all of the various eras of judicially depicted causes of love. Lovers hold everything in common or, in the terms of the *Code of Love*, Rule 24, "Every act of a lover is bounded by thoughts of their beloved." The question that the case law poses most strongly is that of how to determine disputes between parties who hold everything in common, who are intimately bonded, affectively inseparable? Our last case, Zemon's plea, gives a clue. So far as possible, let the lovers themselves decide. Suspend judgment for as long as possible, and then when judging reason justly, which is to say according to the laws of love, the rules that govern amorous and rhetorical felicity. That is the principle that will be traced throughout the various substantive domains covered by the courts of love. Whether the issue pleaded concerns a melancholic lover, a stolen kiss, loss of a lover, violence or withholding of affections, the courts treat it equally and according to what is best for the domain of love. The lovers are indulged, granted time, offered justice in its most antique and purest form. For the justice of love in the end asks only that love be kept alive.

Figure 3 *Cosi de ben amar porto tormento* (Thus I bear the torment of loving well)—*Emblemata amatoria* (1620).

2
Erotic Melancholy

The first judgment of love, reported by Plutarch, was concerned with lovesickness. That is fitting enough. The laws of love address the ailments of desire, the disputes that arise, and the path to their cure. The essential question posed is that of how to find joy through pursuit of desire. Love, the one overriding emotional necessity of human life, can cause untold suffering. The troubadours were indeed forever tabulating the wounds of relationship and the degrees of pain engendered by unfulfilled desire or loss of love. Does a lover who is too afraid to declare herself suffer more or less than one who has been rejected? Or again, does a lover whose partner dies suffer more or less than one whose partner is unfaithful? The answer given by the courts of love was always the same: the greatest suffering is experienced by the lover whose loss most impedes their current path toward the joy of love. Thus, for example, the unfaithful lover whose continued presence reminds the former beloved of his loss causes greater pain than the lover who dies. A radical view. Much in favor of the living though not disrespectful of the dead if you recollect that under Rule 7 of the *Code of Love*: "When a lover dies the survivor is required to wait two years before taking another lover."

The learned doctors, the lawyers of love, devised their amatory laws precisely so as to have available and known rules by which to determine all species of dispute—emotional, practical, moral, or medical—that could arise between lovers. Suffering, the pain that went variously by the name of erotic melancholy, lovesickness or heroic mania, was the enemy of love, the nemesis of enjoyment, and so was a prime subject matter of the law of love. The jurisdiction of the laws was over an emotional territory. They sought from the very beginning to regulate the path of erotic enjoyment. Joy—*joi, jeu*—was a term that connoted both play (*joculum*) and happiness (*gaudium*), the jovial and the jocastic, the rules of the game. As the troubadour Marcabru confesses in a moment of frustrated observation of animals in the mating season: "These small creatures couple together out of love, their joy follows a straight path while ours strays, for among us, everyone cheats."

Gay science sought to codify the properly poetic and so also ethical path of erotic exchange. Joy was to be prized away from the jaws of sorrow. The territory of love was to be constantly expanded. Laws were devised that everywhere held open the prospect and possibilities of augmenting love and engendering joy. Each name that was added to the register kept in the Chancellery of Love was a victory and a cause for celebration. The treatise on *The Laws of Love* that was compiled at the beginning of the fourteenth century by the legally learned troubadours of the Gay Consistory of Toulouse had as its goal the revival of the poetic life of the senses. According to its preamble, the laws were designed explicitly "to educate the ignorant, to curb the mad, to calm the besotted, so as to map the path of a jubilant and joyful life at the same time as putting anger and sorrow, the enemies of gay science, to flight."

The primary source of the laws is desire. It is the motive force behind all amorous encounters, and it drives the formulation of the rules that get codified. To love is to write. Through correspondence and poems we send the letters, the signs and rhymes of intimacy and obsession. That is why the laws of love are on their surface poetic conventions, grammatical rules, stylistic and aesthetic norms. They govern the modes of communication of desire, its passage between the lovers. The purpose of the laws is thus to fashion an eloquence, a rhetoric and conversation that attends to the avenues of successful communication and allows for the expression of passions in constructive, progressive, and positive forms. Eloquence, the expression of love, was best or happiest when effective and reciprocated. Thus gay science itself gains its practical definition in terms of the rules for composition of persuasive desire. That was the originary promise and the purpose of rhetoric. That was the design of the justice that the poets and orators who sat as judges in the courts of love sought to render. Poetics was the law that lay at the base of the invention of the social. It was poetry after all that brought people together, and more specifically in our case drew the couple to love.

Rhyme, assonance, melody of form, urbanity of content, and lightness of expression were the desiderata that the rules promulgated. The lover was a poet. The lover was on a quest. He or she sought to find (*trouver*) a love, and the laws were composed to aid that quest, to overcome the impediments in its way, to bring it to its proper enjoyment and consummation. Pleasure, happiness, and joy were intrinsic to the territory or jurisdiction of desire, they were the rewards, the end or outcome of the search for love. This is an essential point and can be made most eloquently by turning to the case of the melancholic lover, one of the decisions reported in Martial d'Auvergne's *Judgements of Love*.

The case was heard in the High Court of Love. It involved a woman petitioner and her male partner. She sought an order against her lover on the grounds that he had so changed since their affair began as to be unrecognizable to her now. She requested either that he be enjoined to return to his former state or that she be released from their amorous compact. The facts were as follows.

The petitioner had first met the young man some months previously. He was at the time "the happiest, most joyful and playful person imaginable." She was attracted to him precisely because he was kind, gregarious, generous, and outgoing. She fell in love with a man *à la mode*, a fashionable and freethinking gentleman of consummate style and wit. After only a few months, however, the man that she had fallen for had disappeared. In his place was a most morbid and melancholic excuse for a lover.

The defendant's mood seemed to have changed totally from joy to sorrow. He became reclusive, distracted, and sad: "It was as if life now bored him." He was world weary and misanthropic. He seemingly lived now in a melancholic reverie that was impossible to reach into. The petitioner goes on to list his faults. When spoken to, the young man would go into a daydream before answering in so distracted and irrelevant a way as to indicate that his thoughts were entirely elsewhere. When she gave him flowers, he would tear them to pieces and throw them to the ground before they had even left her hands. When music was played he would begin to sigh and tears would come to his eyes. If she tried to talk of love, he would turn the conversation immediately to death or tell some longwinded and pointless story. He was cold when it was hot, and hot when it was cold. He had become quite contrary. She no longer recognized him; he was infuriating, and she felt her love draining away.

The melancholic lover's defense was to plead that love had changed him for the better. He had got religion. Now he wanted to live solely and singly in the service of love. According to the Christian tradition, the loves of this world are but the shadows of a much greater and otherworldly desire. The loves of the living flesh were to be shunned in favor of the suffering and pain that brings the believer to salvation. He had chosen to mortify and so purify himself in the name of love. This meant that he should live for suffering, that he shun the company of women, and that he seek by all means to make up for the time he had lost in the worldly pursuit of desire. Each day his flesh was to be mortified in furtherance of the spirit. He continued by saying that both material wealth and physical enjoyment were meaningless to him. He thanked the petitioner for her good will and kind graces in the past and asked to be released from his promises of love. The time of their love was over for him and indeed he regretted it. He concluded that whatever the Court determined was a matter of indifference to him. Judgment could neither change his pursuit nor threaten him. He did not fear punishment nor would death hold any sting.

The woman responded by saying that the young man was living a dangerous fantasy of otherworldly love. If he gave up his possessions he would regret it later in life. If he abandoned the love of the living, his days would become a living death. She said that she and many others cared deeply for him and prayed that the Court in its sovereignty would command him to return to amorous health.

His reply—his replication as the lawyers call it—was succinct. He regretted the escapades of his former life. Nothing any longer moved him. He hoped to die.

The Court deliberated at great length. It reviewed the facts and the law. The determination arrived at was that the melancholic be ordered a rest cure—the exact words being that he should be "put out to grass" (*mis aux herbes*). Specifically, the defendant was sentenced to one month's imprisonment in a garden. There he was to take in the lushness of the vegetation and the beauty of the flowers. He was to remain alone and to avoid all melancholic company. By these means the Court hoped that he would rediscover his dreams and reanimate his fantasies. The petitioner was also ordered constantly to keep the image of her lover in her mind, to fantasize, to imagine a renewed love. She was to visit him as often as possible in his garden prison and there engage him in amorous dialogue and read to him from erotic texts. If after one month this cure did not succeed, then she was free to seek a new love, and he to pursue his religious passion.

The judgment literally offers the therapy of desire. Disjunction is remedied by conjunction; depression by flirtation; quietude by fantasy or the promise of passion. It might not work, but the law dictates that the lovers try to re-eroticize the relationship before abandoning it. Nothing would hurt so much as acknowledging the loss of the defendant from the register of love. It is also a highly emblematic case. Each element is rhetorically as well as legally significant and a brief analysis of the judgment can draw out its crucial themes.

First the question of jurisdiction. This is both an internal question, a matter of mood, and a question of competence and territory. Start with the latter. The laws of love are always introduced in the context of a heterotopic or liminal space: a green sward, a riverbank, an arbor, a flower garden, a dream. To these we can add the feminine space of the court and later of the alcove or *ruelle*, the dressing room, the corridor, and the bedside. They are variously sites of passage and transition. Their encounters are marked by that curious conflation of seriousness and play, work and leisure, intimate and social that still holds true of the space of travel, of stations, airports, planes, boats, cars, or trains. Note first then that the laws of love take jurisdiction over the liminal space where desire encounters convention, where hedonism mixes with mundane plans, and where the prosaic encounters the poetic. These are the in-between moments of greatest decision, of life changes, and while they may conventionally be viewed as private they are in fact far too important to be left to prejudice or chance. They have their own science and laws.

The garden is thus representative of jurisdiction. It is the rhetorical figure of *topographia*, or description of place. The garden indicates the invocation of another law, that of nature, of the first Venus. It is a common figure and one that is often joined with dream. The judicial sentence that orders a sojourn in a flower garden is neither aimless nor purely recreational. It seeks explicitly to reawaken the subject's fantasies; it is designed to reconnect him to his dreams. Put it like this, an act of passage is necessary for entry into the jurisdiction of the laws of love. It requires a shift from one face of law to the other, from prose to poetry, from the municipal to the natural. It is a law of nature that is being applied and nature is its context.

A brief aside on this very point. According to one critic—Bloch by name—the Courts of Love flounder "on a tedious no-man's land between pseudo-document and literary text." No lover him, one might say, even a touch blocked, but his metaphor is telling. Think it through. No-man's land, *niemensland*, is the space between. It is an eminently social space, a momentary interlude, an event even that promises life amid the horrors of war, hope in the face of mortality, play in place of mutilation and death. No-man's land seems pretty apt as a depiction of the space between lovers, between poetry and prose, pragmatism and imagination, and that is so even without entering the gender dimensions of his metaphor. And of the tedium one might simply say "as in a dream," *te deum*, for you, the God of love. Take an early example.

Case 5 reported by Capellanus is brief and to the following effect. A knight loved his lady unstintingly and took the greatest pleasure in the physical consolations of love. But while he enjoyed her embraces, she did not return his affections. Eventually, dispirited, he sought to leave her. She, however, wished to keep him as her lover and refused to release him from his promises of love. The case came before the Court of the Countess of Champagne and her impromtu judgment was stated thus: "The attitude of the defendant is thoroughly deplorable. She wants to be loved but refuses to love in return. It is idiotic for someone to demand from others what she refuses to bestow in return." An easy yet illustrative case of the principle that the territory of love obtains only for those who make the commitment to love. The figure of the garden or in this case of a woman's court marks a threshold of competency, a step beyond the prosaic or ordinary law, an openness to affect and imagination. Those are historically attributes though now somewhat obscured of the art of law, the *ars iuris* in the antique and expansive sense that is being recollected here.

The last case illustrates among other things that the laws of love belong to a reciprocal space, an "in between" of relationship, a nexus of promising. It can serve to remind us that the laws of love form a voluntary jurisdiction. It is voluntary in the sense of being predicated upon the willingness of both parties to participate—usually *in camera*, or without being named—and in the sense of touching upon desire. In both senses, the threshold of competence is imagination. To return to our case of the defendant melancholic lover, we can note that he was expressly sentenced to his floral imprisonment for didactic and recuperative reasons. He was to meditate on flowers, the very symbol of gay science, the defining attribute of the doctor of amorous erudition. The flowers of gay science were the figures of knowledge of the laws of love—*gay saber* as it was originally called. This leads to a second point of significance. The time out or judicial sentence of recuperative leisure was to be accompanied by texts and readings. The Court ordered that all melancholic literature was to be jettisoned and only erotic fables and verses were to remain. In addition, the petitioner was to visit, read, and recite to the prisoner.

The question is one of importance. What matters in life? What constitutes care of the self? Living well? And the answer, according to the laws, is both ethical and amorous. Its dictate is that you follow your desire, and that you learn to love well. I will be a little esoteric here. If the rules of rhetoric generally teach the art of speaking well, then the laws of love teach the art of loving well. *Ars bene dicendi* leads directly to *ars bene amandi*. At the level of writing and specifically of writing love letters we can also note that the compilers of the proper forms of letter, the *ars dictaminis*, referred to the *ars epistolandi et amandi*, meaning the art of corresponding and loving, as the proper description of the rules of inscribing and sending the inscriptions of desire. And both are arts of justice, arts that render words and loves justly. It is this indeed that Nietzsche, in his later philosophy of the gay science, remarks upon as erudition *in eroticis* or learning to love. And remaining with names that begin with the letter N, Nabokov later observed that anyone can describe the world as it is, but it takes art to make it into something beautiful. As the gloss to the judgment in the case of the melancholic lover observes, choice of text is important. Scholars who read only esoteric texts become sad and removed. They die a little through the inhalation of the dust of dead letters, the ashes of authors long gone.

That is not to say that either law or study is irrelevant to love. The erudition that Nietzsche proposed is one that is gauged to long observation, to attention, to repetition and refrain until we know the beloved so well that their absence would hurt us. To learn to love, to acknowledge and observe the laws of love is a lifelong endeavor, a path, a quest, a mission. We moderns, as Freud liked to point out, tend to be somewhat unconscious about the path to love, whereas the troubadours devoted enormous energy, time, and travail to the proper pursuit of amorous fulfillment. Love was the structuring feature of social life. It was the most important of the forms of knowledge, the most practical, the hardest. This and more is reflected in the codes and the laws. Their most distinctive feature was precisely that they were literary and legal. They had a dual aspect that is well represented in the Court's order that the petitioner read erotic verse to the defendant. The poems were letters of desire, both law and writ, and each in their turn enjoined reentry into the space of relationship that the melancholic lover had quit.

The reference to texts stipulates a return to the correspondence or art of loving. Because this in the end is volitional, it depends upon desire; the judgment is not mandatory but rather a suspension of mandatory judgment, the institution of a time of texts, an interlude during which the Court hopes that the lovers will come to attach the drives described to the persons, the bodies, that enunciate them. These texts are love letters, they are in early legal terminology original writs, personal writs, *me ipso* as they used to say, or in the name of the reader and sender. The lines, the verses and other texts of love, termed the *linea amoris*, refer not just to writing but also to the steps that have to be taken toward love. It is not to be sudden or artless. It has to be done well. There is a knowledge to be learned. Erotic erudition constitutes a law. It starts, Step 1 according to Capellanus, with looking. It moves to conversation.

The third step is touch. The fourth is kissing with the lips. The last step is coitus or consummation.

The sentence to imprisonment in a flower garden where the defendant was to read and to be read erotic verses dictates that the lovers find themselves through writing, inscribe themselves in texts, and so enter the jurisdiction of love. More could be said on this epistolary justice. Indeed more will be said. The case law is stuffed, as we will see, with cases revolving around correspondences, letters sent or sent astray; messengers who die, postal carriers who are captured; messages that are stolen, mistranslated, or misplaced. We will come to those. For the moment this is just the place, the just place for noting that law and love meet in the epistolary space of letters. There the love letter is the original writ, the muse, and the law. It is very Pascalian. Act as if you love, read erotic texts, and soon you are likely to find yourself in love.

Finally, third point, to state the obvious in all its glory and glamor, the case of the melancholic lover institutes a gay law. The Court was petitioned because the defendant had lost his humor, abandoned all company, and fallen into the bleakest and most recalcitrant of moods. He was lost to love and either he could be revived or his death to mortal desire would have to be acknowledged and recorded. Without joy there was no love, and without love there was no law. That is simply because law, or any system of norms for that matter, applies to a territory and to the subjects that people a territory. The realm of love and the laws of love have their application to lovers. It is at root our choice, though the laws will have their say. Consider a late case. It is from the anonymous Chaucerian work, *The Court of Love*.

It is the first case heard by the Court. Emblematic again, significant of jurisdiction, entry point as it were to the portals of desire. The Court convenes on Mount Cithera, where Venus and "blind Cupid" hold their hearings. The charge is brought against a clerk, one Philogenet—meaning a learned man, a scholar. He is accused of willful negligence, of having been absent from the domain of love for 18 years. The defendant confesses that his intentions had always been good but that every time he had encountered the possibility of love, "shamefastness" or modesty had overcome him and had chased him away.

Venus brooks no excuses. Philogenet is sentenced—"for that I was lettred, there I red"—to study the twenty *Statutes of Love* and then to swear undying allegiance to them. The judgment again takes effect through texts. Philogenet has to read the edicts of Eros, the diktats of desire, and through that rite, through the kiss of the text, reaffirm that he is a subject again, that he has rejoined the territory of the heart. Prime among the statutes, the first rule, was the oath of obedience to the jurisdiction of love, the declaration of faith in Venus and her laws. By the fourth Statute he was to commit himself, on all occasions, to "stirring folk to love." He was also, and this is specified in detail in Statutes 6 to 9, himself to love, secretly to honor and patiently serve a lover of his own. In all, the statutes read and sworn, he was to "own his passion" from now until his death.

Joyful wisdom, gay science, laws of love, the new rights and laws—they are all terms for indicating a mundane desire, a love of the world. What is imparted is a degree of pleasure, an eros or amorous commitment that is part of the business of life and of the commerce of the realm. One law on another, a mixed jurisdiction or double sentence that strives, if norms can strive, to appropriate the erotic space of the social and address how we love as a question of art and of law. In the end, however, I fear that questions of jurisdiction, of being and belonging, are somewhat technical, a little legalistic and so the main point needs repeating. These are questions of the avenues of desire, the paths to joy, the possibilities of pursuing laughter, or accepting the charge, the energy and demand of a happy life.

In or out, subject or stranger, the case of the melancholic lover illustrates a choice of jurisdiction, a question of one law or the other. In the terms of the Statute of 1400, the choice was between being enrolled in the Register of Love or of being erased, expunged, banished. Sorrow was its own punishment, regret or the absence of joy just recompense for leaving love. Hence the law's concern was primarily, which is to say initially, with the interface of pleasure and pain, joy and sorrow. So long as the subject sought love and did not infract any of its laws, then they were within the jurisdiction. Loss of subjects to other jurisdictions, to religion in particular was fiercely contested. Thus in the case of a lover who became a monk: Case 37 before the High Court of Love in Paris, as reported by Martial d'Auvergne.

The petitioner was a woman who had entered a contract of love with the defendant. They had given themselves to each other, and in the proper form of the love affair as then practiced they had sworn that whatever adversities came their way they were committed to each other. The alliance was made and the promises were sworn before witnesses and their love was consummated. Not long after the affair had begun, the lovers quarreled. It was, the petitioner claimed, a minor tiff, a trifling matter, but the young man stormed off. Without consulting his lover, without any cooling-off period, in fact without any communication at all he went impulsively and joined a religious order, the

Cordeliers or Friars of St. Francis, so named for the many-knotted rope that they wore as a belt round their midriff. Every medieval lover's worst nightmare. Loss of the beloved to a religious order, whereas today I suspect it would be loss to commerce or work, a more fluid yet nonetheless insidious abandon.

The petitioner sought closure. Her specific request was that the defendant be ordered to come out of the monastery and either renew their vows of love or expressly release her from her promises. She wanted to be free to love or if needs be to love again. If it was really the case, then she wanted to hear from him that his new and spiritual love had once and for all replaced his desire for her. As the *Code of Love* Rule 17 puts it: "A new love drives out the old."

The *Cordeliers* answered on behalf of the young man. They stated that his initiation into the Order was now complete. He had taken his vows and renounced the world, and the last thing he needed now was to be assailed by his past follies, old lovers, or other amorous indiscretions. Specifically, the vows taken by the novice included a promise to renounce all relationship with women. He had sworn never again to look upon or speak to a woman. It was too late to go back on that promise and it was obviously implicit in his vows that he renounced, ended, and was done with his relationship with the petitioner. There was no need to repeat such a clear and incontestable conclusion. The defendant had abandoned both life and love, he had turned his back upon the world and upon women alike.

In her reply, the petitioner argued first that in her experience it would be dangerous to place too great a weight on the promises that the defendant had made, either to her or to the *Cordeliers*. He was prone to impulsive behavior, he had been known to break his word. She simply wanted him to face her and explicitly state that it was over, that his word was naught and her promises thereby released. He should come before the Court and in the rite appropriate to termination tear up their love letters and undo their vows.

Judgment was as follows. The *Cordeliers* were ordered to bring the defendant into the Court. They were permitted to blindfold him so that he did not have to look upon his previous lover, but that was all. The Friars were then to leave the Court and the young man was to make his statement to the petitioner. So ruled.

An observation or two. There are competing jurisdictions of love. The Church placed Capellanus's treatise *On Love* on the list of banned books in 1277. The laws of love were for a long time explicitly heretical. Their jurisdiction thus clashed with that of the Church. Both had a stake in the souls of their subjects. Love now or love later was seemingly the choice, and it was the distinction of gay science to propose the former: love now, love long, love well.

The heretical character of the laws of love explains to some degree the somewhat obscure history of this jurisdiction. The pursuit of pleasure, consummation, or joy were diversely seen at various times as subversive, pornographic, heretical, feministic, sodomitic, satirical, or worse. Their history is thus not so much obscure as obscured. There is no reason now for those constraints, those Blochs or obstacles, to continue to impede a knowledge or observance of such a project and its laws.

Then again, the precarious historical status of the laws of love explains as well the voluntary character of the jurisdiction. The Courts applied a natural law and sought not to compete with other modes of rule so much as to supplement and hold open the possibilities of desire in social life. These are laws that are all about potential; they do not subvert but rather offer a radical promise, a heterotopic aspiration within the most mundane of institutional settings. Joy now or joy later. You choose. And if the choice is now then the cases and other laws of love will tell you how. If not, then go mope. A final case, heard by the High Court of Love in Paris, makes exactly that point.

The petitioner was a man who had long been in love with the defendant woman. He had offered her every kindness, had served her wishes loyally, and had in every way displayed his affection for her. She ignored him and showed neither affection nor any intention of favoring his entreaties. Neither his nor anyone else's. She stated boldly that she was immune to love and that as long as she lived she would resist all amorous advances. The petitioner suffered horribly. He had lost his heart and could find no way of reclaiming it. He petitioned the High Court seeking either that the defendant be ordered to entertain his advances or, failing that, she be required to act in such a way as to remove herself from his desires.

The defendant argued to the contrary that she had observed over time that those who fell in love suffered both injury and infamy to their name. It seemed to her that the service of love was a form of self-delusion, a trick that did untold harm. She therefore had decided a while ago to remain free. She had not and would never succumb to love as long as she lived. As to the petitioner's second request, that she somehow disappear from his thoughts, that was a matter over which she had no control. She was not in possession of the key to his heart nor could she do anything about amorous thoughts that were in her view the product of vain fantasies and the madness of lust. He would have to cure himself. For her part she would remain free and would continue to resist all pleas and advances. Thus stated, she requested her expenses.

The Procurator of Love, who joined the petitioner in this case, presented the next argument. Never to have loved was a crime against nature and desire. Those who had not loved were scarcely alive. It was as if they had not yet arrived. They were lost to the pleasures of being. Lovers, she continued, enter the domain of joy. There is always some pain in our pleasure, there is anxiety as well as enjoyment, but no one in love has ever complained of a lack of goods. The currency and tokens of love were priceless and timeless: a lock of hair, a letter, some other sign, the memory of a dance together. Look at the face of a woman in love. It is alive, happy, benevolent toward others, content in itself. Compare that to the face of someone who refused to love. It is gray, unexpressive, withdrawn from the world, and insouciant of both appearance and conversation. Your average married couple—back then, of course, when marriage was generally a property exchange without reference to desire. The Procurator ended by urging the Court to order the defendant to swear that she would open her heart to love, and so at least try to join the domain of earthly powers.

The defendant responded that nothing in what the Procurator had argued moved her in the slightest. She remained determined to have nothing to do with her suitors. The Procurator then requested the Court to order that she be banished from the realm of love, and shunned by all of its members. Those who encountered her were to rush and publicly wash their hands as a sign of distancing themselves from her ignoble cause. Notwithstanding the above injunction, the Procurator also requested that the Court order the defendant to try to help the petitioner recover his health. She was to greet him warmly when they met. She was to smile at him with her eyes and her lips. So long as he remained lovesick, she was to think of him and try to coax him back to health.

The defendant responded that she had renounced love and that none of the above stipulations were relevant to her. She was outside the Court's jurisdiction, and the Court could neither make requests of her nor order her to do anything. Even if she was subject to the laws of love, nothing would be changed. Love was a matter of will. It was volitional and so it made no sense to try to force her to love. She had said that love was not to her taste. That was the end of the matter.

After hearing the arguments on both sides, the petitioner in his replication said that he did not want any order made against the defendant. He desired her to remain free. She should do what she wished. For his part he had tried everything to forget her. He had embarked on voyages abroad, he had joined pilgrimages to holy places, but nothing could expunge her image from his mind. He would continue to languish. He would likely die still loving her.

The Court listened to the arguments. They took the case under advisement and after long deliberation concluded that the defendant's renunciation of love had to be determinative. She had placed herself outside the jurisdiction of the Court and no order could be made in relation to her. On the other hand, all those who were subject to the laws of love were to treat her as an outlaw both to desire and to joy. She was not of the territory. She was to be ignored by everyone. No one could dance with her at carnivals or on public holidays. No one was to offer her gifts or give her dresses. She was to be left alone. As for the melancholic lover, he was to dress in mourning and he too was to shun her. Once his heart had let go of her image a little, he was to seek relationships with other women. So ordered.

Desire circumscribes a voluntary jurisdiction. That said, the case was heard. Arguments were made and positions were stated. The lover had his day in Court and was forced to recognize that those who do not wish to play, do not wish to play. There is no forcing someone to be happy any more than love can be formally enjoined. The laws of love recognize thus that gay science, erotic erudition, does require a willingness to learn, both patience and study. Time and process can lead the will to love, but love cannot be willed in any instantaneous or involuntary manner. On the other hand, the petitioner could be helped to let go of his infatuation. That seems clear from the arguments and from the judgment. Mourning was necessary. Freud would have approved. A ritual was needed so as to enable the lovesick petitioner to release some and maybe eventually all of the charge that attached to the lost object, the recalcitrant beloved. The simple expedient of dressing in mourning was the avenue chosen by the Court to help the distressed lover acknowledge and release an inappropriate love.

It is no small thing to die to love. The laws of love indeed are designed precisely to avert that fate. It is its own punishment or, as one doctrinal work poetically puts it, those who contradict "the law and power of love" run the risk of "punishment worse than that of Narcissus." In the pre-Freudian terms that we are dealing with here, that means that they become lovers of shadows, the enamorata of ghosts. They become lost to the world. In contemporary terms they would likely receive pharmacological treatment. Viagra or maybe Prozac. The laws of love, however, provided an alternative stratagem, symbolic rites of connection or of expression of loss. Relational cures. The significance of such rites deserves a few parting words.

The case law on erotic melancholia, the determinations of lovesickness, revolves around an initial decision to participate. The jurisdiction of love governs voluntarily. Its injunctions are directed to its willing subjects. They are subjects of a law whose mechanisms of enforcement are symbolic rather than physically coercive, and collective rather than merely individual. Everyone subject to the jurisdiction is affected by the various pathologies and symptoms that emerge in disputes. For this reason the lawyers of love, the Advocates and Procurators, are frequently joined to disputes, and the judges themselves issue orders that are aimed to augment the interests of intimacy, the dissemination of desire, as well as to adjudicate the individual case. For the most part judgment is in fact suspended. The law will literally provide a forum, it offers the litigants a space within which to attend to their relationship or acknowledge its dissolution. The law of love imposes the enactment of the rites of passage of desire that make up the intimate public sphere.

Like all legal systems, the principal function of the laws of love is to provide the discursive parameters for dispute. These laws disseminate the rhetorical rules of the gay science within the realm of relationships. According to the Statute of 1400, it was skill in poetry, oratorical ability, the talent of speaking well that was to govern the selection of judges. Their task was to speak justly. Wherever possible, just speech, the eros of verse, the eloquence of well-turned phrases would bring lovers together and indicate in intimate yet public ways how melancholia could be dissipated and desire reborn. That way lies joy, the path of a hedonic life.

Figure 4 *Te stante virebo* (While you stand, I flourish)—*Emblemata amatoria* (1620).

3
Purloined Love Letters

The logic of the purloined love letter is that desire is everywhere to be seen. It ends up in all the most obvious places but we tend to overlook it. If you remember Poe's story, the detective Dupin, never leaving the broodingly narcotic atmosphere of a private library, located the missing love letter without lifting a finger. It was there for everyone to see. Its concealment lay in its not being concealed. Dupin laughed at the police and outwitted them in their searches by following the deeper law, a poetic justice in which desire held pride of place and maximum visibility.

Stating the obvious is not a bad place to start. The *Code of Love* recommends it. The initial signs of love, specifically of 'falling' in love, are easy to discern, and hard to hide. Rule 15: "Every lover tends to grow pale when their partner looks at them." Rule 16: "A lover's heart beats faster at the sight of the beloved." Rule 23: "The stress of love makes it hard to eat and sleep." To these empirical laws we can add the various other insignia of love. Tears, blushes, palpitations, stammering, perspiration, heat. All are bodily signs and all are pretty visible or easily apprehensible through smell, taste, or touch. It is perhaps for that reason that Ovid, from whom most of these markers are taken, recommended inscribing love letters on the body of an intermediary. The erotic message ought to be erotic, not to say visceral and palpable.

The laws of love govern the social presence of desire, the passage of intimacy through public spaces. The enactment of love thus requires first and most prominently a set of rules governing the communication of desire, and ensuring safe passage of intimate missives through extimate spaces. The message has to be prized away from the body of the lover and transmitted to the beloved. That requires writing and in an age where love was the antithesis of marriage, where the affair was heretical and most usually illicit, this necessitated the use of messengers. The laws had therefore to address most urgently the best means of keeping the avenues of communication open and the message safe. The laws of Venus had to trump the laws of men.

The first and overriding law was that the messenger be selected wisely and be true to the message. The *Precepts of Love*, by Rule 6, thus stipulated care in the choice of messenger: "Do not share your love with too many confidants (*secretarios*)." The word itself, the medieval Latin *secretarius* actually means a secret place, a site of the hidden, and so by extension it came to mean a confidential representative. The secretary was a confidant who carried intimate messages and could be a cleric or a friend or a simple courier who specialized in secret delivery. Their role, before the advent of a mail service, let alone the communicative profusions of the web, was constitutive of the domain of love. Without the letter carriers there would be no possibility of love, the avenues of passage of desire would be closed except for chance encounters and momentary infatuations.

The most important and celebrated of the cases of love reported by Capellanus concerns precisely this issue of fidelity to the message. Judgment 16 heard by the Court of the Countess of Champagne concerned theft of a message. The petitioner was in love with a woman but circumstances prevented him from conversing with her at any length. He had been able fleetingly to indicate his desire but there had never been an opportunity to arrange for a meeting. He decided therefore to employ a confidant to relay his affections to the woman, to allow her to declare hers in return, and to arrange to meet. The confidant agreed to undertake this solemn office of courier. Far from delivering the lover's message, however, the confidant took the opportunity of conversation with the beloved to press his own claims. Despite his promise of confidence, he abandoned his role and the message he was carrying and instead declared himself in love with the woman to whom the unwritten letter was addressed. Pure fraud one might think but the woman complied with his ruse. Although she was aware of the deception, she listened to his importuning and soon afterward became his lover "fulfilling everything he asked of her."

The petitioner was enraged by the deception and went to Court. The facts stated, the case was pleaded. So important was its subject matter that the Countess of Champagne summoned 60 women to adjudicate. The determination was both simple and poetic. The confidant had broken the law, the woman had equally acted basely and immodestly in consenting to the love of a messenger: "She did not even blush when consenting to his villainous demands." So far so good. Less obvious was the sentence.

Rather wonderfully this condemned the treacherous defendant to a love that he thoroughly deserved: "Let him enjoy his love, the evil fruit of his betrayal, and let her enjoy a lover that she richly merits." Both are thereby sentenced to the purgatory of their mutual affections. They are at the same time sequestrated from the love of anyone else. Having broken the Code they are condemned in perpetuity to their purloined love. They are struck off the Register of Lovers, erased from the Book, and so banished from the domain of love, exiled and excommunicated.

Why so many judges, so severe a determination, so harsh and unusual a decree? The answer lies in the dependence of love upon the truth of the message. Put it like this, the message is part of the lover's body, it is a visceral sign, an affective thing. It is the token of love, a good, a gift. Under the rules of love, it is usually sent unsigned so as to safeguard the secrecy of the affair, and thus it depends in a double sense upon the fidelity of the confidant messenger. It is their office, their role to deliver the name of the author as well as the thing, the message or letter itself. The 60 judges were needed for emphasis, to symbolize the enormity of the crime.

The theft of the message, its non-delivery or more precisely its arrival in a perverted form was not only breach of a promise of delivery. It was that, of course, but it was more. The theft of the correspondence was a hermeneutic betrayal, a fraud against the principles of love. We can make the point with a play on words. To love is to write, and to write is to love. That is the lesson of rhetoric and of the art of writing. Thus the homonymy of right and writing, of law and writ that we witness in the medieval word *rectorica* that precisely combines rhetoric and right. By the same token the word notary, the term for someone who notes and inscribes letters and symbols was originally a legal designation. What was noted had to be true. That was the law from the beginning. It was the law because society depends upon the truth of its instruments—*de fide instrumentorum* or we have to believe in our codes, our symbols and writing—according to the antique law. It was the law because the notary was a confidant, a trustee of the inner person, of the soul.

The significance of the decision, of the sixty judges, of the numerousness of the Court, lies in its inscription of a first principle. Rhetoric, the rules of just speech, the laws of love precede secular law. No secular law without a prior love of words and the domain of correspondence that attaches to them. On the other hand, love does not depend on law. It precedes it. So one might say, although it also needs to be observed that love is and has its own law. It is a point made through the very charge of the sitting and of the determination to excommunicate the culprits who had purloined the petitioner's message. Theft of the missive was not simply grand larceny, a heinous intrusion upon their intimacy, an undoing of the domain of love; it was also a threat to the constitution of the social. If the passage of intimate messages could not be trusted then no communication was safe, nothing could be believed and neither law nor love, neither intimacy nor polity, would be possible.

We have to be able to believe our instruments and historically that meant faith in the system of messages, in words and their carriers. A later case, Judgement 41 in Martial d'Auvergne's *Judgments of Love* makes the link between writing and loving explicit. The importance of this decision of the High Court of Love is equally signaled by the manner of the case. The Procurator General of Love joined the petitioner in making the complaint. That this was necessary signals again that the matter disputed was essential to the proper functioning of the jurisdiction of love. The facts were the following.

The petitioner was a young man in love. The defendant was a close friend of his, with whom he shared many intimacies. The two men were inseparable and the petitioner placed every confidence in the defendant. He shared the secrets of his soul, including the narratives of his love life. The defendant listened attentively and comforted his friend who suffered much from a distant love or *amour de loin* for a certain very beautiful woman. The defendant seemed to attend most empathically to his friend's suffering and longing. He offered him every aid available to him, his money, his body, his services as a confidant and courier. The defendant eventually elicited the name of the woman from his friend. He then used that knowledge and everything else he had learned about the woman to try to seduce her himself. He courted her, made her promises, gave her gifts, all of which acts were contrary to the laws of love.

The *coup de grace* came in the form of a false letter. The defendant, unbeknown to the petitioner, went to a monk who owed him a favor. He persuaded the monk to forge a letter under the seal and in the name of the petitioner. In this false missive, the petitioner tells the woman that their affair is over. He says that she is no longer important to him; that she is unworthy of his love, and other hurtful, damaging, and utterly false things. None of this, needless to say, remotely reflected the petitioner's sentiments, nor would he ever have conceivably said such things.

The letter was delivered by the monk. On reading it the woman fainted and for a while was sick in bed. She had no way of knowing that the missive was false, she believed the source and suffered as a consequence. The defendant nursed the woman through her illness and in that manner managed to intrude subtly upon her good graces. By the time that the woman had recovered her health, she and the defendant were lovers.

Knowing nothing of the forged letters, indeed being incapable of thinking any such things of his beloved, the petitioner approached her in his usual manner when they next encountered. She turned her back on him and walked away. When he pressed her, she said she would rather burn in hell than give him the pleasure of a single kind word. On subsequent occasions when they met, she and the defendant would publicly mock the petitioner and then hurl abuse at him as he walked away. He could make no sense of her behavior and eventually went to Court to demand an explanation. It was in explaining her anger that the woman produced the false love letter and the present case emerged.

The defendant was ordered to appear in Court. He fled to the sanctuary of the monastery and the case was heard in his absence. After listening to the complaints and reviewing the evidence, the Court judged in favor of the petitioner. The letter was ceremonially brought into Court, shredded and then burned. The woman was ordered to renounce the defendant and to make amends to the petitioner. The defendant was ordered, *in absentia*, to walk barefoot with a torch outside the woman's house and publicly declare that he had falsely, wickedly, and without justification deceived and betrayed his friend. He was to confess his guilt and beg forgiveness. He was then ordered to pay a fine of substantial proportions.

So great was the gravity of this case that the monk was also ordered into Court for his role in the betrayal. There it was declared in his presence, once and for all, that in matters that touch upon love, no one should ever entrust their missions or missives to monks. The monasteries were not the proper avenue of the mixed messages of secular love affairs. If lovers desired not to be deceived then it rested upon them to choose a scriptorium and delivery service appropriate to love.

The decision comes toward the end of the era of gay science and its historical context needs a little unpacking. The medieval monasteries were the original scriptoria for most forms of documentation. Charters, cartularies, writs, and obligations were all originally most likely to be inscribed by professional scribes in the monasteries. The Church kept something of a stranglehold upon the training of scribes and to a large degree upon the production of writings. The faith that was to be placed in instruments was a literal faith in a Christian order of inscription. Capellanus, to take the obvious example, author of the most important early collection of amatory cases, was a chaplain. Abelard and Heloise ended their affair in cloisters. It would not have been surprising that a monk would have inscribed and delivered a love letter. But things changed. The love lyric was also declared heretical, the spiritual and secular laws started to compete with each other, and a domain of mixed or physical love emerged in the face of Church opposition.

Judgement 41 illustrates a shift in the social location of love. Formerly an offshoot of the Church's hold over the laws of Venus or the doctrine of love, the laws of love had over time become an increasingly secular endeavor and the domain of love established its own territory, its own intimate public sphere, its own post and postings. These remain tied up with an earlier doctrine, and love will always be both a spiritual and secular affair, but the emphasis in the case in question has clearly shifted to the need for sites of inscription and modes of delivery that are free of the Church and as yet separate from affairs of state. Neither ecclesiastical nor royal governance were necessary to the passage of desire, indeed they were perceived as impediments. The laws of love belonged to an expanded class of the literate and the literary, defined now as much by competence as by status or position. The laws of love formed their own jurisdiction, they became an alternative relay, a new form of post.

Returning then to the question of the purloined love letter there is a shift between the decision reported by Capellanus and the later Judgment depicted by d'Auvergne. In the earlier law there was a simple theft of a message. A perversion of meaning. Non-delivery of a very personal kind. The confidant abandoned his office and pressed his own claim. In the earlier case, the confidant was an agent of the sender, and the message, the letter, was an oral missive inscribed in the memory of the messenger. In the later case, the confidant employs an intermediary with the power of writing not only to inscribe a false message but also to append a forged seal. What is at stake is more obviously the public sphere of desire and the media of its passage. The personal has become a degree more public. The spheres of intimacy and publicity have mixed in a new way, and the era of the postal relay of love letters is upon us. Love becomes a writing system. A discourse. And that is a much more complex semiotic event than the previous state of affairs. The personal relay of the confidant messenger now comes face to face with the expansion of the laws of love to a more general social terrain. What was a more or less secret, and by and large aristocratic pursuit, shifted into a broader social sphere. Anyone with access to writing could engage in correspondence, in the back and forth of love letters but, as the last case shows, there has to be faith in the instrument, be it scribe or interpreter.

Move to the end of our era, the 1650s and the shift in the mode of the post is close to completion. For the *précieuses*, love was a literary affair and correspondence was its emblematic form. For these advocates of amorous ethics, the love letter was the principal medium of desire. It was both avenue and expression of love, and epistolary hermeneutics; the interpretation of correspondence became the key instrument of the love affair as also of its laws. No gay scientists these, it has to be said. The Jansenists of love were more serious than the troubadours, and more explicitly political than the legally learned authors of *Las Leys d'amors*, but their aesthetic practices and norms were very similar so long as different circumstances are taken into account.

The love letter back then, in the mid-seventeenth century, was the missive form of the love affair, the secret correspondence through which desire reigned. It had something of the ambivalent status of the intimate email today. It was an affective message placed in a public medium. An interiority given its passage by a social host. Then and now the host too has an interest and often will own the message. The rules that govern sending and delivery are thus of crucial importance. They are the constitutional law of the intimate public sphere, they are the norms that govern the passage of desire between the lovers. A case from the very end of our period can illustrate the stakes.

The defendant was an urbane and successful man. He fell in love with the wife of a merchant. He endeavored to spend as much time as he could with the merchant's wife and over time they became enamored of each other. The husband had a head full business and paid little attention to his wife but even he eventually noticed how distracted his wife had become. Matters came to a head when he by chance discovered the couple *tête á tête* in a park. He became obsessed with his wife's infidelity and watched her constantly. When he couldn't watch her himself, he employed a servant to tail her. She was forced by the husband to tell her lover that she would not see him again.

The defendant did not believe her; indeed the enforced separation simply had the effect of inflaming his desire. He had to devise ingenious ways of communicating with her. He took to disguising himself as an old woman begging for alms and when his beloved approached him he would hand her notes complaining of his unhappiness and suggesting ways of meeting. On the occasion in question the wife acceded to his request in an unusual way.

The husband was due to go on a business trip outside of Paris. His wife could not come and so he left his servant with strict instructions to observe her every move. When the day came the defendant was to dress in the official uniform of a courier and await the departure of the husband. Once he had left, the defendant knocked on the door of their house armed with a pile of paper folded to look like letters. The top piece of paper was addressed to the merchant. The servant opens the door and is handed the letter addressed to the merchant. The servant gives this to the wife who then searches unsuccessfully for coins with which to pay the courier. She finds a bill of large denomination and sends the servant out to get change.

Once the servant has left, the wife sends her lover up to her room. She then awaits the return of the servant and tells him that she found some change in another pocket and so she has paid the courier and he has left. She then attends religious service with the servant in tow before joining her lover. The lovers spend the day together. Enraptured, the defendant refuses to leave when night falls. While the advisability of staying is still being discussed, the husband returns. The defendant has no choice but to leave by the window and thence to climb into the garden of a neighbor. The adjoining house is owned by a lawyer and when he discovers the defendant in his garden he challenges him, assuming from his disarray that he is a thief. The defendant cannot explain his presence without betraying his lover and so he remains silent and is arrested and charged.

The wife petitions the Court seeking an order that the defendant, here represented in his absence by a Procurator of Love, be allowed to name her and so escape imprisonment. The Procurator argues that this is inadvisable. The law of love enjoins secrecy where property and secular law are involved. The lover had knowingly taken the risk. He should not sacrifice the petitioner so as to save himself. That would be to prefer *amour propre* or self-love over declared love and that could not be tolerated. Those who take the risks of love must accept the consequences. The Court agreed and the defendant was enjoined to silence. If that seems harsh, we also later learn that the defendant was a friend of the Minister of Justice and that by way of special pleading his sentence was reduced.

The case is complex, though the logic is plain: follow the letter. It is the letter that makes desire possible, it is the letter that gives entry into the space of intimacy, and it is the letter that allows the consummation of love. According to one of the earliest treatises, Estienne du Tronchet's *Love Letters* of 1569, the love letter is indeed the virtue and the necessity of love. The letter has the power to open the space of affection and encounter. Nowhere is that more clearly evidenced than in this thoroughly allegorical case. Here the lover is his own courier. What he carries is a blank page. The folded blank page with a name and address is the archetype of the love letter; it is a salaam or token allowing admission. What the courier in fact carries is himself. He is the bearer of his own desire. The uniform and the letter are first and foremost formal items, pure symbols, empty signifiers that provide the means of transmission, safe relay through public space. After that, after the possibilities made available through correspondence, love is what the lovers do.

The image of the lover as a courier, a postman carrying folded sheets of blank paper again comports very well with the logic of the post. If the story of the purloined letter teaches us that the letter is where you think it is, in the most obvious place, then here the proper construction clearly places the letter in the bed chamber, its message in the bed: blank sheets leading to the sheets plain and simple. Or borrow from Freud: a flourish of the pen was all that was needed. Or some such. What is interesting is that the correspondent is the lover and the letter delivers him to his desire. The letter literally gave the lovers what they long for.

There is also an important matter of legal interpretation raised by the circumstances of this case. The blank letter signified much more, and in a much more real way, than a merely textual missive. One can note initially that to signify nothing is to signify sex, the big O, zero, Shakespeare's vaginal nothing, the path to love. One of the questions raised is that of the relation between the support of the sign and the thing signified. According to the old law, the sign or the image carried by a tablet or canvas, the letters on a page, belong to the artist or author and not to the owner of the tablet. The image painted or the imagination conveyed, either by brush or pen, by picture or words, had priority over the material through which it was transmitted. It was called the doctrine of accession in Roman law, and it entailed that the thing gave way to—acceded to—the image. In our somewhat histrionic case it is very clear that the letter gives way to the person. It is a clear case in point of the antique law. An explicit instance of what du Tronchet had termed the sanctity of desire and so of the precedence of the spirit of love over its material transports. And the same holds true of the love letter that simply signals the desire of one absent through image and word. It is not the paper that in the end matters, it is desire that seeks to get through. That was the theory.

The last point is perhaps not entirely clear. It is a touch esoteric, a little abstract, a mite legalistic. Consider then another example, a case from the annals of the great Jean Donneau de Visé, last name curiously pronounced "weeze ay" according to an old soul I met on the Quai Malaquais some years back, and in any event a veritable hero of the long term of the laws of love.

Again the issue was posed in the context of a married couple. Here indeed we witness the slow movement toward romantic love between spouses. But that is a separate issue. The couple were the assonant Celie and Celian, male and female versions of the same name. Celie was a *précieuse,* a woman of taste and erudition. She was a Latinist and she especially enjoyed conversing about the classics in Latin. Her skill in philology and criticism was well-known and attracted admirers. One such was Thersandre, who after meeting her corresponded with her for some time in fluent Latin. His Latin was good and Celie found herself falling for him because she found him to be "almost as loveable as his Latin." The letters became amorous and Celie took to keeping Thersandre's missives in her chamber.

The husband Celian, who was at that time traveling, received an unsigned note warning him that his wife was in love with one of his friends. Celian decided to investigate and returning home searches for letters in Celie's rooms. His logic is simple. If she is in love, there will be missives, and sure enough he finds a letter left carelessly among her things. The letter, however, is in Latin, a language that is unknown to him. He is none the wiser for his discovery until he recollects that one of his friends, Thersandre no less, is familiar with Latin and can probably be persuaded to translate the missive without exposing Celian's fear that his wife has been unfaithful.

Much to his surprise, Thersandre is subsequently accosted by Celian and asked to translate a letter for him. Surprise gives way to astonishment when Thersandre discovers that the letter is one of his own that has been discovered by his friend, her husband, in her room. He conceals his shock and takes some time to read the letter. He then tells Celian that it is nothing, merely the text of a polemical lecture delivered by the Polish ambassador attacking the policies of the French King. Under the pretext of returning the letter to its owner, Thersandre writes a note to Celie explaining that she may be questioned about the ambassador's speech and engages the relieved husband in conversation until the servant entrusted with delivering the note has returned.

So far so good, but Celie subsequently tires of Thersandre and begins a new correspondence with a younger Latinist, one Cleobulle. Celian again begins to suspect that Célie is having an affair and this time shares his suspicion with his friend Thersandre. The former lover is also somewhat jealous and suspicious. He suggests to Celian that he again purloin one of Celie's letters. This he does, and Thersandre has his suspicions confirmed, Cleobulle's letter is full of romance. Unwilling, however, to divulge this to Celian, Thersandre says that it is indeed a love letter but Celie has not yet acceded to that importuning. Thersandre later confronts Celie and in the process of discussion lets slip that he has read one of Cleobulle's love letters.

Celie throws Thersandre out. She then writes a letter to him in Latin, which she leaves in her room. Celian finds this letter and takes it to Thersandre to translate. The latter reads it and only narrowly avoids becoming apoplectic. The letter pretends to respond to an importunate request of Thersandre's. It berates him for his infidelity to Celian, his betrayal of friendship, and his base attempt to seduce her. Thersandre reads the letter, changes color, and then stammeringly tells Celian that Celie has consummated her relationship with Cleobulle. Pure spite. Celian, however, does not know this. To the contrary, his worst fears are confirmed, and he returns home in a rage to confront Celie.

Celie remains calm. She prizes from her husband that the source of his anger is the letter that Thersandre has just translated. She asks to see it. Reads it slowly, and then tells Celian to go and get it translated by a Professor of Latin she knows at the University. Celian does so and learns that far from being a love letter, the missive in fact exposes Thersandre's attempt to seduce his wife and records her chaste and unblemished reply.

The question of love posed is whether it is Celie or Thersandre who has behaved worst. Which of them is to be held in breach of their promise of love. At first instance Thersandre succeeds, but on appeal it is Celie who is vindicated. She followed her desire and that is justification enough for her new correspondence. Inversely, her new love is certainly no excuse for purloining her love letters. It is the worst of offences against the epistolary realm of love.

The love letters in this last case convey a series of messages. Their theft is equally multifaceted. Start with the untrustworthy Latin. It is a sign of the ethics of love, a marker of entry into the domain of the laws of love. It is a sign of secrecy that will protect the lovers. It is the device that holds them together when circumstances force them to part.

The first rule then is that the letter establishes the virtue of the correspondent, the ethical attraction of the potential lover. It is a site of justice, both the testament and the incident of love. The *précieuses* in particular insisted upon the epistolary character of the love affair. For them it was always a question of the aesthetic discrimination and literary felicity of the correspondent. A man who couldn't write wasn't worth the postage, let alone a tryst or encounter. If they couldn't write, they couldn't love. And similarly if their conversation was flawed then they likely lacked the spirit of love. These were matters for judgment, serious questions to which the latter-day court of the alcove had to provide answers.

Recollect that in the last case Celie fell in love first with her correspondent's Latin and only latterly with his person. If the correspondent knows

Latin and specifically the *ars amatoria*, the erotic verse of the classics, then he or she will of necessity know the Statutes of Love and submit to their jurisdiction. Latin is here a sign of virtue, though obviously it is not the only one. In other cases it would be felicity of vernacular expression, the measure of the meter, the tone of the text, the ode less traveled. Doesn't matter which, the point is that a language is devised as between the lovers and a judgment is formed on the basis of their expression. The rule is set out in detail in Estienne du Tronchet's textbook. The love letter establishes the qualities of the potential lover, their virtue and their passion. No love without letters, no letters without love. That is the maxim and we find it repeated persistently then and now. Each new love is a new correspondence. It is through epistolary exchange that the lovers enter into the domain of love and become subject to its justice. To that we can add that there have to be records, the *lex scripta* of intimacy. These are love's writs, exchanged between the *belle-lettrists'* of desire, each lover an author, each letter a law.

The second rule is that the correspondence be secret. Latin is thus a sign, albeit an archaic sign of the desirability of hiding love from exposure. There are concentric spheres of intimacy but the degree zero is the space between the two lovers. Epistolary space establishes the justice of the plea, the eloquence of the enamorata, and will ideally open on to "express love," encounter and embrace. According to the laws of love the risk of harm to other potential lovers as well as the danger of the lovers being apprehended by a jealous spouse dictates that as far as is possible the letter be encoded. It should come unsigned according to the very earliest laws. In the *Statutes of Love*, enacted in the *Court of Love*, the second law is "Secretly to kepe Councell of Love"; and by the eleventh law "Thy signes for to con [know] ... secretly to bring." Evidence enough that where Latin is used it has as one of its functions the secrecy of the message, and that as far as possible it keeps the lovers' identity concealed. That is at one level because the love letter is for the correspondent's eyes only. It is written for and sent to the lover. It is for the lover to judge it and not for other eyes to scrutinize without cause or invitation. At another level, as an injunction to hide one's desire, it is a slightly curious rule, a period piece, but it does also have a certain continuing resonance in the office affair, in the surprise encounter or *coup de foudre* where it is anyone's guess where the love will lead. There are consequences to exposure and so initially at least it makes sense that the love be kept between the lovers, it is their affair.

The third rule is in many ways the best or at least most contemporary. The lovers must keep writing. If the pen goes dry then love too has run its course. That was the theory. Correspondence was the stuff of the love affair, it is its virtue, its intimacy, and now we learn it is also its duration. The rule is discussed by Francois Callières in his *Lover's Logic*. The letter gives a portrait of the lover. Like a portrait it is also the sign of the lover that can be turned to when the lover is absent. If time threatens to efface the image of the lover from the heart of the beloved, the love letter is the stay or remedy for that erasure of desire. In an ancient definition, the love letter conveys the desire of one absent to the heart without voice. For Callières, correspondence is similarly necessary so as to keep affection aflame, desire present, and love alive. The love letter "unites in an invisible chain what time has suffered to be broken."

Enough norms. Never mind the rules, what about the principles? Don't steal love letters. If you do, then don't read them—it will only do you harm or cause you pain. The law governing purloined love letters indeed turns out to follow closely the much-analyzed logic of Poe's detective story. The missive encodes desire. The letter transmits the soul, the better part, the imaginings of the lover. What then is stolen if the letter is purloined? At one level nothing. A blank piece of paper. Words directed elsewhere, and addressed to another. But then the crime of false letters—what Bartolus terms *crimen falsi*—or the theft of a missive alike concern something more than the letter. What is at issue is greatly in excess of the simple theft of the material of correspondence, the physical substrate of the missive, the paper or words. What matters is not the thing but the image. The crime is against the image, and what is in issue is an assault on imagination, theft of a fantasy. Purloining of an image is a spiritual offence. The proper term for that betrayal of the integrity of epistolary space, for that intrusion upon the domain of love, is sacrilege, a taking of the law of love into your own hands, playing author, pretending to be the correspondent. It is a crime against the state of intimacy as such, for nothing could be worse than arrogating to yourself the signs of a soul that belongs to another.

A final point. Parting words. The relevant theory is that any fraud relating to correspondence, and here specifically the theft of letters, destabilizes not only the relationship in question but also the intimate public sphere as such. The law states that it is through letters that desire is opened up, rendered ethical and subject to justice. For justice to be possible it is necessary to believe in its instruments, the epistolary writs, the love letters themselves. If they are forged or stolen then not only are the lovers brought down, but the very instruments of the laws of love are infracted. Where faith is gone, where the instruments of transmission, the words themselves, are compromised, then likely as not love too will die. Du Tronchet put it best. Love letters are the means of generating love. They facilitate the declaration of desire, the expression of inner inventions and imaginations. They make the intimate visible. As the laws of love dictate, love letters have their own reason. To steal them is to deprive us of that reason and to take away its law.

Figure 5 *Ni mesme la mort* (Not even death)—*Emblemata amatoria* (1620).

4
Contracts of Love

The contemporary meaning of the word contract is somewhat dry and narrow. It tends to refer to a corporate tool, a pre-printed document that lawyers are wont to describe by means of the curious figure of dealings "at arms length." By this they mean that the parties communicate insouciantly at a distance, without touch, rather than, as the choreographic figure of being at arms length might suggest, at the extremity of the ambit of touching. Close, but just out of reach. The modern contract thus circulates generically and it doesn't matter between whom the agreement is made, nor indeed whether it is performed. All that matters is that someone will either do as they promised or be made to pay. Happily, however, such an impersonal notion of distant contracts and their abstract obligations, is a relatively recent concept, a mere vestige of an earlier form, a vague shadow of the contract as practiced within the laws of love.

The older meaning of contract is much more intimate: to contract is to draw together, to relate, and most emblematically of all, to marry. Lovers make promises and there must be faith in promises, trust in agreement or else how could compact govern amity, and contract conquer law? That was what Henry II legislated, and that was the principle that underpinned the lovedays that took the place of royal court and its lawdays throughout much of the middle ages. So allow for just a moment of detail, a hair of the dogma, a whisker of erudition. Go back a bit to the roots of the practice and we find that laws of love were adjudicating agreements, remedying breaches of promise, and invalidating unconscionable terms long before secular law had got beyond the pre-contractual devices of stipulation or unilateral declarations of obligation.

Consider then the word contract. It derives from the Latin *contraho* meaning to draw together. The classical connotation was that of bringing into company, of getting together, of assembling persons or things. Contract was gregarious rather than constricting. In medieval Latin the primary meaning of the word is "to marry," and when the common law author Bracton first refers to contract, his reference is to the "public contract of marriage." That is how it all starts. So there you have it, *in nuce*, in a nutshell, to whit that the art of contract is the art of the primary social bond, the formation of the family, the institution of the intimate public sphere. Marriage has, no question about it, a public and proprietary face but as we have seen throughout, the real action lies in the shadow of the family, in the love affair, in the *alliance d'amours*, or promises of love, that come to be interpreted on lovedays and in the courts of love.

As with commercial contracts we begin, good students that we are, with questions of formation of agreement and then move to matters of interpretation. The contract of love was a formal exchange of promises and it was ideally accompanied by "tears and kisses" in front of witnesses. The compact of love was thus a ritual of amorous possession that was closely aligned to the rite by which individuals took possession of property in front of witnesses by means of "livery and seisin," simply meaning by going on to the land and holding up a handful of earth in front of witnesses. That indicated, symbolically, that this is mine, and will be jealously guarded. By the same token, tears and kisses indicated a mixing of the two bodies, an exchange of fluids that joined the two lovers and mutually marked their souls. As the troubadours put it, there was a bonding that took place through promises but was expressed through the emotive marks of touch. Bernard de Ventadorn, for example, writes of how "it pleased you to grant me such honor that day you sealed your love with a kiss." And Pierre Vidal, similarly promises that "I have put in you all my firm hope, all my heart and all my trust, and made you my lady and my lord." A dramatic declaration, a stringent commitment and, as we shall see, a complicated contract to interpret. Remain, however, with the question of agreement itself. It was through the exchange of promises and then the rite of embracing that the compact was formed.

At the level of doctrine, common law also offered the theory that what we mix ourselves with becomes our property. The fifteenth century Lord Chief Justice Fortescue offered the example of the good honest perspiration that falls to the ground when tilling the soil as justification for claiming the property so tilled as our own. It is ours because we have mixed ourselves with it. It is in me and I am in it. That was the theory. And so for lovers tears and saliva will do the same thing. As the poets put it, I lose my heart. It now exists over there, and his heart inhabits me. The exterior representation of that exchange is the mixing of *pneuma*, of breath and spirit. Put it like this, taste leads to consumption in the theory of kissing. The lips are labile. And tears run in rivulets, thus also marking the fluidity or collapse of a boundary. Joining together, sealing, and so crossing the limit of the body is the signature of desire.

Back to contracts. The promises of love are ideally exchanged in person. The tears and the kisses are reciprocally given. The lovers are joined in the realm of love. They promise to desire each other and can only be freed from those promises if either desire or the lover dies. One or the other, but that was it, no other excuses or grounds for escaping the promise of love. Thus in a case heard before the Court of the Countess of Champagne a woman petitioned the Court to be released from a contract of love by virtue of the seeming desertion of her lover. He had been abroad for over two years. A confidant of the absent lover indignantly opposed her petition on the ground that there was no evidence that the missing lover had abandoned her, nor that he was abroad for anything other than the most noble of reasons, in the service of the State.

The woman's argument was that her lover had gone abroad and had now been overseas in excess of two years. According to the *Code of Love*, if a lover dies, the surviving lover can take a new partner after a two-year period of mourning. Rule 7. Clear as day. And by analogy, someone whose living partner has been away for over two years should surely also, *a fortiori* in the jargon of secular lawyers, have the right to move on? To this she added that not only had her lover been abroad, he had been silent. She had not received a single letter, no messenger had come, neither gift nor greeting from her beloved since he had departed. And so, she suggested, both precedent and reason supported her claim to be set free of her amorous alliance.

The Court heard these and further arguments before withdrawing and then pronouncing the following judgment. Mere absence is insufficient ground for ending a relationship. More is needed to justify such breach of promise. Specifically, clear evidence of infidelity or of some other amorous transgression is required before a lover can legitimately move on and look for another partner. The lover's absence was in this case hardly frivolous. He was engaged in an honorable expedition, a noble cause, and the petitioner should appreciate and support that enterprise. Furthermore, the absence of any letters or messengers did not prove anything. His love might well be too valuable, too precious to entrust to a stranger or risk in a letter. If the messenger betrayed him, then their love would be exposed. If the letter was lost or opened by others, then the secret of their love would fall into potentially harmful hands. So the recommendation of the Court was that the petitioner await further news or the return of her lover. In sum, she should keep her promise, and be faithful to her contract.

Contrary to later secular law, which generally takes the view that you can keep or abandon an agreement indifferently, according to nothing more ethical than a callous calculation of costs, the laws of love dictated that promises should be kept. Faith in the promise was essential to the domain of love. A promise was not nothing. A promise was a sign, it was an act, and constituted a gift. A contract of love was thus an exchange of physically invested or visceral intentions. More lewdly it was a mixing of fluids and desires. Once the exchange had occurred then according to the laws of love the lovers were intertwined in the most literal or physical of senses: I am in the beloved, and the beloved is in me. Him or her, man or woman, who cares? It is in other words the same thing. Loss of property in the self engenders a greater identity, that of the relationship, the community of lovers. It is the space in between, as Martial d'Auvergne later termed it, the felicity of coming together, of being three: I, you, and us.

The contract of love was clearly no small matter. There were numerous social and spiritual risks attendant upon a formal alliance of love. Similarly, granted the degree of commitment, the lovers should not commit lightly. Love is another country, one might say, and things are done differently there. So do not go lightly into that bright space. According to another judgment, this time handed down by the Court of Queen Eleanor of Aquitaine, the contract was the product of the exchange of both words and signs. The two went together or no agreement was formed.

The case involved a knight who sought the love of a noble woman. She refused his advances. Then he sent her some really quite decent gifts and she accepted them with alacrity and something akin to greed. Despite taking the gifts, there was no change in her attitude and she continued to ignore the petitioner's advances. His promises were deflected, his offer refused. He came to the Court and argued that his gifts were obviously tokens of love—they were in accordance with the law's definition of appropriate amorous presents and could only properly be accepted as such. A gift in the service of love, a salaam or loving exchange could not be accepted without also accepting the promise that accompanied it. An interesting argument. The gift was a symbol and could not be kept without also accepting what it signified.

The judgment of Queen Eleanor was in favor of the petitioner. In her opinion the woman was bound either to refuse the gifts offered to her or she should return them. These were not simple donations, they were given with a view to love, they accompanied an offer of relationship.

To accept the gifts but refuse the request was to act unethically. The defendant appeared to have behaved meretriciously and the case was judged accordingly.

As in all matters that attach to or are adjudicated by the laws of love, it is in the end affect that governs and here it is the joy of exchange that determines agreement. An amorous gift is either part of an agreement of love, an affective bargain, or it is a benefit conferred with the intention of engendering or furthering a relationship. It is in such cases given in good faith and must be accepted in such a vein or not at all. If the other party intends no relationship, if no contract is entertained, then the gift must be returned, or in the language of law, restitution should follow. The decision offers an early insight into the doctrine of unjust enrichment in relation to matters of the heart. It is interesting that the doctrine was developed in the laws of love centuries before its advent in relation to benefits conferred in secular contexts. We may indeed argue over whether love conquers law, but it cannot be disputed that love precedes law both as a matter of the history of forms and very often in terms of the substance of precedent. There is no place for unjust enrichment, bad faith profiteering, in the map of the heart. By the same token, if the gift is taken in good faith but things don't work out, no harm is done, no faith is broken, and no restitution should follow. So it was held in a case heard before the Court of the Reformer General of Abuses of Love.

The complaint was laid in respect of an unsuccessful amorous adventure. The petitioner was in love with the defendant. He had on several occasions, when the opportunity presented itself, pleaded his case with her. He had given her numerous gifts: rings, jewels, six yards of the finest damask silk, two gold canes, a statue of the lamb of God in gold, and many other things. He gave her these gifts and she listened to his declarations but as time passed she cooled toward him. She made no promises. A while later she seemed to tire of him and became steadily less receptive to his advances. He asked the Court to order her either to agree to his pleas or to return his gifts.

The defendant argued that the petitioner had proved himself to be immature and unworthy of her love. She argued first that as a matter of principle, a lover who asked for his gifts back was an unspeakable character, unworthy of love, and should be banished altogether from the realm of love. In the alternative, she said that the petitioner, who had endlessly sought to entreat her in public, had put her at risk of exposure, and had acted generally in a gauche and inappropriately extrovert manner. She had listened to his pleas, she had been open to his approaches, but in the end she felt he was too demanding, too needy, and was trying more to buy her affections than to win her heart. Finally, she pointed out that she had never asked for any gifts and indeed had not wanted to take them but for the tireless persistence of the petitioner. He had made her accept these trinkets and other goods. She had done so in good faith and had even had the cloth he had given her made into a dress that she had worn in his honor and out of affection for him. Eventually, however, she had tired of his advances.

Relying upon the earlier case law, the petitioner argued that when gifts were given in the pursuit of love, they should only be accepted if the recipient intended to enter a relationship. Anything else was bad faith and should be punished. At the very least she should return the tokens of a love that left her cold.

The Procurator of Love joined the action and argued that love could not be bought or sold. Gifts were one thing, promises were by and large another. The petitioner was at fault. He had acted improperly in supposing that gold, silver, or jewels could buy the heart.

The defendant replied that she had wanted nothing of the petitioner. She did not care for him or for his gifts. No one could persuade her to love with money or gifts. Not all the jewels in the world could alter the inclinations of her heart.

The Reformer General held that the defendant was free to keep the cloth and silk that had been used to make dresses but should return the statue, the rings and jewels. That was not all. The petitioner was also condemned. He had tried to buy the love of the defendant and that was a crime. His offence was against love itself and he was ordered to pay damages in the amount of double the value of the gifts he had given.

The decision was appealed to the High Court of Love and was reversed in part, upheld in other particulars. As regards the behavior of the petitioner, the High Court fully agreed that he had behaved badly and that his plea was redolent of an attempt to buy love with money. That was objectionable and the sentence to pay damages should stand. As regards the female defendant, the conclusion of the Court was that she had behaved justifiably. She had not asked for the gifts, nor had she promised to love him in return for them. She had kept an open mind, she had listened to the petitioner, and she had in good faith eventually turned him down. She was at liberty to keep his presents and do as she wished with them. There was no reason for restitution.

It is an important decision. It renders with clarity the distinction between commercial contracts and amorous compacts or the liaisons of lovers. Both are exchanges. Both indeed are bargains in which promises are reciprocated but only in contracts of love is the promise its own consideration. It is both aspiration and substance, word and thing. The High Court's decision makes clear what was perhaps only implicit in the judgment of Queen Eleanor's Court, namely that the promise is greater than the reward, and that an amorous contract is formed by the exchange of will and not by the transfer of things. Thus bad faith could be grounds for returning things given outside of any promise or contract, but where things have been given in good faith and taken without any venal intent, then like words they must lie where they fall. Love is not merchandise, promises of love must be given freely and that means in this instance free of ulterior bargain, bribes or other venal lures. Gifts within the domain of love are tokens of affection or signs of desire but they are not given and cannot be accepted as any kind of means of purchasing affection or reducing love to money.

The upshot is that amorous contracts are formed differently. Like the old spousals *de futuro*, or contract of engagement, they are all promise, election and volition rather than transfer or *quid pro quo*. The different rules governing formation are matched too by distinct rules of interpretation. The hermeneutics of the courts of love offer much by way of invention and eloquence of determination.

The usual form of dispute relating to contractual agreement concerns whether or not performance matches what was promised. Thus if we agreed that builders are to use pipes of Reading manufacture in the house being constructed then failure to do so will be breach of contract. The offending party will have to pay, unless that is they can show that the pipe used was of the same quality as the pipe promised. In which case they are free and clear because the tribunal will point out that in effect the promisee got what he bargained for. Substantial performance is sufficient because it is not the letter but the spirit that must be followed, not the form but the intention. That is true too of the laws of love. More so, in fact, because their principles are all to do with equity, with fairness and its proper consolations.

A case concerning livery and seisin, meaning transfer and possession in love came before the Court of the Women Counsellors of Love in the Chamber of Pleasure. A fine sounding forum, indicative indeed of a subsisting hedonic space within law. The complaint was brought by a lover against his beloved for failure to keep her promises. The arguments were as follows.

The petitioner complained that he and the defendant had not long ago entered a contract of love. They had performed the traditional ceremony of amorous liaison before witnesses and had sealed their commitment with tears and kisses. The promises thus solemnly exchanged were that they would love each other their entire lives, until death, and that nothing would come between them. To ensure that their love lasted, the couple also promised that they would never do anything that would displease the other, and that what one wanted the other would consent to. Such were their freely given promises. A fair exchange but how, one might wonder, were the terms to be put into practice?

The petitioner's complaint to the Court was that soon after the exchange of these promises the defendant had started behaving quite strangely toward him. When he encountered her in public and greeted her warmly, she acted as if she had never met him before. She would pay scant attention to him in company and seemed much more interested in talking warmly with other men than conversing with him. It seemed to him now that everything he said and did displeased her. When he approached her, she would move away. When he became flirtatious or playful she would push him away. His advances seemed to annoy her, and she would mock his protestations of love. All of these rebuffs, he argued, were wrongs and constituted breaches of her promises.

The petitioner's legal argument was that the contract of love was predicated upon reverence for the lover. The meaning of the promises was dependent upon an implicit commitment to treating the beloved as the exclusive object of one's attention and affections. The promise to have no other lover implied not only a physical fidelity but also an affective loyalty. This meant that the lover would only have eyes for their beloved. Whatever was said between them was to receive the greatest attention. When meeting, the warmth of their greeting should exceed that offered to others. By the same token the complainant argued that whatever the enamorata said should be attended to as the most interesting, amusing, and insightful of statements. Inversely, the lover should pay relatively little attention to the jokes or conversations of other men.

The defendant replied that the first and only principle of liaison was that love be voluntary, a product of pleasure and joy and nothing else. Love did not know duty. The relevant maxim was to be taken from Cicero *amor enim voluntarius est*: love is rooted only in desire. Basing her argument on this classical principle, she argued that it would be wrong to feign the affections that the complainant wanted. If he bored her or displeased her then she should be free to express her disinterest just as if she found others interesting, pleasing or witty she should be free to enjoy that too. The petitioner, she said, was interpreting her promises of love much too seriously. He was becoming too wrapped up in himself and his thoughts and so giving way to unrealistic fantasies and rather paranoid imaginings.

The contract of love, according to the defendant, should be interpreted in hedonic fashion. Its purpose was to improve the spirits and to increase the enjoyment of love. It should be performed in that manner, according to the principles of desire, and thus she was not only free to accompany others, she should be encouraged to enjoy youthful flirtations and witty exchanges. The law of love, she claimed, clearly dictated that following one's desire was the greatest of amorous goods. The contract of love was an agreement and not a form of slavery. It depended upon her will and if that changed then so too must her promises be reinterpreted in light of that change. She could not be expected to love the petitioner forever if her heart or pleasure dictated otherwise. As the petitioner had rapidly proven himself to be rabidly possessive, unreasonably jealous and annoyingly dull, she was well within her rights to ignore him and indeed to send him away until such time as he appealed more to her. She argued finally that his complaint was itself a breach of his promises. It displeased her and so infracted the spirit of their agreement.

In his reply, the petitioner repeated that the defendant had not kept her word and so was in breach of her amorous agreement. To this he added that he did not wish to prevent her enjoying the company of others but he did ask that he be greeted as special and assured that she loved him more than her other friends. As to his complaint itself breaching the agreement, he pointed out that she had breached first and it was her infidelity that had given rise to his petition.

The Women Counselors of Love then heard 12 witnesses speak to the relation between the parties. After the testimony had been heard, after questions and cross-examination of the parties, the Court judged in favor of the defendant. The petition was poorly formulated and legally weak. He was unreasonably depressed and his demands were excessive and overbearing. The defendant should love as she pleased without fear of promissory sanctions or of contractually imposed duties. That was the affective right of all lovers; that was the freedom of the heart that the *Code of Love* promised.

The decision was appealed to the High Court of Love. Here the arguments were heard again and the Court examined further proofs of their promises. Gifts that had been exchanged, a gold necklace in the form of tears that the defendant had given him and that he always wore, a gold charm in the shape of a heart that he had given her, dresses and other clothes that had been exchanged, letters that had been written. All these and more were introduced as evidence of a loving relationship. In light of such evidence the Court amended the earlier judgment. The complainant was correct in claiming that the defendant had denied their love and so broken her promises. In entertaining visits and accepting gifts from other men she had overstepped the boundaries of the promises she had made to the petitioner and had in effect evacuated the agreement. The Court now declared that the liaison was officially terminated and costs were awarded to the petitioner.

The contract of love promises priority to the beloved. It is a subjective commitment, a symbolization of desire as well as a declaration of faith. It does not preclude disparate pleasures, nor the company of others, but it does limit such enjoyment and exchange within the bounds of the promise to keep the beloved foremost among friends. In treating others as potential suitors, and in accepting secret visits and gifts that fell within the declared definition of tokens of love, the defendant had acted contrary to the spirit of their agreement. The point is an interesting and important one with respect to the interpretation of intimate contracts.

The defendant was not wrong to claim that love entails freedom. Nor was she in error in asserting that the purpose of a contract of love was to symbolize and seal a hedonic relationship. If the pleasure dried up then true enough the relationship had failed and in time could be terminated. Desire governs all. She was also correct in claiming that it would be wrong to treat the agreement of love as a form of servitude. The lovers retain their independence. Their agreement is based upon mutual desire; its interpretation is according to reciprocal affections. All that could be accepted by the Court but with one limitation. The agreement entailed that the parties never act in a way that would threaten the intimacy between them. According to the law of love, the contract creates a space in between, a third place as it were, a realm of relationship that endures between the parties but does not belong to and cannot be defined by either one alone. The space in between is precisely a shared realm of affect, a domain in which imaginations and other energies can grow. It was in acting contrary to that space in between, in behaving as if there was no shared intimacy, no zone of mutual imagination that the defendant had broken the agreement.

The contract of love is an agreement of principle and its interpretation is a matter of degree. Just as an aside, another case heard before the Court of Flowers concerned a similar point but in a lesser degree. The parties were young lovers and had formally sworn to be faithful to each other according to the laws. The dispute arose because of the behavior of a female lover in relation to other friends.

The petitioner complained that despite her promise to give him her heart, despite her protestations of loyalty, her solemn oath that there would be none but him, it seemed that she was easily distracted by other young men. She continued to enjoy the company of others, she would entertain, and most threatening of all she would accept gifts of flowers, fresh bouquets, exotic orchids, foreign floral designs and more from other men. He wanted the Court of Flowers to forbid her to wear, disport or accept any flowers except those that he had given her.

The defendant woman claimed that she had behaved joyfully, sociably, amiably even, but had in no way broken the spirit of her agreement. She was happy, and she shared that happiness in her encounters. That was all to the greater good of the cause and if anything should make her more desirable to the petitioner and agitate his amorous fantasies anew. All told, her behavior should be commended. The purpose of the agreement was to expand their love, augment their desire, and increase the intimacy between them. If the knock on effect of that was exuberance, intensity, flirtation and even a little charge in her encounters with others, then that was all to the erotic good.

The Marquis of Flowers deliberated and held that the contract could not properly be interpreted as precluding the pleasures of social interaction. The promises that the defendant had made did not prevent her from enjoying herself. She was free to laugh, to play, to wear violets, to carry flowers, to accept bouquets as licit incidents of jovial interaction. She was free to please herself in entertaining and being entertained and none of this was prohibited by the promises she had exchanged with the petitioner. Her agreement was to be interpreted liberally and loosely because the contract of love was a civil commitment and should be understood both lightly and purposively. Flowers after all are a currency of communication, of civil exchange in the realm of love and should be accepted as such and no more.

Contrary to modern legal wisdom, the contract of love was not to be understood as being "all in the detail." Remember St. Paul and the Christian doctrine of love? The letter kills but the spirit gives life. Not a bad metaphor in fact for the principle of amorous agreement: insufflation, kissing draws relationship onward, it gives life to desire and so long as that possibility between the couple is maintained then they are free to indulge in whatever pleasure or company they wish or in the more ancient terms, they could play as they listed. It was not the minutiae, the *ipsissima verba* or very letter of the agreement that was in issue but rather the bigger picture, the third place, the intimate space in between the lovers, the spirit of the agreement itself both as it touched and as it allowed for touch between the parties. It was the amorous principle of agreement that had to be maintained and the details counted only insofar as they acted upon the principle of affective commitment itself. It is a point that is well illustrated in another decision involving an action for rescission of a contract of love.

The action was brought in the Court of the Minister of Justice in matters of Love. The petitioner and defendant were lovers. The complaint was that the contract was usurious or as we would now put it, the bargain was unequal, and the agreement unconscionable. The petitioner argued that in matters of love both reason and law prohibit the exploitation of either party. Desire makes us vulnerable and can lead us into unfair bargains. That was what had happened, so he claimed, in the instant case.

The petitioner complained of love at first sight. He had become enamored of the defendant at their first meeting. In the throws of desire, enraptured by the sight of her, he had sought to do anything and everything he could to win her good graces. He had showered her with gifts and gratuities. He had made numerous promises. In particular, he had sworn and obligated himself to do the following. Every public holiday he promised that he would come early in the morning with a group of minstrels and wake her with a serenade. He would then give her a hat made from the finest silk. Each first of May he would give her a new dress in whatever color she chose. He promised that every month he would bring her a new frock made to her design. All this he had promised and faithfully performed, for a very long time, to the letter.

Now he was tired of his commitments and sought release on the basis that while he had loyally and willingly carried out his promises, she had given him next to nothing in return. For all his labor and ardor he had received the recompense of a single kiss. He claimed it would be quite unfair to insist upon any further performance. He should be released.

The petitioner based his argument upon the inequality of the exchange. He had promised a great deal, and had performed for several years. It was hard to find minstrels, it was expensive to hire them and it was both tiring and often dangerous to his health to be outside in all weather to serenade the dawn outside his lover's rooms. Similarly, dresses were costly, and the services of tailors had grown in expense. All of this in return for a solitary kiss seemed like the worst of bargains, indeed like no bargain at all.

The defendant took a different view. She argued that the petitioner was quite mistaken. The pleasures of love had to be earned. It took time, care, and attention on both sides. That said she did not feel that she had unduly gained from the bargain. And this for three reasons. First, she had not asked for anything. The petitioner had pressed these promises upon her, he had pleaded with her to accept his offerings, his tokens of love, and she had eventually agreed. Second, what was promised in matters of love should be performed in a spirit of generosity and neither time nor adverse circumstance should diminish one iota the pleasure that the petitioner should take in performing these services. The greater the burden, the better its representation of desire. And then finally, and most crucially, the tokens of love, these merely material gifts, were symbols of an interior affection, a volition or commitment that exceeded all property and was of far greater value than base goods or venal intentions. He got what he wanted and it made him want more. That is the very definition of a successful kiss. She concluded as follows.

The kiss that she had given the petitioner could not and should not be measured against either the services or the things that he had given her. A kiss, freely given, accompanied by the heart, was worth more than all of the goods in the world. It was literally priceless because it betokened joy, the end and purpose of all love. The kiss was the ultimate symbol of affect within the domain of love. It was a spiritual entity, an aspect of the soul, and it signaled a desire that transcended property and promised much more, an affective space and intimacy in between the lovers. The kiss, and here the classics can be quoted, is the greatest of all goods that can pass between humans. It is to be prized above all mundane measure, it has no market value, it is incomparable and cannot be bought or sold, bargained with or assigned a numerical status in the accounting of love. It is its own beginning and its own end, sufficient in itself, utter and complete in its own expression.

The arguments so heard, judgment was given for the defendant. In the law of love it was plain, a matter of first principles in fact that the kiss circulated according to an economy of its very own. It was a good in itself, indeed the greatest of goods and should be recognized as such. Thus the kiss bestowed was more than adequate compensation, better indeed than what the petitioner had given and it mitigated against the honor of love to dispute the worth of the defendant's embrace. The Minister of Justice's decision was affirmed on appeal.

The logic of the case is highly significant. The promises that lovers make are to be interpreted according to the extent to which they augment desire and so draw the lovers together. The formal contract of love had as its founding principle the symbolization, witnessed and sealed, of a space of desire and possibility of joy as between the two lovers. These were promises that were to be kept according to the spirit of agreement and not by way of observance of the letter. By the same token, the contract of love was to be interpreted according to the mood of the promises and the tone of performance. Their measure was the fulfillment of their purpose, their contribution to the possibilities of extending relationship and nothing more.

The core of the amorous contract is the value of the promise of love. The promise is to be interpreted in such a way as to give sustenance to the desire that underpins it. So too the cases amply illustrate that it is this libidinal purpose that drives the development of doctrine. Insofar as affect is generally seen as being outside the market and intangible it has to be the promise rather than the exchange that is the subject matter of interpretation. What matters is not the accumulation of wealth but the progress and expansion of relationship, of the space of desire between the parties and anything that falls short of that, anything that threatens to diminish desire or negate love will be condemned.

Returning to the earlier case law and the Court of the Countess of Champagne, the point can be made by reviewing the very first judgment of love reported from her Court. The first case is of course exemplary. It is definitive in principle of what is to follow and it is in consequence most appropriate that it addresses precisely this question of what a lover promises when she promises and how it is to be interpreted.

The case concerned unrequited love. The petitioner was besotted with the defendant. He became obsessed with her and even though she refused his advances he continued to suffer the pangs of love. Eventually she acceded to his pleas in the following manner. She told her suitor that she was aware of his suffering and acknowledged his persistence. She then said that the condition of winning her love was that he make her a firm and unbreakable promise to do whatever she demanded. He was also and equally to promise that if he ever in any way broke this promise he was to be utterly deprived of her love. He agreed to this and made the promise. The defendant immediately ordered him to abandon his quest for her love and never again to sing her praises in the company of others.

The lover kept his promise and struggled to remain silent. He succeeded in keeping his word for several months until he was present at a discussion in which he heard some other women gossiping about his beloved, slandering her name, and lowering her reputation. At first he held his tongue but eventually he broke down and harshly rebuked the vile calumniators. He refuted their insults and defended her name vociferously. When she heard what had happened, the defendant informed the petitioner that he was from then on to be wholly deprived of her love. All hope was ended because he had broken his promise.

The Countess of Champagne held that the agreement was far too punitive and was badly made on the part of the defendant. She had held out the prospect of love and had bound him to her through an agreement that should never have been abused in the manner she devised. Her potential lover had done nothing wrong. He had defended her name in public and in a thoroughly admirable manner. In that the purpose of the agreement was to facilitate love, the defendant had acted wrongfully and judgment was given accordingly against her.

Two principles of interpretation seemingly emerge and both are unusual. The first is that while lovers are free to promise anything at all, including the harshest of penalties and the most exquisitely painful delays to love, all these promises are to be interpreted *ab amorem* or through love. This means, as in the last reported case, that where promises potentially have deflationary or apotropaic consequences they are to be interpreted otherwise and in accordance with the furtherance of love. The most outrageous seeming amorous agreements are perfectly valid, so long as they meet the single threshold requirement of being amenable to a good faith interpretation that offers or expands the possibility of love. Validity, in other words, was not the issue. The question was not whether, as in modern law, there was consideration or cause for the promises but rather and only whether the exchange of commitments could be interpreted as envisaging a space of future relationship, of desire, of joy as between the promising pair.

The second principle is a development, though a subtle one, of the first. In general language we are held to our promises because of the intention or volition that they express. This is in the end a singular view of agreement because it depends only upon what the promisor manifests in his or her promise. The conditions of exchange are simply conditions of enforcement; they are not the criteria by which the promises are interpreted. Commitment is abstract and singular in secular law but not at all so according to the laws of love. Under the latter and more amorous principles, the promise is everything, but it is everything to the other. Put it like this, it is nothing in itself but rather depends wholly upon its rapport with and meaning for its recipient.

It is a radical theory. According to the laws of love an agreement is to be interpreted according to a theory of response. This departs the normal scene of legal interpretation. Utterances are usually gauged to enunciation. What the speaker means is the criterion that is manipulated to interpret a promise or other statement. This can involve analysis of the status of the speaker, the site of enunciation, institutional, or professional support for the statement but it will seldom incorporate attention to what the auditor wanted to hear. According to the cases of love this addresses the question of interpretation backward. What truly matters is the future of the relationship, the project, and so the first criterion of interpretation should be the question of reception. What do the words mean to their recipient? How will the beloved hear these promises? What might this mean to a lover? The question of interpretation then depends not upon what was intended but upon what was received.

A last example from the later code of Coquillart's *New Laws*. It is a curious case moved before the Court as a disputed question of love or *quaestio amoris*. A married woman is keen to have an affair and becomes enamored of an eligible young man. Concerned about keeping her love secret, she enters an agreement with her chambermaid. The chambermaid, and recollect this case is being heard circa the end of the fifteenth century, is permitted to romp—to kiss, hug, embrace, and touch—with this potential lover in a secret place. The question is whether this is an enforceable contract, a legitimate pact? Should the chambermaid be entitled to insist upon enjoying herself according to the agreement or should she be restrained on moral grounds? The answer given is that while the old laws would have viewed this agreement as dubious, the new laws interpreted such a pact purposively and generously. In matters of love, agreements were not to be interpreted *stricti iuris*, or according to the letter of the moral code, but rather according to desire. The agreement was entered into for good reason, to protect the secrecy of the lovers, to guard their honor and so expand the possibilities of their relationship. For these reasons the contract was held to be good and enforceable.

The case is an interesting example of the flexibility or even eloquence of the laws of love. They allowed for exceptions. The rigor of strict law, *dura lex* as they called it, was to be mitigated by *benignitas* or kindness. Everything was to be interpreted according to the cause of love, the law of libidinal economy or *nomos* of desire. In such terms or enwrapped in the hermeneutics of desire, the function of the contract of love is to generate spaces of intimacy. These are the windowless sites of encounter, the alcoves, the dressing rooms, the corridors and parlors, the spaces of passage and abandonment that allow for amorous openings. The amorous compact functions to establish a zone of intimacy, a hidden space between lovers and potential lovers. Indeed all lovers are also potential lovers because eros has to be regenerated, imagination deepened, fantasy repeated, mind and body opened. For this to happen requires a zone of intimacy, the availability of spaces of communication and caress.

The *alliance d'amours* draws the parties together; it contracts a space between the two and then interprets their agreement from the perspective of the zone of intimacy and imagination that exists between them. The question to be posed in interpreting the agreement is thus not, or at least not immediately, what was intended or indeed what was said in any generic sense but rather how can this promise be heard so as to fuel fantasy and to augment or help intimacy grow. It is a matter then of using the contract to construct a world, a hidden yet licit space of desire, a shadow zone where minds and bodies open to each other.

How ever thou the Viper take,
A dang'rous hazzard thou doſt make.

ILLVSTR. XXXIX. Book. 4

THis *Figure* warnes us, that wee meddle not
With matters, whereby nothing may bee got,
Save *harme* or *loſſe*; and, ſuch as once begun,
Wee may, nor ſafely *doe*, nor leave *undone*.

Figure 6 *Utcunque* (However)—George Whither, *A Collection of Emblemes Anciente and Moderne* (1635).

5
Amorous Wrong by Words

According to the *Edicts of Love*, a set of amorous ordinances promulgated in Paris in the late 1660s, the greatest of all the wrongs against love was nonchalance. Lack of concern, insouciance or indifference distanced the lovers from each other and blinded them to the delicacies of attention, the patience and care that erotic liaison requires. Nonchalance, literally lack of heat, not only meant that the heart had grown cold, and the ear waxed over, but it also reflected an inattention to love that the *Edicts* condemned in terms of a mental slackening, a loss of intelligence, a stupidity that was both shameful and disassociative.

The *Edicts* were promulgated at the very end of our epoch. They were in large part a response to the Fronde, the French Civil war of the mid-seventeenth century, and that perhaps explains why the principal torts, the delicts of desire that they sought to remedy concerned indelicate love, lack of eloquence, and a general tendency to prefer physical consolation to the art of building and sustaining love through conversation. Consummation without relationship was depicted as an oxymoron, it was denounced as debauchery, and dismissed as mere venereal amusement without art or inspiration. Love was engendered otherwise, through the slow growth of tenderness, through time spent tête à tête, and more generally through observance of the proper procedures of love, the rules of amorous rhetoric, the art of engendering erotic inclinations.

There were 28 Edicts and all of them were directed at remedying the decline in erotic manners, the loss of style. Of particular concern was the tendency toward episodic physical attachments that lacked not only duration but also respect. According to Edict 12, all attachments that failed to observe the proper stages of coming to know the other, that omitted the moral necessity of attention to intimacy were condemned as lacking in amorous character, as being "in the highest degree distasteful" and to be repudiated as "shamefully nonchalant." The *Edicts* here reinstate one of the primary principles of erotic art, the conjunction of the lyrical and the legal, a care for words that translates also into concern for the subject of love.

The laws of love had always required much more than a general *caritas* or love of the world, they dictated delicacy, and ordained that the lovers follow the protocols of liaison, meaning that they take time, offer attention, and eventually, through the long term of encounter and conversation come to know the heart of the beloved. At the core of the love affair was a genuine fondness, a care for the hidden desires and inarticulate needs of the other. Enjoyment of love might have a pinnacle in physical consummation but that was the end, the repeated end, of a long process of learning to attend to and care for the pleasure of the other. Consummation came as a climax, as the expression of love when words finally and briefly ran out. Note then that physical enjoyment comes after words and not before them. It is the end of conversation and not its substitute or displacement. That was the thrust of the courtly lyric, the subject of the promulgations of the Gay Consistory, and the prime concern of the *Edicts of Love*. This duty of concern, the obligation of intimacy, the requirement of attention to the protocols and other procedures of the art of love can be traced to the very beginnings of the tradition.

The love affair was from early on defined as being a work of art, a matter of eloquent self-expression governed by the rules of rhetoric and the principles of poetic presentation. Love was first an affair with language, a poetically defined adventure, and its laws were directed to keeping the space of words open. Take an early example, a *tenson* reported by Bertolme Zorzi. It records a dispute between lovers over the use of words. The plaintiff complained that the defendant had been indiscreet. He had "babbled" about her and specifically, in singing her praises, had let slip for all to hear that she had granted him her favors. Such a confession was dangerous to her reputation and harmful to the secrecy of love.

In his defense the man argued that the complaint was unfounded. He had acted joyfully, he had done no more than praise his lover and she was wrong to listen to the rumors that those jealous of love or protective of convention will always spread. To give credit to slander was to detract from the intimacy and imagination of love. Zorzi reports that the *tenson* was resolved in favor of the loquacious lover: it was held that he had neither babbled nor betrayed the secrets of love. He had been over-zealous perhaps, indiscreetly passionate maybe, but if desire led to an outpouring of words, to an excess of poetry praising the beloved it was blameless. He should be excused his excess. There was no evidence that the defendant intended anything other than to give expression to his love and as the lawyers put it back then *animus injurandi* or intent to harm was a condition of any action for a wrong caused by words.

Zorzi's case illustrates well the paradox or double bind of the courtly lover. The art of love is embodied in eloquence, rhetorical skill and expression, an efflorescence of words, and yet at the same time secrecy was essential to the successful pursuit of love and to the conduct of love affairs. By the time of the publication of the *Precepts* and *Code of Love* in the late twelfth century, the dual axioms of secrecy and expression, of discretion and care, structure the import of amorous law. The first of the *Precepts of Love* reported by Capellanus enjoins lovers to be generous. They should give, and that includes giving praise and opening to words. It is also clear, however, from the *Precepts* and from the *Code* that secrecy is equally essential to the duration of love. The lover is enjoined to fidelity and this includes not exposing the secrets of love because, Rule 13 of the *Code* declares: "Love does not often survive being voiced abroad."

The tension of the *tenson*, the paradox of the *Precepts*, can be explored further by looking to the later formulation of the law in the Statutes of Love. The first substantive Statute dictates the lover "... Secretly to kepe / Councell of love, nat blowing every-where / All that I know ..." and further enjoins that "slaunder" be exiled. So stipulated, one might imagine the Statutes to favor circumspection or at the most a taciturn public recognition of the pleasures and pangs of love. Not so. By Statute 4 lovers are ordered "... To purchace ever to here, / And stiren folk to love, and beten fyr / On Venus awter, here about and there." Of which one could plausibly remark that if love is spread "here about and there" the danger of exposure is necessarily increased. Indeed how hard is it, as medieval cautionary love tales were so fond of pointing out, to follow a noisy lover to the source of his or her expressions?

A partial solution is offered by Statute 11: " ... Thy signes for to con / With y and finger, and with smiles soft, / And low to cough, and always for to shon, / For dred of spyes, for to winken oft, / But secretly to bring a sigh a-loft," and so on. The signs of love were motions of the eye, wiggles of the finger, soft coughing, winking, puckering of the lips, and the like. Love was best encrypted or kept out of the domain of obvious visibility. When making public declarations of love it was best to erase all markers of identity, to hide the names and to stir up affect by suggestion and flirtation. The nominate eloquence of love, the true words, were best kept for zones of intimacy: for the conversations of the corridor, the verbals of the vestibule, the orality of the alcove. Failing that, if such spaces are unavailable, the law dictated that the lovers adopt the airy and innominate code of the courtly lyric in which the beloved is praised in conventional form: round cheeks, full lips, generous curves, easy blushes, golden hair, white skin, full breasts, and more. You've read that kind of thing and, allowing for changes in the cultural perception of beauty, it still gets written. And on the other side, less often perhaps, convention dictates of the male lover that he is tall, dark haired, with aquiline nose, fleet of foot, bold and strong. Either way, the altar of Venus is there for the taking, and love's praises are sung.

The initial duty of care is that of attention to words and to the consequences of enunciation. By the date of the *Edicts* this has come to be formulated in terms of the art or aesthetic of conversation—the "air galant" of Madeleine de Scudéry—but it was always the case that words, the usages of love, were the messengers of desire, the outward markers of erotic attachment, prize and wrong. The duty to take care of the beloved, to protect and praise love singly and severally, nominally and notionally was evidently law from early on. A duty to care, to attend, also necessarily implies the possibility of breach, the danger of nonchalance and other torts of desire, which start of course with the harms caused by words.

The Court of the Ladies of Gascony was convened to hear a particularly heinous case. A lover had willfully and basely revealed the most intimate secrets of his love. He had exposed the name of his lover and according to the report given by Capellanus, "the whole army of Love" demanded that his transgression be punished to the maximum so that no precedent for such dereliction of duty be set for others to follow. A unanimous Court decreed that the defendant be banished forever from the domain of love. He was to be utterly deprived of all hope of future love and whenever present in society was to be an object of contempt and ridicule. If any woman ever defied this decree, as for example by giving him her love, she too was to be banished and subject to the hostility of every woman that she subsequently encountered.

The harm of exposure was not simply that of revealing the name and intimate details of an affair but also that of bad conversation or offensive use of words. The remedy was similarly discursive and symbolic. The offender was to be subjected to the *risus acri*, to ridicule and ostracism. The offence constituted a harm to the lover whose name was revealed but it was also an infraction of the *Code of Love* and was dangerous to the very basis of the art. If we use the proper legal terminology for this kind of harm, his words constituted both *infamia facti* or allegation of an immoral life and *infamia canonica* or a spiritual crime. In that he could not but have intended to harm his lover, banishment, the amorous equivalent of excommunication—amorous outlawry—was the appropriate injunction. The women of the Court were done with this dangerous braggart, this incontinent knight.

Being a little philosophical about it, one might say that just as there is a sincerity condition for serious speech to be possible, so too there is a felicity condition of erotic eloquence. This can be defined in terms of the levity or *bel esprit* of love, meaning a knowledge of its laws, an appreciation of its figures of proper expression. It is what I coined as *rectorica*, the juridical principle of gay science, which proposes that the best speech, indeed just speech is the most felicitous. In praising a lover, in writing letters, or in speaking well of desire rhetorical appropriateness dictates the proper use of figures of speech that will encode the name or protect the parties. Erotic felicity means poetic skill. Recollect that according to the rules set out in the *Laws of Love* and repeated in the Statute of 1400 it was oratorical ability that qualified the judges to determine disputed questions of the heart. Poetic competence was what allowed for the proper interpretation of the law.

Moving forward in time, chronographically, from the Gay Consistory and *Las leys d'amor* to the slightly later judgments recorded in Mahieu le Poirier's *Court of Love* we can observe with a certain glee that the very first of the complaints of amorous injustice heard, to the accompaniment of smiles, "joy, and laughter," by the Bailiff of Love concerns again this matter of the proper use of words. A jealous man accuses his lover, and all women, of being unfaithful, deceitful, and dangerous. He asks the Court to acknowledge the criminal extent of women's capacity to destroy men and ends by requesting that the Court follow local custom and sever the offending woman's nose.

It is an extreme and aggressive plea. It causes the Bailiff to blush and he subsequently pronounces a judgment that roundly condemns the complainant. Only extreme malice could have motivated the plea and only the malicious would listen to such calumny against a lover and love itself. The complaint was adjudged false and badly made. The complainant had slandered his lover. He had "lied through his teeth." So held, and it is worth pointing out that this judgment establishes the condition of possibility of the subsequent decisions. All are predicated upon a respect for the intimacy of attachment and the honesty and honor that subtend desire. Just to repeat this point, to delay momentarily so as not to have passed on too quickly, the key consideration is that the libidinal economy of the love affair is predicated upon a willingness to accept the art and other protocols of love in good faith. If love is justice in speech, erotic eloquence, intensity maintained over time, then any act or assumption that attacks the intimate space of this rhetorical possibility is unjust and should be condemned.

The same crucial point can be made by observing that poetry is linguistically complicated. Erotic eloquence is highly figurative. The lover oftentimes cannot point too directly to the enamorata and the symbolism of expression is greatly increased when it takes the form of writing, of notes, gifts, and correspondence. What has to be remembered is that this rhetorical inscription of love, the use of signs to encode expression is itself in large measure an erotic device, a manner of creating a zone of intimacy within a generally recalcitrant if not always directly hostile public sphere. It is a point that can be made by reference to another decision of the Bailiff of Love in what is described explicitly as a great cause. The question posed is whether, out of loyalty, one should hide love. Time and circumstance obviously influence the answer to such a question, but posed as a matter of doctrine the answer is clear. Love should be expressed, the benefits and pleasures of eros should wherever possible be extolled and the social space of desire expanded.

That or something to that effect. What the Bailiff of Love states is formulated cautiously. Love should be hidden from those who will gossip or slander the lovers. As the *Code of Love* anciently declared, secrecy is desirable where disclosure will be dangerous or the lovers harmed. By the late fourteenth century when Poirier was writing the social space of love was somewhat broader and bolder than were the prevalent practices when Capellanus was reporting. For the Bailiff of Love only extreme threat could justify concealment of freely given love. Even then, the duty of the lovers was to try and demonstrate the virtue and wealth of love. Wherever possible they should seek to declare their affections and seek to value and acknowledge each other. Hope should prevail over ill will, and the levity of poetry, of rhythm and rhyme should conquer adverse judgment.

Poetic passion trumps timorous concealment. That was the law. Speak out wherever possible, honor and embrace your desires. Act ethically and eloquently. The two are twins. *Jouissance* and justice; rhetoric and right. And that remained the precedent in matters of the heart for the rest of the tradition. There was a duty to speak out, an obligation to declare love, and so too a licit impetus to expand the intimate public sphere through speaking well of the amatory arts. Later case law can bear this out to the end of our period and beyond.

Case 28 before the High Court of Love involved a complaint brought by a woman against her neighbor. The wrong complained of was malicious gossip, slander to the neighborhood and persistent harm to her reputation. The petitioner came to Court and pleaded that the defendant held her in the lowest esteem. Whenever she was visited by her lover, or by anyone else of the opposite sex for that matter, this neighbor would spread the news abroad. She would tell everyone in the vicinity. She would gossip incessantly. She would come to her window and loudly proclaim that she could see the couple and knew that they were up to no good. She would throw pebbles at the visitor when he left. She would speak ill of the petitioner whenever she could, and as if that were not enough, whenever the petitioner wore a new hat or dress, this foul-mouthed neighbor would say that it was a reward for her incontinent behavior. She asked the Court to issue an injunction prohibiting the defendant from speaking ill of her ever again.

The defendant's reply was that she had not spoken ill of the petitioner except to the limited extent that she had reason to do so. The petitioner had moved into the neighborhood. It had previously been quiet and reputable but that had started to change with the petitioner's arrival. The petitioner was greedy, she had too many visitors, and she accepted too many gifts. All of this had sometimes annoyed the defendant and she had spoken out. At the same time, she pointed out that the petitioner had spoken rather unflatteringly of her and in turn deserved punishment though the defendant was happy to let God decide what that should be rather than imposing upon the High Court of Love.

Replications and duplications completed, the Court pronounced the following judgment. The window from which the defendant shouted and threw pebbles should be walled over like a condemned space. Beyond that whenever the two ran into each other they should not speak except to praise and honor the other. So ordered upon pain of confiscation of property or incarceration.

It is an interesting judgment. Consider first the phenomenon of the walled over window. They can still be seen quite commonly on older buildings and the usual explanation is that the windows were walled over because of window taxes. For economic reasons and aren't they always the simplest? But here we have a judgment that suggests that some of these walled windows or erased apertures were part of a rather different economy of visibility and intimacy. Within the domain of love the intimate is that which is not overlooked. It is a social space of invisibility and has as its core a shared interiority that is walled off in some manner from the rest of the world. This zone of the intimate can be momentary, it usually is, taking the form say of a brief flaring on the inside of a formal gathering, an intensity exchanged in an alcove or vestibule, a note slipped into the pocket of a friend during a pause in proceedings at a work meeting.

The point of the precedent is that this invisibility of intimacy requires the protection of names and the maintenance of non-disclosure even where the zone of intimacy is overlooked. The right to light, as lawyers say, does not come without obligations and in this case the neighbor had abused that right by overlooking and intruding upon the zone of intimacy by word and by deed. It was a double wrong.

One can also note that the judgment in Case 28 was a strong one in terms of the doctrine of duty of care. The usual rule of law is that if someone moves into a neighborhood their interests are subject to the prior claims of the established residents. You take the vicinity as you find it and if that means that you are overlooked or subject to the observation and commentaries of a neighbor then you have to lump it or leave it. Not so, however, in the domain of love. The intimate public sphere is always precarious and ever dependent upon the discretion of observers. The alcove is always overlooked but in the law of love that means that the passerby literally overlooks, she refuses to see, her gaze is turned the other way. The rule is that you look lightly, you pass over, you see what you will always see again.

The window overlooks an intimate history, whereas the mouth opens onto discourse. Apertures both and equally requiring rules of opening, a rhetoric of seeing and of speaking. A further case can add briefly to our account of the duty of concern in the use of words. A suit was brought by the Procurator General of Love after the imprisonment of an elderly woman for slander, or more precisely "by reason and because of certain ill-sounding words she had spoken, or let slip from her mouth."

The Procurator General claimed that he had interrogated the woman and that she had confessed to having made a practice of going to social gatherings, parties, receptions, banquets, and even bridal showers and there, out of hate and spite, she would declaim the ills of love, vociferously deplore the sovereignty of desire, and try to persuade people to leave.

The petitioner sought corporal punishment for the woman so as to make an example of her to others. For her part the defendant argued that she regretted her words. She had been angry and had not intended any serious harm. She had spoken lightly and despite herself.

The Court found for the petitioner and held that the defendant had committed a tort. She had spoken offensively and was ordered to wear a placard round her neck declaring that she had offended and wounded love through loose words and ill-considered speech. Or words to that effect. Translation of medieval French meter is not entirely my thing. It is, as I was saying, a little bit of a lost art. Not something lawyers do so much of these days, and more is the pity if I can put it like that.

The two cases illustrate not only a certain pathology with respect to others, but the closely guarded parameters, the jealousy if you will of the realm of love itself. It is the question of the map, of the recognition and unseen visibility of the *carte de tendre* or territory of the heart. What is most interesting to later conceptions of the spatial presence of desire is that it was a rhetorical domain that was protected, language that was first encouraged or enjoined according to its hermeneutic impact upon that third social space, the shadow public domain of intimacy and the variegated affairs of the heart. The duty of concern, the affective obligation underpinning speech was exhortatory. Any speech that would lower the standing or contract the spaces of liaison was to be condemned as a wrong, as slander against the realm of the heart and whether general or specific was to be condemned in doctrine and refuted in practice.

These are themes that steadily grow in importance as the republic of love and letters expands. They reach a jurisprudential crescendo by the end of our period, the latter part of the seventeenth century, but the signs are there to be extracted from earlier case law. Another example, this time taken from the *New Laws* promulgated by Coquillart in the 1490s.

The case involved the servant of a young, beautiful, and much sought after woman. Each time a potential suitor appeared on the scene, the defendant servant would take money from them and then tell her mistress that this suitor was the one. She would paint a picture of a dramatically desirable individual. She would claim that the poorest wretch was a man of great honor, good looks, fine clothes, wise and generous. Her mistress would get aroused. She would arrange a meeting and go to the tryst with gifts in hand and great anticipation. She would strew the suitor with amorous attention only to discover that he was dishonorable, ugly, dressed in rags, uneducated and miserly. She would return in tears and empty-handed. The servant would laugh silently at her mistress's woes.

It was held that the servant had abused language and engaged in a sordid economics, or to use the proper word she was a pimp (*macquerelle*). It was held that she had acted maliciously, engaged in false and fraudulent counsel and she was ordered to give all the money she had gained from her deceptions to her mistress. Her wages, on the other hand, were to be paid "to the spaces of intimacy," now and always. A poetic disposition and a remedy that nicely illustrates the scope of the positive duty of concern. The use of language was to be gauged according to its capacity to bolster the intimate public sphere. Slander and misrepresentation are both amatory wrongs because of their incursion upon the shared space of desire. If rhetoric, skill in words is the scaffolding upon which liaison is built, then misprision or abuse of words is the greatest of all threats to erotic fulfillment and the most strongly condemned.

Underlying the actions against the verbally incontinent and the maliciously inclined is the all-important impetus to protect and expand the zone of intimate affairs. The question, legally speaking, is always that of facilitating the conditions of liaison, of generating poetic spaces, and generally encouraging erotic exchange. These are all matters of rhetorical governance, of the artistic use of words, and of the proper knowledge of the procedures, the stages and intensities of desire that oratory or poetry will generate. On the underside, unproductive and undesired, are the false uses of words, and specifically the maliciously uttered invective. And the word malice is here well chosen. Its Latin root *malitia* actually means unfruitful, barren, and leading to nothing. The malicious use of words breaches the duty of concern because the words are used fruitlessly, without end, without erotic progeny of any kind.

Love is an intensity of feeling. The laws of love teach that language is the tensor, and rhetoric the agent of its use, of contraction and release, spasm and dilation, according to one's orientation or whim. Our last case can usefully illustrate this very issue. Heard before the Parliament of Love, in the town of Paphlos, the action was brought by one Artaminte against Ligamon.

The petitioner's complaint was as follows. The defendant Ligamon had courted Artaminte and declared his love for her. Not only had he protested his affection for her innumerable times, he had also bestowed her with gifts and other tokens of his love. She learned subsequently that even when she was not around, he would talk about her incessantly to whomever he met. She was also told that while he undoubtedly delighted in singing her praises, he would also sometimes say things that were hurtful and unflattering. She could not understand how he could speak in such contrary ways: "If he loves me then why say insulting things about me? If he hates me then why praise me?" Artaminte concluded her pleadings by asking the Court to enjoin Ligamon from ever talking about her again.

Ligamon responded that he had never said anything good or ill about Artaminte out of malice, but only ever out of love. He praised her because he burned with desire for her, and if he had spoken ill of her that was because his love was extreme. Love inspires the greatest and most violent passion; it generates excess, irrational feelings, and loss of self-control. His love had led him, he argued, constantly to think and talk about his lover. He was not the master of what he said but he did know that he would much rather speak ill of Artaminte than not speak of her at all. He could not help himself, he wanted to keep talking about her for all eternity and more. He concluded by saying that even if he had spoken harshly and at times unfavorably about her, he had never said anything very bad. The harm was not great. He concluded by asking the Court to order Artaminte to listen to his protestations of love.

The Advocate General of Love joined the case and pointed out that there was no dispute of fact. Ligamon accepted the case as Artaminte had pleaded it. He noted next that whatever Ligamon had said had been said out of passion and desire. What separated them, the "differend" between them, was simply the question of whether or not love could excuse verbal excess. Love he then opined could well excuse strange linguistic usages and all variety of extraordinary statements. This in part exonerated Ligamon. His crime was hardly a great one, the mitigating circumstances were significant, the insulting things he had said were not so serious. All of which led the Advocate General to recommend to the judges that they act leniently. Ligamon should be pardoned this time. He should be ordered thenceforth to speak only well of Artaminte. If he reverted to speaking ill of her he would be enjoined from ever seeing her again.

The judges followed the recommendations of the Advocate General. The reasons are plain. The lover's duty of concern is a mechanism of investment, a requirement of engagement, the overriding desideratum of involvement. As between the lovers, this duty is coincident with watching over the enamorata and caring for her. Rhetorically this positively requires composition: the writing and recitation of verse, the *ex tempore* praise of the beloved, the owning and expression of passion as the Statutes of Love had earlier put it. Granted that there are often torments, pains, and other manias associated with love it is not too surprising that the lover on occasion complains, bemoans, or denounces the trials and tribulations of desire. This may lead to things being said that are critical or dismissive of the beloved but so long as they are said in the greater cause of erotic fulfillment then no significant harm is done.

Note here the understated yet radical acknowledgment in the Advocate General's argument that love is sometimes violent. If nonchalance is the enemy of passion, if the icy cool of indifference is the antonym of heat and desire, then some element of violence, at the very least an illocutionary force, an emotional assault are frequent incidents of intimacy and factors that require their own interpretation. The laws of love neither denounce force nor claim some unrealistic zero tolerance for violence. The criterion of judgment is different. Where words wound, the issue to be adjudicated is simply whether or not that wounding is or can be made productive. This is a question that is best evaluated from the space in between the lovers and, as in the last case, can take the form of assessing whether the insults promote or diminish the prospects of love. By the same token, if words have injured the vista of the love affair then what remedy will best rekindle it.

Violence, excess, and hurt through words are treated hermeneutically. The laws of love address the harm that language can cause in the rhetorically appropriate manner, indeed justly. The words are placed back in the context of an expanded conversation. They are interpreted within the flow of relationship and they are judged according to the future of the love affair. From this perspective the violence that words can do, the intimate hurts that occur, are dealt with as aspects of dialogue. Verbal force may well express the passion of desire, and if it does not, lashing out through words, the force or violence of expression still evidences an attempt to communicate. The laws of love latch on to that communicative substrate of verbal excess and seek through interpretation to bring it to its fullest possible expression. And slander gains a new definition. It refers not to injurious words as such, but to hurtful expressions that fail to contribute to the zone of intimacy or that actively diminish the possibilities of the love affair. Such unproductive words are potential breaches of the duty of concern that lovers bear. They are nonchalant, and as the *Edicts of Love* remind us, nonchalance is the greatest of all wrongs against the realm of heart.

In ſtudioſum captum amore.

EMBLEMA CIX.

IMMERSVS ſtudijs, dicundo & iure peritus,
Et maximus libellio.
Helianiran amat, quantum nec Thracius vmquam
Princeps ſororis pellicem.
Pallada cur alio ſuperaſti iudice Cypri?
Num ſat ſub Ida eſt vincere?

Figure 7 *In studiosum captum amore* (A legal scholar overcome by love)—Andreas Alciatus, *Emblematum libellus* (1531).

6
Delicts of Desire

The *Edicts of Love* proclaimed that nonchalance or lack of concern was the primary wrong in matters of the heart. The initial application of that principle came, as we saw, in the domain of words. Rhetorical injustices, abusive words – *cacozelia* – would prevent liaisons being formed, or would undermine and harm amorous affairs in progress. Purloined letters, false reports, corruption of messages, and malicious rumors all intruded upon the rhetorical space across which erotic communication took place and the love affair became a possibility. Slander was the first and greatest of amorous harms not only because it wounded the lover purposelessly but also because it threatened the condition of possibility of the love affair. Malice infracted the felicity condition of liaison: the requirement that words be playful and amorous, socially light and emotionally loaded. Formulate it as a principle: the positive duty of the lover is playful and poetic, their words are either erotic or nonchalant. If the latter then they are to be condemned. Plainly enough the same criterion applies to harm by deed or, as in the next case to be discussed, by interposition of the body.

A judgment taken from the *New Laws,* Part I, *de iure naturali,* of natural law, can provide an initial illustration of this principle. Coquillart records an instance of *infamia* that involves a domestic servant who out of jealousy betrays her mistress's love. The complainant was young and pretty. She had a lover whom she was in the practice of meeting in the garden behind her house. The chambermaid, who was also young, attractive and open to love, knew of these secret encounters and was jealous of her mistress's good fortune. On the day in question, late in the afternoon as the shadows lengthened, she saw her mistress's lover slip into the garden in the hope of a chance tryst. Rather than inform her mistress, the chambermaid went and waited in the spot where the lovers habitually met and embraced. Using her knowledge of their meetings, the gloaming and a pretense of modesty to her advantage she frolicked with her mistress's lover and lured him into a sexual encounter.♥ A classic bedtrick, except that it took place in the garden rather than the bedroom. I would call it a trick plain and simple, were it not for the case that in the argot of sex a trick is often a synonym for prostitution.

The question before the Court was that of what punishment was appropriate, and what restitution necessary, in response to this theft of love? Under the old law there was no question that this was a flagrant offence and as far back as the *Precepts of Love*, Rule 3: "When someone is having an affair with another it is wrong for anyone who knows this to try to seduce them." Such conversion of love was aggravated by the fact that the trickster was the servant of the injured woman. It was a double betrayal and under the old law it was designated "grand treason," an amorous iniquity and an offence punishable by corporal penance. Under the new law a somewhat different position was adopted. The offence was so cruel, the act so infamous, the disloyalty and abuse of good will so extreme that the only proper determination was banishment from the household and sequestration from love.

Games have rules, and those of love require levity for sure, investment in the erotic excitement, in the masquerade of desire, but also commitment to the enterprise of liaison, to the domain of intimacy, and to the felicity of amorous communication. For all of the doctrinal discussion of pure love as opposed to mixed or carnal expression, the subtitle of Capellanus's foundational treatise was most often given as *On the Art of Honest Love*. Pleasure, as the contemporaneous Occitan *Cort d'amor* puts it, is *bon legistes*, a good lawyer. And so too, by amorous custom and use, intimacy had its laws. There was a duty of concern, a condition of felicity that required recognition and respect for the rights of lovers and here for the space between the enamored couple. It was the defendant's non-recognition of the in-between of relationship, her intrusion upon an emotional terrain, and specifically her extraction of a desire intended for another through misrepresentation that constituted her principal offence against the new laws. She evidenced a narcissistic indifference, a blatant nonchalance with respect to the amorous concerns of others.

It is important to acknowledge the doctrinal basis of the duty of concern in this case. According to the law as set out by Capellanus and others, there is no harm in occasional and spontaneous expressions of lust.

♥I am relying here upon the context and John Farmer's chrestomathic *Vocabula amatoria* in translating "ceste *provision*" as the act of sex.

The treatise is very clear on the point. If a couple encounter each other by chance in a secluded place and overcome by lust lie together, that is not against the law. Realism and respect for the natural law of desire mitigated in favor of allowing that such encounters will occur and should not be stigmatized. There were, of course, limits to such libertinage. The *Code of Love* Rule 29 stipulated: "Someone who engages in excessive sensuality is not usually in love." Later law greatly expanded that principle. Love was built through conversation, it grew rhetorically, it belonged within an intimate history, and its growth was an effect of dialogue over time. All of which implies an art and genre of amorous discourse that incites desire through rhetorical rules and stages it according to a grammar, the protocols of the laws of love. Outside of such poetical progress, erotic expression is generally likely to be unjust or at the least indelicate and best forgotten. That is the theory. It proposes an ethos of rhetorical honesty, felicity of discourse being the condition of good love.

The theory is that we perform desire through a pattern of exchange. We don't repeat because we love, rather we love because we repeat. Repetition, performance over time, attention to detail leads to what Nietzsche termed erotic erudition, or what we might in the vernacular now call conscious love. It is something more than a *coup de foudre*, passion at first sight, pheromenes, hormones or genes run wild. Felicitous intimacy is a result of the eroticization of discourse over time. It is a rhetorical construct, an epistemic project, a mode of listening and responding, of concern and attention over time.

Start with the temporality of repetition. It requires spaces within which intimacy and attention, poetry and response are possible. That is why the courts of love were so often taken up with the question of the proper spaces of desire. The salon, the alcove, the boudoir, chamber or vestibule, the arbor or grove, the lovers' lane, are all alike indicative of amorous location. They are "microtopic" spaces, zones of intimacy and erotic possibility secluded within the social, publicly visible yet curiously overlooked. The microtopia allows for the relational within the professional, the intimate within the institutional. It constitutes an amorous version of bound space, the term that Husserl used for socially undisposed yet aesthetically valuable space. It is in any event, let us predict a little, within the microtopia that the felicity conditions of desire are best met.

Auvergne's *Aresta amorum*—like all law prior to the contemporary era published first in Latin and only later in a species of French—include a brief report that makes this point. Judgment 47 concerns a nuisance that intrudes upon the evanescent space of love. The case is brought by a representative group of lovers—*galands amoureux*—against a group of ambulant waffle makers and pastry cooks whose efforts to cook and sell their products in the public space where lovers went to meet caused considerable distraction to amorous pursuits. The smells and especially the smoke were unpleasant as also was the surveillance of intimate space by merchants. The petitioners' requested that the vendors be ordered to cease and desist from cooking and selling their wares in the vicinity of this lovers' lane.

The respondents argued that they were simply trying to make a living. Their métier was cooking, and to survive commercially they had to follow the populace and sell their wares. Nobody, they added, would want to eat a cold waffle and so if they did not make them close to where the consumers were located they would lose their sale; a culinary plea that might well appeal to a French court.

The petitioners' responded in some detail. The cooking carts blocked the path that the lovers would stroll down. Worse still, the fumes from the cooking were acrid and would get into their eyes. Eyes watering from smoke, or worse still closed against the fumy vapors, could not look on the beloved. If sight incites desire then the intrusion of the waffle making upon the visibility of what were already often-fleeting presences was a considerable harm. It was suggested strongly that the vendors should go elsewhere to cook and sell their wares.

The High Court heard the arguments and determined in favor of the petitioners. The space of love was not a commercial sphere and it followed clearly that it should not be intruded upon by merchants. Their activities inhibited love and were therefore to be condemned. More than that, it was to be observed that the public zones of intimacy were spaces for the carnival of love. According to Roman law, Benoit de Court points out in his commentary on the case, days of carnival were holidays. They were free of commerce—*dies festis non mercandum*, to put it in the proper jargon. By analogy, the social spaces of intimacy, the microtopias of desire, were equally festive and ought to be similarly free of commerce. A strong argument and in this decision a winning one. The vendors were ordered to go market their wares elsewhere in the city. In its commercial spaces, among the crowds, and away from all alcoves and other intimate locations.

The separation of the amatory and the mercantile might be questioned today by the more hardened proponents of law and economics. The goods of love, they could argue, are credence goods and can be subjected to cost benefit analysis like any others. That is not necessarily untrue and the decision reported could be reconstructed in terms of the inefficiencies of amorous exchange engendered by the presence of merchants. That, however, would be a misunderstanding of the relevant economics. It is certainly true that the case raises issues relating to the free circulation of desire within the libidinal economy but the relevant *nomos* or law is not mercantile but curatorial. The issue is that of concern, and specifically the investment of concern in the microtopia of liaison. They ignored the discursive economy of desire, they intruded nonchalantly upon the erotic space of exchange, and for that reason they committed a wrong.

The principle again is clear. According to the laws of love all those who come into contact with the social spaces and practices of amorous liaison must recognize both the rhetorical art that governs erotic encounter and the duty of concern incumbent upon every act that intrudes on the zones of intimacy. That said, the bulk of the laws govern the internal dynamics of intimacy and intercourse. The rules on wrongs are subtle and at times counterintuitive to contemporary sensibilities. The duty of concern may be a subjective duty but it is circumscribed not by the intention behind an act, nor by the foreseeability of the result, but rather by the effects of the act upon the respondent and upon lovers collectively. Thus it was not the desire for love that was a wrong in the case extracted from Coquillart's *New Laws* but rather it was the theft of that love from another when the defendant well knew of the prior relationship. Similarly it was not the preparation of food in the latter case that was a wrong but rather the effect of the practice upon the space occupied by lovers. Concern can occasion prediction, it may be reckless to laugh at the attributes of a lover or to douse them with water, as later cases will show, but the issue at which amorous justice is directed is that of actual response and how to bring it into dialogue with the missive or act at its origin.

The principle of amorous effect can be illustrated by the tenth of the *Questioni d'amore* reported by Boccaccio in the mid-fourteenth century. The question is posed by Ascaleon to Queen Fiammetta. Shortly after the death of her husband a very beautiful and much admired woman was unjustly accused of a crime. The charges were brought by the family of the deceased. By dint of false evidence the magistrate had no choice but to find the woman guilty as charged and so, according to the law of the day, sentenced her to death by fire. He suspected, however, that there had been some injustice in the accusation and therefore imposed a condition on the sentence. When the time came for the sentence to be carried out, she would be spared and set free if she could find a defender who would combat and overcome a proponent of her guilt. If her defender lost then she would be burned as per the sentence.

The woman had two male suitors who subsequently learned of this condition. The first to hear of it immediately announced that he would defend the woman and took to the field to challenge anyone who proclaimed her guilt. The second suitor was distressed to learn that because of his slackness his rival had acted faster and had already entered the field on her behalf. He decided to go into the field proclaiming the woman's guilt and then allow himself to be overcome, thereby allowing her to be freed. Acting according to this plan he successfully facilitated the escape of the woman.

Both suitors subsequently pressed their claims to the love of the woman. The first claimed that he had risked his life for his love. The second said that he had courted eternal infamy and dishonor so as to save her life. The question posed to the Queen was which of the two most merited her love?

The judgment was for the first suitor. He had risked his life in a forthright manner. He might well have been killed in combat. The latter lover, however, had entered the field knowing full well that he would not die. He had risked the least and so deserved the lesser gain. When Ascaleon challenged this holding on the ground that the second suitor had been the wiser, Fiammetta upheld her judgment. Her reasoning was that the second suitor had acted out of envy. He did not want the other suitor to succeed. Thus, she continued, "although we cannot know it with any certainty" the second suitor was motivated mainly "to disturb the [other] and not out of the love he claimed ..."

The logic is subtle. Jealousy is treated in amatory law as being essential to love. Rule 2 of the *Code* states: "someone who is not jealous cannot be in love." Plain as day. And Rule 21 adds: "true jealousy makes the feeling of love grow." To be jealous is to wish to protect what you have. Envy, by contrast, is defined by the desire to take what belongs to another. It is an illegitimate motive, and it tends toward the diminution of desire. It is a breach of the duty of concern as we have defined it because its effect is to harm another lover. That part of the judgment is well settled. Fiammetta, however, goes on to offer a further justification.

It is not just a matter of bad motive leading to an illicit attempt to steal love. There was also a rhetorical infelicity involved. The art of honest love requires openness as between lovers. Those who inhabit the temporary erotic zones in which relationship are formed, affairs inaugurated, and eros undressed have as their principal duty the observance of the felicity condition of speech. Queen Fiammetta makes the point most directly: "He is a fool who under the guise of an enemy expects compensation for helping another." And she continues to extol the desideratum of showing love through "open friendship" and so without mask or disguise. That much she concludes is true to the law. So held.

The wrong that envy prompts is one that involves taking something away from someone else. Nonchalance detracts from the domain of desire. Both in their way are the effects of an affective infraction. The other cases that decide disputes as to amorous wrongs are similarly predicated upon the emotional consequences of acts, upon affective responses and their evaluation. Case 23 reported by Auvergne nicely illustrates the point with facts that well symbolize the full scope of the wrong of nonchalance.

The case involved a dispute between two lovers. The male complainant said that he had been for some time in the practice of passing by his lover's house at night and calling out his salutations and if possible conversing with her. On the night in question he had arrived very late and had attempted to attract her attention by loudly coughing and clearing his throat outside her window. The moment that she knew it was him below she took a pitcher of water, threw it out of the window and drenched him from head to toe. She and her chambermaid then looked out of the window and laughed at him, a now sorry figure standing sopping. They made his misery worse by mocking him.

Enraged by her actions, the lover made a complaint before the Justices of Love who agreed to investigate the case. Their preliminary finding was that the woman had acted deliberately and wrongfully—with hate and derision—and should make reparation.

In her defense the defendant said that she had always spoken well of her lover. She had ever sought to please him and had never done or said anything that could distress him. She would neither laugh at him nor mock him. She went on to say that when the water was thrown out of the window she had no idea that he was outside. More than that, it was in fact her chambermaid, a young and foolish woman, who had thrown the water out of the window and she was harshly scolded subsequently. She then assured the Court that whatever their conclusions she would never again play any practical jokes upon the complainant. Finally, in mitigation, she pointed out that the water had been clean and, on a hot night as it had been, it may have wet him but it should also have been splendidly refreshing.

In his response, the lover again deplored the action. He had not needed any cooling down that night. He believed that she knew full well it was him—he had coughed several times to identify himself—and she had played an unpleasant practical joke on him. The night should be a time of protection for lovers and she should therefore be punished.

The High Court heard the arguments and determined that if the facts as stated by the complainant were correct then the woman had acted wrongfully. Lovers required especial protection at night. Drenching and ridicule did not make it into that category. The Court ordered the woman and the chambermaid to attend and face interrogation as to their behavior. In the meantime an order was issued requiring the couple to behave reasonably.

Note two things. First that night is designated as a time for lovers. It is its own temporary intimate zone, a microtopia of amorous transmission, a special space of liaison because lovers can pass unseen. Night offers safe passage. According to the laws of love, the nocturnal outings of the enamoured, the covert missions and meetings of the infatuated, were protected by the "Oubliers"—which translates best as the anamnesiac police—the equivalent of a spiritual guard. The secular law in fact also recognized that aspect of the nocturnal. The lawyer and antiquarian John Selden remarks that night is a feminine measure of time, named after female Goddesses, the Greek Furies, but we can expand that and say that in the laws of love night is also an amorous demarcation.

The second observation pertinent to the judgment is that humor must have its place. The practical joke was certainly not a wrong in itself but again, as in all matters amorous, what matters is not the intention but the consequence, the response. It is legally very simple. The joke could be good or bad, that is after all usually no more than a question of timing and delivery, but what is clear is that the respondent did not find the dousing funny. Laughter can't be forced and so, granted their intimate history, concern on the part of the defendant should have led her immediately to make good her dereliction and apologize for the unwelcome surprise that she had jettisoned from her window. It was not good enough to say that she had always treated him well and he should not be complaining. Nor should she deflect the blame onto her companion. Nor, finally, was it appropriate to claim that the complainant was humorless. It is no use flaying a dead joke. In the end humor like love is relational and depends upon engaging the auditor. This she had signally failed to do: *hinc illae lachrymae*, or hence all these tears, as the philosophers were once wont to say.

The broader principle, the take home for the *lex amatoria* is that the negotiation of feelings is delicate and that where the protocols and diplomacy of love are concerned then the amorous subject's perceptions should be indulged so that knowledge rather than imposition or decree will resolve the perceived slight or intimate wrong. Nowhere could it be more clearly stated that the function of the law of amorous wrongs is not to reprimand wrongdoing or punish breaches of the duty of concern but rather the opposite. It is the context of breach, the nonchalance that underlies the wrongful act, the failure of connection that has to be repaired, and conversation restored, for the lovers to be returned to the amity of their affair. The function of the law of love is thus pretty much the opposite of municipal tort. Where common law endeavors to make the plaintiff whole through compensating a breach of duty, an infraction of proximity as they like to call it, amatory norms seek rather to repair the breach and return the parties to intimacy. Where actions in tort tend to evince the terminus of proximity, and compensation there marks a substitute for care, the laws of love seek restoration to proximity, and the continuance of concern once the episode of nonchalance has been reproved and its causes mended.

Another nuance to be noted is that the rules relating to amorous wrong are manipulated not according to the act but rather as a response to how the complainant perceived the act. Running through all the cases is a principle of affective impact whereby the courts endeavor to measure the emotional harm that the incident has occasioned. The logic of this assessment is irrefutable. If emotional states are to be defined, as surely they must, by reference to how the subject feels, then the measure of harm is initially that of simple sensibility: what effect did the act have upon its recipient. The practical joke can be humorously intended and yet it fails, and its jocular character is ignored, if the recipient of the humor in fact experiences it as dismissive, hurtful, or plain aggressive. Affect is the measure and it has to be sanctioned legally or supported in a delicate manner.

In the end it is not right or wrong in any obvious juridical sense that best captures the law of amatory torts. The distribution of responsibility and the reparation of affective wounds require a perspective that sees beyond naming and blaming to what the courts of love called the "differend," the emotional deficit that divided the parties. Repairing the *differend* means taking the long-term position, the perspective of the interior, the aspiration of a future for the relationship. It is the in-between space, the intersubjective or altruistic context of the love affair that determines what is to be done. What matters is the maintenance, so far as is possible, of the affective bond between the lovers because in the end, if that bond fails then the law of love runs out as well. Its very existence depends precisely upon the affect or desire that drives intimate relations. It is the law of their nature, an interior and eloquent norm, a felicitous justice.

That said, there is also a realism that humor implies and that nuisance invokes. As the case law shows, smells can deflate desire, smoke gets in the eyes, and an inopportune dousing can lead to unfortunate responses. These accidents and other intrusions upon the microtopic space of desire have to be dealt with lightly, with good humor as well as emotional insight. Otherwise the parties will walk, either literally or emotionally. That would detract from the erotic bond and simultaneously defeat the purpose of the law, which is to augment the quantum of amorous affairs. The only limitation is the nature of the parties themselves, their emotional capacity, their openness to the reality of liaison as it is to be found in the particular contexts of love. A final case can make the point.

The petitioner complained that the greatest desire of any lover was to see his beloved. It was with such an amorous motive that the petitioner would go every evening to see the defendant. On nights when circumstance kept her from him or her husband's presence precluded her acknowledging him, the petitioner would bid his salutations to the thin air and then kiss the keyhole of her door. It was a simple ritual but one that was impeded by the fact that the defendant had a pet quail, a noisy bird that would shriek warnings to its mistress when her lover approached the door. The noise and consequent danger of detection and later of gossip greatly disturbed the petitioner and on one occasion he had been so startled by the bird that he had injured his nose on the door when springing up in surprise at the quail's cry. That night he had not been able to sleep at all. He wanted to kill the bird but could not because he did not have access to the house. He asked the Court to order the defendant to throttle the bird or at least to get rid of it.

The defendant disagreed. She said first that the bird was not hers but belonged to a friend who loved it dearly. She went on to say that birds live to sing. It meant no harm, it was just following its nature and giving voice to a warning. It would be quite wrong to kill a bird for being a bird.

The High Court heard the pleadings and decided in favor of the defendant. The petition was poorly made. The quail was a pet and should not needlessly be killed. It was following its nature and the petitioner needed to work around that context to his affair. The Court ordered the petitioner to respect the bird and threatened him with deprivation of love if he in any ways tried to harm or abuse the quail.

Benoit de Court notes that this decision has precedents in classical lore, and particularly in Lucretius's *On the Nature of Things*. These tended to the view that the petitioner was protesting too much and acting effete. Don't stick your nose into keyholes unless you are prepared to take the consequences. The High Court was less condemnatory but still took the view that there is a duty to take the lover as she is, in her context, demarcated by the real. She had a bird, a quail and it deserved respect rather than death for being what it was. More than that, the lovers' desires and possessions, their attributes and externalizations should be learned and their whims humored. And then again, more philosophically, the bird is a symbol of levity and love. In losing his lightness the lover relinquished his desire. He was too serious to be properly in love, not playful enough to enter the space of liaison.

The legal principle is the one enunciated already. The law of love addresses the response in terms of the felicity conditions of the affair. The man wanted to kiss the keyhole of his lover's door without fear of detection. He wanted to watch her unobserved. As it happened that was not possible because of the bird, call it an attribute or possession of his lover. Rather than working around that, attending to the details, showing concern for his lover's loves, her birds, her things, he raged against it with avicidal intentions. He was up to no good, acting in poor taste, showing a lack of discrimination and behaving overall as a camel rather than a dancer. Put it in terms of a contrast between the first and this last case. At its simplest, and law is best where it is lucid, the intrusion upon the space of love was commercial and venal in the first of our cases, and there the Court was happy to enjoin, prohibit and expel. Here, however, it was nature that impinged and deserved to be respected. The order of love is the order of things.

And finally, and still on the subject of torts of desire, and harms occasioned by nonchalance: Why record these cases, with their peculiar and burlesque facts? Burned waffles, spilled water, incontinent birds, gossiping neighbors, and archaic and bizarre schemes, are perhaps not the most obvious basis for regulating quotidian amorous affairs. Humorous circumstances, practical jokes or elaborate deceits are not usually viewed as the proper tone of legal facts. But the opposite is also true. The case law that sticks is in fact most often that predicated upon the comedy of the real, the unimaginable coincidences, the truth that is stranger than fiction. More to the immediate point, the comedy of eros is precisely the stuff of everyday amorous disputes, of office affairs, institutional liaisons, of the socially covert workings of desire. The cases are as exemplary as the rules are enduring. Here we are still reading them. That has to count for something. That kind of suggests that they could be law for us.

Figure 8 *Non bene convenit* (It leads to no good)—Albert Flamen, *Devises et emblesmes d'amour moralisez* (1648).

7
The Casuistry of Kissing

Here is an interesting thought. Those who study such things usually break down the meaning of the word philosophy into its Greek roots of *philein* or friend and *sophia* or wisdom. I have done that myself, on occasion, so as to make an argument about friendship and knowledge. It works well enough. It helps make the point that philosophy means amity for ideas. The word *philein*, however, also meant to kiss and so philosophy could equally mean the kissing of wisdom, or the wisdom of kissing. This suggests—does it not?—that the kiss and kissing, proper noun and transitive verb, osculatory theory and practice, insufflation literal and metaphorical go to the very roots of the tradition. Study of the wisdom of kissing may not be how we normally think of the philosophical tradition, it may in fact be a secondary meaning of the discipline, a shadow side perhaps, but it is everywhere present. Kissing is more or less a synonym for community. No sociality without osculation. And then as well kissing is the emblematic sign of desire. As Freud later observed, in those moments of animation that are of the essence of living well we are very keen to taste each other.

Put it like this, whether or not kissing is at the root of the tradition, leaving aside the theory that tasting each other is in some measure the civilized form of earlier cannibalistic practices, the brushing together of labia, the smacking conjunction of lips, the smelling and tasting of the beloved's face is pervasive. It is in the news, it is in the courts, and even the universities are in on the regulatory act. Professors are disciplined for kissing students, gay couples are challenged for public osculation, a seven-year-old boy is sent home from school for kissing a ten-year-old girl. You know the story. The Church too has historically had the greatest of trouble in limiting the practices of kissing. It remains, one might say, a touch involuntarily involved. Catholic priests seem on occasion to have extended the practice of kissing the communion wafer—I am thinking of the rite of brushing the lips over the bread and murmuring "this is my body"—to a broader public sphere of embraces. In sum, we are addicted to kissing but we have lost the knowledge of how to do it well. The justice of kissing, the protocols, the manners, the rules addressed to the different kinds of kissing all belong to a forgotten art. When conflict arises, when kisses are challenged in the workplace, in tribunals, in court, the judges have no law to lean back on. They cannot turn to any established custom or *nomos* to guide them, no memory of a curriculum in the laws of Venus remains to serve them. That needs to be put right. Lawyers are after all historians, practitioners of precedent, inheritors of a rich and plural set of laws.

First note, *prima regula*, the governance of kissing was a central element in Christian doctrine. The kiss of peace—the *osculum pacis*—was the sign of belonging to the Church, to the brotherhood of Christians. More profoundly, the length and depth of kissing was also regulated strictly because in Christian doctrine kissing was an exchange of the spirit, and in heavy kissing, according to the *Song of Songs*, it is Christ who is kissed through the mouth of the other. And in its way that seems an appropriate theory for a religion based on love. The kiss was the mark of entry into the brotherhood of love; it was the sign of a boundary being crossed, of the outside meeting the inside, of the public becoming intimate. And then once inside, now a member of the community, the heavy kiss was the mode of expression of spiritual passion, of soul touching soul, of Christ being reached. That, however, is not my topic. It could be, but the passionate, male to male, mouth to mouth kissing of early Christian doctrine seems a far cry from the erotically disinvested spaces that contemporary institutions pretend dismally to inhabit. In fact I think the distance is little more than a question of the current degrees of suppression of the public expression of desire but these issues have to be approached gently. Softly, softly is the coda of legal anthropology in the West. The relevant maxim is don't muddle the middle classes. What Christian doctrines on kissing do amply and admirably evidence, however, is that there is a long-established frame within which the gay science developed its osculatory mandates, its laws of labial love.

Kissing was one of the most heavily regulated practices within the case law and the various codes of love. Admit if you will that kissing and loving are almost the same. Start with the fact that you cannot love without kissing though you can kiss without loving. Judas, for example, illustrates the latter point. The heart did not accompany the lips. Or that is how Clement of Alexandria puts it in his description of the kiss of the spider. And in a similar vein, the courts of love would also police the integrity of the embrace, the truth of the kiss. In other words there are genuine kisses and false kisses, a distinction that gay science eventually defines in terms of distinguishing spiritual and venal embraces. The kiss was an essential sign, a primary law, and it is in many senses a key point of entry into the doctrine and judgments of love.

To love is to kiss. To kiss is to love. That is the initial axiom of amour, both spiritual and secular. The domain of desire, the territory of the heart, is entered, and that entry is marked by a kiss. The English poem, the *Court of Love* thus starts with the words, *Domine labia,* Lord open my lips. And in a similar vein, to take an earlier instance, the troubadour Bernard de Ventadorn pleads of his lover: "I ask one gift of her: that she break the fasting of my mouth with a kiss." In the troubadour lyric the kiss is a sacral token. It ends the drought of love, the fasting of *amour lointain,* and inaugurates the joy after which the gay science is named. It is unsurprising that the laws of love also recognize the kiss, the *osculum amoris,* as the lawful mark of commencement of the love affair. The kiss must be given in good faith—*bona fe* in the Occitan—and once given could not be retracted. The kiss was the outer mark of an inner belief and prospect, and kissing, according to the *New Laws,* is the lover's rite. The lips promise entry into the body, physical exchange, from one set of labia to the other. By the same logic it was contrary to law to kiss a stranger because "being a sign of love, the kiss is offered as a token of the love to come." And a kiss without such promise was not a kiss at all. It was poison not love, betrayal and not faith. Either that, or as Ovid observed, if kissing led no further this was a sign not of modesty but of ineptitude. Less a question of bad faith than of fumbling.

Once the agreement to become lovers, the contract of mutual desire has been sealed with kisses then the souls of the enamored are bound to each other. Those in love not only mark their amorous bond by kissing but afterwards owe their kisses exclusively to each other. That is indeed one of the most extensively litigated issues before courts of love. The questions are fairly standard. Who can be kissed? Is there a right to kisses? Can kisses be withheld? Can kisses be sold? Can they be taken by force? When is a kiss excessive? When is a kiss too cold? These are the questions that lovers pose, that the procurators of love argue, and that the courts and parliaments determine. The libidinal is labial. The labial, one might say, is labile, and the laws of love had to respond to that in an informed and delicate way.

Start with Capellanus. According to the Chaplain, pure love joins the hearts of the lovers with universal feelings of affection. He goes on: "it embraces the contemplation of the mind and the feeling of the heart. It goes as far as kissing on the mouth, embracing with the arms, and chaste contact with the naked lover, but the final consolation is avoided." This is a recipe for increasing desire and making love last. The kiss, in other words, eroticizes and promises. It is chaste, even spiritual, so long as the promise remains a promise, so long as the purity of love, the exchange of breath does not descend to penetration. Thus the kiss is not simply liminal, a complex and ambivalent marker of the boundary between the pure and the corporal, but it is also temporal and stays till the act of love. It promises what it withholds. It is both erotic and entirely semiotic. It is both portent and prelude.

Our first case illustrates this last point. The kiss is a sign within an economy of desire. It has to be interpreted according to the laws of love. In the first instance it is true or false according to the subjective criteria of what it promises and the desire that accompanies it. Capellanus notes that the kiss is a proper gift as between lovers and according to numerous later lawyers of love the kiss was a proper subject matter of exchange in contracts of love. In a case heard before the Seneschal of Wild Roses, the plaintiff, a soldier, had acquired by agreement with a female friend the right to one kiss per week. Returning sometime later from a campaign abroad, destitute and sick, the plaintiff, with the consent of the woman, had agreed to sell the right to her kisses to a friend, the defendant. The right was duly transferred and the defendant enjoyed her kisses for some months, until indeed the plaintiff recovered sufficient of his fortune to be in a position to buy the kiss back. The defendant refused to offer such restitution.

The plaintiff's argument was that he was the first and most proximately entitled to the kiss. In lineal terms he was next of kiss. He had sold it out of poverty but had always presumed that when circumstances allowed he could, with the consent of the woman, buy the kiss back. His argument suggested that there was a law of inheritance of kisses whereby the first recipient had the best claim to such a kiss. The first in line of descent was entitled to his or her osculatory due.

The defendant argued that there was no equivalent of primogeniture for kisses. A kiss had to pass freely between subjects. If it was transferred for money, as in this case, that was simply a free exchange, *nudum pactum* or naked agreement as we lawyers are wont to say, and so a gift that gave rise to no rights of return to the original donor.

The Seneschal held for the defendant and the High Court of Love on appeal concurred and awarded all costs against the plaintiff. The logic of decision can be reconstructed as follows. A kiss is a token of love and has its value within the libidinal economy of amorous desire. That is what the kiss means, it is a contract in its own right. While it is perfectly possible to make agreements relating to kisses, and equally proper consensually to record and transfer rights to kisses, the laws of love necessarily recognize desire and not compact as the final arbiter of all insufflations. Thus once performed, the agreement was complete. There were no residual rights, no clauses or sub-clauses, express or implied, that would allow the plaintiff to demand the return of the right he had given away in exchange for money. One might say that he got what was coming to him. More profoundly, the kiss lies where it falls.

The importance of deciding the status and proper forms of circulation of kisses is evident throughout the case law of love. The second case recorded in Martial d'Auvergne's *Judgments of Love* offers the inverse of the case just reported. It addresses the manners and degrees of kissing as between lovers. The case came before the Bailiff of Joy. The plaintiff was a rather sickly young man. The defendant was a married woman and his lover. On the day in question, the couple had met and conversed outside the defendant's house. They acted properly for fear of being seen by the husband, and the young man eventually took his leave. While he was still in view, the defendant woman beckoned to him to come back. Thinking she had something further to say he returned. Perhaps she had thought of a time and place when they could meet again more privately. She was standing in the shade of a tree and as he leaned forward to listen to her, she sprang forward and kissed him passionately on the mouth. She kissed him so forcibly that he sprang back and his nose started to bleed. Thinking that he was pulling away from her and rejecting her kiss, she proceeded to chastise him with her hat. Unfortunately when she struck him with her bonnet, her hatpin scratched his nose and bruised his cheek. The cut resulted in an infection and the plaintiff became ill. He asked the Court to order her to make amends, and specifically that she nurse him through his illness.

The defendant argued that the plaintiff was unworthy of her kiss. Rather than complaining he should treasure the kiss and its consequences. He had fallen ill through love. Amorous wounds, she suggested, were honorable marks and they should be prized possessions. In the alternative, she argued that the cut was a chance wounding, an unlucky hazard occasioned by passion. Either way it was to be applauded, and hence the Court should view his response as unreasonable and extreme.

The Bailiff consulted the Doctors of Love on the nature and severity of the wound and determined that just as the mouth was the cause of the injury, so too it should be the cure. He ordered that the defendant woman tend to the plaintiff and each day should moisten her lips and kiss the cut until the poison had gone and the wound was cured. The miscreant kiss, in other words, was to be remedied by further and gentler kisses.

The defendant was most unhappy with the decision and appealed to the High Court of Love. It was brought to the attention of the appellate Court, in the course of argument, that the defendant had indicated in no uncertain terms that if she was required to cure the plaintiff by kissing his wound she planned to moisten her lips and give him a bite that he would never forget.

The High Court confirmed the decision of the Bailiff of Love. In light of the defendant's express intentions, however, the sentence was commuted. She was to make reparation by paying a substantial sum to the Prisoners of Love for their use in holding banquets and developing herbal cures for amorous ailments.

In his commentary on the case Symphorianus traces the relevant law to an Accursian gloss on the *Corpus iuris* stating the principle that playful and lascivious acts merit gentle punishment. It was also a principle of ecclesiastical law that only truly wanton acts deserve harsh retribution. Pursuant to those principles the Bailiff of Love proposed reconciliation through osculation, a return, if you will, to amorous insufflations. Such a remedy, however, can only work consensually. It favors love over revenge, remorse over reparation, but if that is ineffective then the Appellate Court's order of payment to an amatory charity is an eloquent alternative. It is not the plaintiff but rather the cause of love that most required recompense.

The kiss transpires in the case just cited, though this is hardly novel, to be the emblematic currency of the libidinal economy, of the laws of love. We noted already that the contract of love was sealed with "tears and kisses". The kiss was a form of *seisin* or taking possession of the space of desire. It was an intimate public act that marked entry into relationship and it was used both in the courts of love and also in the process of amicable reconciliation that was the distinguishing feature of the lovedays. The kiss counted. It was the first currency of compensation, it brought the parties back together, it gave desire another chance. Thus the case law tended to enforce promises of kisses and would frequently order kisses as compensation for amorous wrongdoing.

An extreme example of that principle can be taken again from a decision of the High Court of Love. In this case the lovers' came to court to dispute the right to a kiss. The love affair had been ongoing for some years. At the time in question, the defendant felt that his lover, the plaintiff, had been withholding love and kisses unreasonably. He had suffered for her, he loved her, he wanted to mark that love with kisses. Happening upon his lover one hot afternoon he took the opportunity of her husband not being present to embrace her. This sudden intrusion surprised her. He was hot and sweaty and she pulled back saying he was in no condition to kiss her. She was embarrassed by his unkempt state and his perspiration and would not kiss him further, not until he was in a more pleasing condition.

The plaintiff brought the case on the grounds that the defendant should be punished for taking the kiss without a request. In matters of love, she claimed, style was everything and he should not have intruded or kissed her without asking. A proleptic *précieuse,* an amorous Jansenist before her time, "avant la lettre," ahead of the game. She was willing to kiss him but reserved the right to do so only when she was in the mood and he was in a state that pleased her. The defendant pleaded both passion and his right to a kiss. They were lovers of long standing, he said, and their agreement or contract of love included her promise of physical affection, of kisses and contact whenever possible. If he had positively to prove his right to a kiss each time he encountered her at a safe distance from her husband then the time of the kiss would never come. Her excuses were frivolous, it was always the wrong time and so he had eventually chosen to alleviate his suffering by acting on his desire.

The Court was sympathetic to the defendant. He had pursued his love diligently and had pressed his cause within the bounds of reason. She had promised kisses and he was entitled, when safely in seclusion, to act with passion and playfully embrace her. Seizing the occasion meant that he might not always be in the most demure or presentable of states. That was not a proper bar to kissing. The Court further held that the kiss so taken was blameless. It also determined that it was neither satisfactory nor a proper fulfillment of her promise. She was ordered to kiss him with alacrity whenever it was safe and he so requested. Thus it was hoped love would grow.

The anxiety of kissing is a complicated and sensitive issue. It is clear from the *Code of Love* that had the woman plaintiff claimed that she did not desire the defendant then his kiss would have been illicit. Desire governs all amorous exchanges and its absence is fatal to amatory claims. Clause 17 of the *Code* states the reason succinctly: "A new love forces the old to depart." Where desire wanes and the remedies of love fail to reignite it, then relationship is over, lovers separate and new love prevails. Amatory doctrine designates this as a shift from distant love to *amor absconditus* or love abandoned. The important point is that desire rather than divorce, the new love rather than the old, is the object of address and of hope. It is enough to love anew. By operation of a law, by an implicit or default rule the absence of love is sign enough of moving on.

The anxiety of kissing, concern over the dress or deportment of the osculating subject is an obstacle to be overcome if at all possible. It is in either event a matter for medical or legal attention, like blushes or palpitations or sleeplessness, and not a necessary ending of love. What the law tries to do is simply to realign desire with practice, love and the lips.

A further case comes from the High Court of Love where the appellant appeals the theft of a kiss. The appellant woman was in love with the defendant, a gallant young man. She was happy in their love and always welcomed the defendant warmly when she met him in public places. On the day in question the appellant was taking a walk with a number of female friends. She had not noticed the defendant who came up behind her. As he approached she thought from his manner that he wished to whisper some entreaty or endearment to her but much to her embarrassment he lifted her hat and suddenly kissed her. This, she claimed was theft of a kiss, public larceny of love and she prayed that the Court prohibit the defendant from ever again touching her in public without clear advance notice. Her reasoning was that such a visible display of love was inimical to those who might witness or hear about it. Others who loved her would be rendered sad, her husband might learn of it and feel slighted. It was best, as the laws of love constantly iterate, to keep the signs of their love away from public view. Clause 13 of the *Code of Love* is explicit: "Love does not usually survive public exposure."

The defendant argued to the contrary that he had stolen nothing. He had indeed approached his lover with the intention of telling her something but just as he was about to do so he slipped and in falling his lips brushed his beloved's ear, caressed her cheek, and fleetingly tasted her lips. This was no kiss but rather happenstance, a marginal benefit, a chance reward. He had done her no injury, caused no wound, and should be held harmless.

The Court pronounced judgment in favor of the defendant. The relevant principle was easily stated. The defendant lover's surprise planting of a kiss had been an innocent and admirable expression of affection. Lovers should not be threatened by attention nor embarrassed by the public acknowledgment of their desires. In the absence of any positive evidence of harm being occasioned by this kiss, it could stand without censure and indeed deserved praise for its courage and attention to desire. That said, the relevant rules of osculation are in accord with the principle as stated.

First, kisses between lovers are to be encouraged. The only real measure of the legitimacy of the kiss is the desire that drives it. Provided that affect and mouth are in accord, then the kiss is commendable. Second, while kisses are the stuff of amorous expression there is little need for circumspection. The presence of friends or others in public space is no proper bar to osculation. The more visible the love, the greater the social territory and public space of desire. Third, sensitivity limits the above rule only to the extent that the husband or just possibly a competing lover are present and the kiss may unnecessarily inflame or wound them. Fourth, assuming that the kiss is legitimate under Rule 1, that is to say that it is exchanged between lovers and expresses an honest desire, then it cannot be theft unless it goes too far.

If the kiss is in public and is taken by surprise, law dictates only that it be limited in duration and depth. There is always a little element of the arbitrary in general rules but here is how it was formulated. Where the kiss is in public and without notice then it should be neither overlong nor excessive. The question of length is one of degree in the discretion of the court. The matter of excess has clearer markers. The kiss was illicit if the hands wandered below the waist or onto the breasts. It was theft if the brush of the lips turned to biting. Then it became larceny—"larrecin publicque," or *furtum manifestum osculum* as Symphorianus puts it. The law of love decrees that on surprising your lover in public, you can kiss but you can't consume. Options should be open. Stay or go, stop or continue, chaste or lascivious, becomes a question of negotiation, of intimate intimation.

The New Laws, under the third heading *Of Presumptions*, is in accord with the earlier law. The specific case concerns a young man who, having been permitted to kiss his lover, squeezes her buttocks. According to old law the presumption here was that the man had acted illicitly. Under the new law no such presumption was to be made. Each case was to be evaluated on its specific facts. That said, the law tended to view kissing as one thing, an oral adventure, and hands wandering over erogenous zones as another and more extensive embrace. The crucial question was whether or not the complainant indicated, however discreetly—and all lovers know how important it is for appearances to be kept up—that the approach upset or angered her. The slightest indicator, the smallest sign of disapproval was all that was needed.

Such rules provide an important and useful map of the intimate public sphere of kissing. They are educative for the young, comforting of the anxieties of parents, and potentially highly probative for resolving disputes as to erotic encounters in the workplace. End if you will in current affairs. With a celebrated case of a professor kissing a graduate student. The details of this case have been elaborated elsewhere and at some length and so the bare details will do.

A female graduate student, Dana Beckleman, was infatuated with her professor, her dissertation supervisor, Professor Jane Gallop. Beckleman from time to time let slip her desire for Gallop. Erotic notes and essays on love were sent, and conversation occasionally got down and dirty. The couple would go for coffee and occasionally for drinks; they got in the habit of lightly kissing in greeting and parting, though nothing beyond that was done. At least not until a very public conference of gay and lesbian graduate students. Late at night, at a post conference disco, Gallop decided to leave and in front of a large number of participants kissed Beckleman goodnight.

This kiss is a famous one. It lasted a minute or more. According to the complaint that Beckleman later made, Gallop had said, "Aren't you going to kiss me goodnight?" Beckleman proffered her mouth expecting a peck, whereupon Gallop galloped: "she mashed her lips against mine and shoved her tongue in my mouth and just sat there." Beckelman goes on to say that she was feeling vindictive at the time, there had been an upsetting interaction earlier that day, and so she decided spontaneously to kiss Gallop back: "I was angry and hurt and I saw kissing her as a form of revenge, a way to manipulate her desire knowing I would never go any further."

Gallop claims in her defence and in a book—*Feminist Accused of Sexual Harrassment*—that the kiss was purely semiotic. A didactic performance. An epistemic insufflation. And she claims too that it took her by surprise. Realizing that this was no ordinary kiss she decided it must be a performance of sorts, a feminist enactment of desire as knowledge, a dramatization of lesbian lust and of its infraction of university norms. Not a bad argument but equally not a very relevant way of addressing the nature of the kiss.

Start with the details and move to the motives. According to the laws of love the kiss could be criticized on several rather peripheral grounds. It was not a particularly sensitive sounding embrace, it was a touch inactive or indecisive on Gallop's part and under the discretionary rule governing length of kiss, it was arguably though certainly not necessarily too long. The real question, however, is whether or not the kiss was salacious and so illicit under the second criterion that prohibits biting. Here it seems evident that if the parties were lovers then the kiss was thoroughly reasonable. There was no biting, no excessive consummation or consumption. The issue is a much deeper one. It is epistemological. Was this an honest kiss?

There was certainly charge and desire between the parties. They had a flirtatiously erotic relation. Beckleman talks of the kiss as being on her part "more vindictive than reciprocally sexual." It is a significant choice of words. Vindictive has its root in to vindicate. At one level this means to set free, so that Beckleman was seemingly seeking to liberate herself, or in legal jargon she wanted manumission: the Professorial tongue would allow her to let go of her desire. Take this longing from my tongue. At the same time, we have no choice but to note that the kiss was also sexual, it was interlaced with anger and desire, hurt and love. It is not unequivocally a dishonest kiss; it is simply a complicated one. And Gallop too acknowledges confusion. She didn't start the explicitly sexual aspect of the kiss. She may have wanted to, but aware of the context she opted to view the osculatory exchange as a perfomative, as a mode of enacting and so teaching the character of lesbian knowledge as desire and transgressive practice.

A kiss at cross-purposes is not of itself an illicit exchange. If Beckleman is to be believed in saying that she would never go any further than the kiss, she might be questioned as to betrayal or even treason according to the laws of love. The doctrine is pretty clear. The kiss *ab ore* or on the mouth is, according to Capellanus, a promise of further and more extensive embraces to come. Here then, by her own confession, Beckleman admits that anger made her provocative and duplicitous. She was teasing her professor, acting out her frustrations, using her mouth to communicate a complicated and probably unsuccessful message. That said, however, it is evident that there was ample desire underlying the kiss. It was not a promise made to a stranger but rather a promise partly intended and partly withholding or opaque. Surrounding evidence and earlier encounters suggest that there was sufficient desire, though it may have been mixed with anger and jealousy, to constitute an honest embrace. But jealousy here I think is the key.

According to the law of love the public kiss should avoid wanton hurt to others. Granted that neither party had a lover or spouse present one might think that they were free to kiss at length and as they liked. The furor created by the case and the complaint that followed, indicate something different. It is true that these are mad times; that all erotic exchanges are subject to bizarre and restrictive criteria and codes of professional and workplace conduct. That may be part of the issue but the laws of love suggest something more profound.

A professor, to quote Robert Louis Stevenson, is a person of distinction, someone who has manifestly achieved recognition, an authority figure, and sometimes (too infrequently I fear) an object of veneration. Gallop herself, in discussing this case points out that transference, the displacement of an earlier love onto the authority figure is common in academic contexts. The good teacher is often an object of desire and has both to live with that, learn from it, and use it in their teaching. Students are likely to have momentary or lengthier infatuations with teachers. And, to be brutal about it, vice versa. Think of the statistics on marriage between professors and students. It runs at about thirty percent. Something erotic is going on. That is for sure.

Return now to the decision of the High Court of Love in the last case reported. It seems unlikely that Gallop would be held to have stolen a kiss but it does seem clear that she infracted a lesser rule. Recollect that the law of love dictates that kissing should be avoided where another lover is present and may be unnecessarily hurt by witnessing an extended osculatory exchange. As is well known, and as Gallop acknowledges, students desire professors, and some or many of those present were likely infatuated with or at least desirous of the attentions of Gallop. She was a famous professor, a hip leader of a new theory movement in academia, and so likely always to be in the student eye. And quite possibly also in the eye of her colleagues. The entire conference context was one of transference. Multiple transferences. She should have known that others would be hurt. She should not have kissed Beckleman lengthily in front of her peers. Not at least in that non-pedagogic context. Her actions were over the line.

I don't think one can plausibly interpret the laws of love as likely to have held Gallop guilty of larceny of a kiss. Her offense did not rise to a crime against love. In fact she was trying quite commendably to promote and expand the realm of public desire to lesbian couples, to older and younger partners, teachers and students. She just did it in a questionable way. She infracted a minor rule. Let's say that she lifted a kiss, took it out of context, flaunted it too publicly, and so failed to pay her way as a teacher and lover of knowledge. She was in the wrong. Not because of the kiss per se, but rather because of the transference present in the context. All those other students who might be or were in love with her, they would likely be hurt or threatened or put in their place.

No matter the outcome, what is truly relevant is that the laws and cases of love provide a language in which to address a charged and emotional dispute as to manners and powers such as are raised by institutional figures kissing. The laws provide a mechanism and process for addressing intimate public acts that today are at best excoriated administratively and at worst legally and by means of lawyers' usual emotional aphasia. The High Court had an array of tools, a map of kissing, both experience and reasons that applied to the detailed practice of osculation. Such rules and coda are nowhere studied today. That is unfortunate. It is our loss not theirs. In fact, if philosophy can be taken in a secondary sense to mean the wisdom of kissing then the High Court of Love was more philosophical and quite simply wiser than courts today.

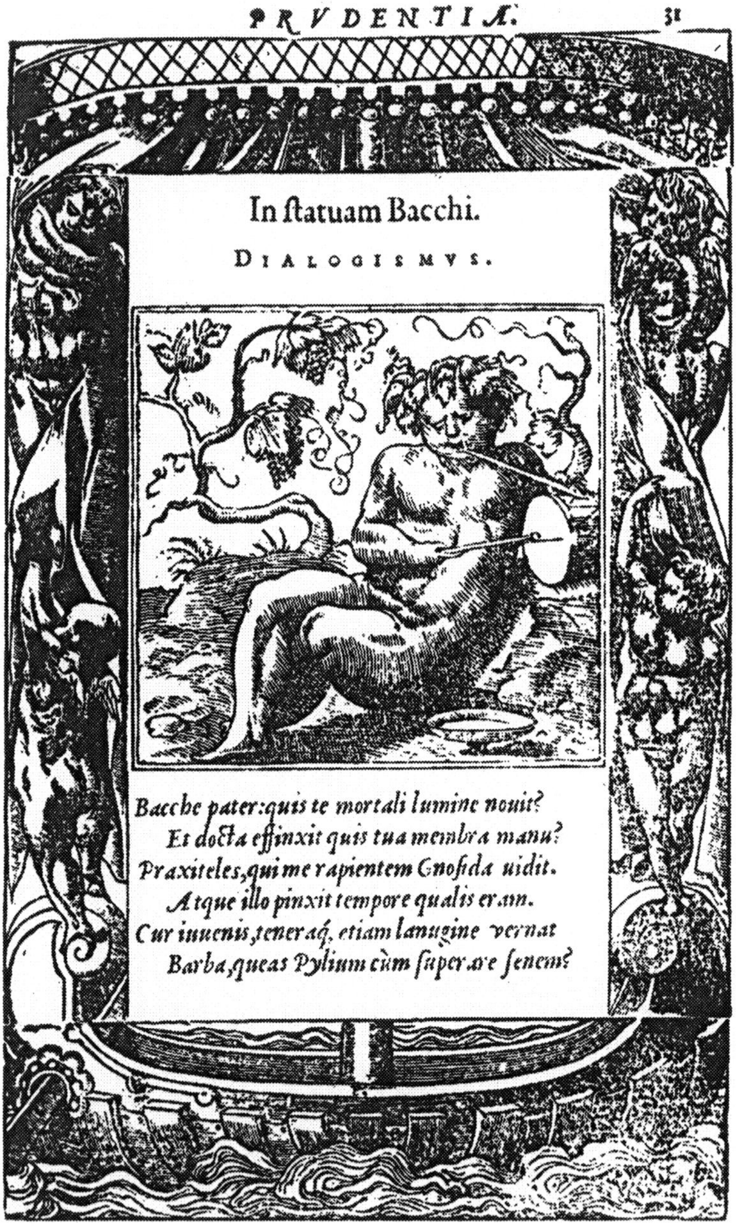
PRVDENTIÆ. 31

In ſtatuam Bacchi.

DIALOGISMVS.

Bacche pater: quis te mortali lumine nouit?
Et docta effinxit quis tua membra manu?
Praxiteles, qui me rapientem Gnoſida uidit.
Atque illo pinxit tempore qualis eram.
Cur iuuenis, teneraq. etiam lanugine vernat
Barba, queas Pylium cùm ſuperare ſenem?

Figure 9 In statuam Bacchi (on a statue of Bacchus)—Andreas Alciatus, *Emblematum libellus* (1531).

8
The Dolorific Calculus

There is a very simple principle that underlies all of the laws of love. It is that desire hurts and fulfillment brings relief. As simple as that. As complex as that. Pain and pleasure, beginning and end, the history of love is the quest for release from the fond sufferings of hope or the less dulcet frustrations of an unattainable amour. In between the great passion and its satisfaction is the distance traversed, the trajectory from lack to fulfillment, from the pangs of hope to the joys of expression. The founding charter of the Gay Consistory, the mid-fourteenth century learned and legal council which inscribed and published the most comprehensive of the laws of love—*las leys d'amors*—expressly dictates as much: "Pleasure and enjoyment are the sole purpose of the Gay Science and its laws." To the end of producing such happy climax the laws set out the rules of amorous dialogue, the poetics, the eloquence and good taste that best leads to love's expression, its enjoyment, its fulfillment. The rhetorical rules of the gay science—the earlier troubadour's *dreit d'amor*—dictate the means of transforming desire into fulfillment, lust into communication, and so they map the path from inside to outside, from conception to fruition, or in the terms of the precious Madeleine de Scudéry, amorous cartographer, from danger to the delicacies of genuine affection. But first things first. Love starts, the treatises all tell us, in agitation, anxiety, suffering and pain. First comes Cupid's dart, a wound, a blow, a certain mania or madness.

The philosophically oriented *Treatise on Love* by Capellanus begins, page one, first proposition, emblematic definition, with the statement: "Love is an inborn suffering resulting from the sight of and immoderate thinking about an image of the other sex." We start the journey toward love with a specter, a face, a visual trigger that subsists in the form of an unrequited fantasm of the object of desire. Thus the ambivalence of the common English "I want him, her, them, it," meaning simultaneously I desire and I lack. Want hurts. Love begins in suffering, a solitary lust, an interior excitation, a compulsion, palpitation, fever, obsession. The *Code of Love* thus sets out numerous physical indicators of falling in love. Rule 15: "Every lover tends to grow pale when their beloved looks at them." Rule 16: "The heart of a lover beats fast at the sight of the beloved." Rule 23: "Someone in love finds it hard to eat and to sleep." And Rule 30: "A true lover clings constantly to the image of the beloved." Four rules that together indicate serious trouble, physical discomfort, a danger to health and a threat to well being. This is the stuff of lovesickness or, to use the proper medical phrase of the time, erotic mania, the agitation and disturbance of a new desire.

The anonymous *Treatise on Perfect Love* that came in part as a response to Capellanus compounds the sense in which suffering is intrinsic to the birth of love. The author of this short juridical tract lists 23 disputed questions of love or *quaestiones amoris*, and of these a full seven are concerned more or less directly with the sufferings of lovers, with a dolorific calculus, with sighs and pain. An initial example, Question 3: "Why is it that at first encounter true lovers become pale, numb, unsteady, and often mute?" The answer is that on first encounter love, which governs the whole spectrum of the soul, absorbs all the energies of the afflicted party. A new love spreads into the deepest interior of the heart and disturbs all of its functions, physical and spiritual: "the tongue refuses to speak, the eyes to see, the ears to hear, and all the other parts of the body become dysfunctional. So much so that if love is delayed long, the body, deprived of its strength and functions, will waste away." The contraction of erotic mania is a signal danger, a matter of life and death. And like most matters medico-legal this malady or wound requires classification, measure, and explanation.

Turning to the last of the questions of love posed in the *Treatise* we find what is perhaps the most direct of analyses of the physiognomy of lovesickness. "Why is it that a lover who quarrels with his beloved and is then denied the pleasures of amorous intimacy will often fall so ill as to be in danger of dieing, and with blood spilling from their mouth?" The answer is that the sudden loss of love is a sorrow that penetrates the inflamed heart. The dual intensities of love and loss tear the heart apart and place the deprived lover in danger of death. At the same time, the release of this disappointed heat in the form of sighs will often so dilate the arteries as to rupture the veins in the chest and blood will in consequence flow from the mouth like water from a spring. Which doesn't sound good and cannot by the seems of it be very easily cured.

I suspect that erotic medicine has both progressed and regressed since Gilles of Rome, the probable author of the *Treatise on Perfect Love*, composed his various explanations of the norms of true love. And blood is always a metaphor, a sign of an emotive cause, of disturbance, harm or dilation. The point to be drawn from these various and diverse calculations of the physical impact of falling in love is that the laws of love start with a rupture, a rending of the body, a symbolic collapse that ushers in the various customary norms of erotic erudition, an amorous pedagogy and law that will fill the gap or heal the wound that love has brought. That is why the pallid lover, the trembling aspirant, the teary eyed suitor is a fit subject of medical diagnosis and of legal education. That or the alternative of interment, as most famously with the troubadour Jaufré de Rudel who fell in love with the Countess of Tripoli without ever having seen her. He simply liked what he had heard of her. He wrote songs to her. He joined a crusade in the hope of seeing her but fell ill on the boat and was carried on a stretcher to Tripoli and left for dead at an Inn. The Countess heard of this and came to see him. Jaufré, recovering his senses momentarily, died in her arms.

If falling in love can cause a suffering even unto death—if unrequited desire can lead to a nihilistic posing of the question: "What is the point?"—then the first act of the medico-legal practitioner has to be that of diagnosing the degree of the harm, the extent of the suffering endured by frustrated or abandoned lovers. The dolorific calculus is the flip side of the Benthamite felicific calculus. One measures sorrow, the other happiness. Polar points on the same hedonic scale. Different moments in the history of a love affair. But nonetheless these are two faces of the same event, two points on the map, beginning and ending of the love affair. That is how it was viewed and the poets and other theorists of amatory law were full of cases, doctrines, norms, and other explanations of the extent of the suffering endured by unfulfilled or jilted lovers. These were the subject of amorous histories, of the annals of gallantry, the emotional histories of the Court, of salon and society, of rollick and rupture.

What are the degrees of pain, who suffers most and how is that suffering to be accounted, how remedied? These are staple questions of love, constant referents in the *demandes d'amour*, and frequently pleaded for resolution before the diverse courts of love. Is it worse to love in vain or to be rejected? Does someone whose lover betrays them for another suffer more than one whose lover dies? Is it better to experience love and then lose it or never to taste love at all? Does someone who dares not voice their love for fear of rejection suffer more than one who declares a love and is rebuffed? The answer to that, incidentally, according to

Poirier is that the former suffers more dolorously. At least the lover who tries and fails, has declared their love, knows the answer, and can in theory move on. Or, take a last example, a question of amorous felicity just for a change: Is it ethical to pursue a spontaneous lust? If a couple suddenly, by chance encounter and instant arousal, consummate their desire, are they to be censored according to the code of love? The answer to that is no, so long as it doesn't happen too often. Rule 29 of the *Code*: "Someone affected by excessive sensuality is usually not in love." But in moderation spontaneous intimacy, where occasion both prompts and allows, is to be tolerated as a fact of love. There is a much more extensive jurisprudence, a labyrinthine casuistry and with it an ethics that seeks to limit suffering either, as in the last case, by allowing a sudden fulfillment, or as in the next case by demanding of lovers that the fostering of hope of future fulfillment be authentic and in good faith.

The question arose in the first case of love reported by Capellanus. The complaint was that the defendant woman had gratuitously inflicted amorous burdens so as to taunt the complainant suitor. The facts were reviewed earlier in relation to contracts of love and their proper interpretation and so can be summarized briefly. The woman's promise to her suitor was: "you must agree to bind yourself completely to my will and promise to obey all of my commands and simultaneously agree to be utterly deprived of my love if you act to the contrary." The suitor so promised. The woman then commanded him no longer to seek her love and never to praise her in public again.

The suitor broke his promise. When he heard others speaking ill of her in public, he came to her defense. He both denounced her defamers and sung her praises. She treated this as breach of promise and told him that he was never again to seek her love. The Court of the Countess of Champagne heard the case and pronounced judgment for the plaintiff. Quite aside from issues of interpretation according to the principles of love, it was unjust to destroy the hopes of a lover when all he had done was seek to protect her honor and name. She was in bad faith and had acted unethically precisely because the law of love treats it as a first principle that all actions be directed toward the augmentation of pleasure, the expansion of desire. The judgment seeks to facilitate felicity and limit suffering. The dolorific calculus may be a fact of life, a sad reflection of the injuries that distance, convention, status, and preference can bring, but wherever there is choice, then the denizens of the domain of desire must exercise that choice so as to limit the suffering of other lovers. That is the broad principle at play in most of the rest of the case law and doctrine concerned with the causes of suffering and the remedies for despair. Take a look, have a gander.

The advocate and notary Alain Chartier in *The Book of Four Women* provides a fine and elaborately staged illustration of this somewhat quixotic classificatory enterprise. Four women debate the suffering caused by their particular plight. One had lost her lover in war, at the battle of Agincourt. The second woman's lover had been taken prisoner by the English. The third had not heard of her lover since the battle. The fourth woman lamented a lover who had run away from the field of battle. Who had suffered most? The answer was that the third woman scored highest on the dolorific calculus. She had to live without knowing whether or not her lover was alive or dead. She suffered twice, a double uncertainty, a bipolar pain: she had to mourn him as if he was dead and she had to mourn him also as if he was lost but still living. Each was its own kind of suffering and the uncertainty exacerbated both, she could neither act as if freed by his death nor attend to the hope that if lost he might return. Of the other women, the first was free to take another lover and so could in time recover her joy. The fourth woman was also at liberty to take another lover without moral blame. The second woman could live in the hope of the escape or release of her lover. The third alone suffered without remedy and suffered most.

Chartier's *Book* provides a significant systematization of the earlier tradition and it is interesting that the discussion explicitly begins by invoking the courts of love and staging the debate so as to banish melancholy—*pour oublier melencolie*—and to lighten the heart with joyful conversation. Suffering expressed and measured, exteriorized and subjected to analysis was easier to bear, closer to remedy than the trembling and solitary experience of the first shocks of thwarted desire. The same point can be drawn at length from Guillaume de Machaut's *Judgment of the King of Bohemia*. This poses an exemplary and frequently repeated question of love in a lyrical and legal manner. Who suffers more, a man whose lover has taken a new partner or a woman whose lover dies? The various commonplaces and precedents of the laws of love are rehearsed and rebutted, reviewed and reprised.

The two melancholic lovers debate their history and their suffering. The woman had been happily engaged in a love affair for roughly eight years. They had been as one, his joy was her joy, her desire was his wish, and there was nothing that could come between them. Then fate intervened and her lover died. She was cast into the depths of a blinding sorrow, an inconsolable loss. Ahead of her there is only bleakness and emptiness: "My days will be dark and full of woe; my hopes will remain unfulfilled; and my grief will be hard and unremitting, for I must ceaselessly grow pale, tremble, blush and quake, grieve, weep, sigh and moan, and shudder in the dread of despair." All her pleasures reversed, she wants only to die. At which, final flourish, persuasive peroration, enactment of ending, she faints.

The man's story by contrast was that of having fallen in love with a woman whom he sought to serve without reward. His was a pure or we would say platonic love. He worshiped his beloved and "the sweet image of her face was so imprinted in [his] heart that it remains there ever, and has never left ..." The magnitude of his love was the measure of the extent of his loss when his lover abandoned him by falling for another man: "Fortune the traitor, who behaves differently towards each of us" renounced him and his grief was so great as to leave him wishing only for death. Time, he argues, only augments his grief, his growing desolation: "When I see her love another and have no care for me ... my love nearly drives me mad." His sorrow runs so deep that he could elicit no pleasure even from remembering their former love. He rather "lies vanquished in the blind alley of memory," and seeks only to die.

The King of Bohemia hears the lengthy arguments and then sets out a judgment according to the relevant law. He starts from the premise that both the pleasures and sufferings of love are visceral, they gain their first and greatest expression in physical affections, in bodily feelings, in embrace. Being a carnal affection "its desires and essence all incline to pleasure" as expressed through the presence of the beloved. Thus if a lover dies and their soul leaves their body then over time love will diminish and so too the suffering of the survivor: "Since she will not see him again ... she will forget him; for the heart will never love anything so much that it won't forget it after separation."

As for the man, he continues to suffer. If love is a carnal affection its access to the heart is through the beauty of the beloved and hence through the eyes. The man still sees his unfaithful lover: "Love enflames him night and day, and he will not and cannot forget his loss." In consequence, "he languishes in great folly, madness, grief and delirium, in great jealousy, and in danger of losing both life and soul." Concluding that "he who is closest to the fire burns the most," the King gives judgment for the man because he has to live with the presence of his loss. He suffers the most and the remedy, in time tested manner, was that he be the guest of honor at a banquet and then detained a week in the company of the Court, humored, praised, cheered, and then sent on his way with gifts and good wishes. The hope being that this treatment would tip the scales from sorrow to felicity.

There are cases that decide this question of love differently. The Court of the King of Navarre, for example, records a judgment on this issue, appealed from Bohemia, to the opposite effect but the reason was largely the weakness of the arguments made by the lover who had been betrayed. They became absurd and in consequence the King was forced to allow that in the instant case the woman whose lover had died had suffered most. The dolorific calculus is much more specific than the felicific scale, and for all that the logic of love is general the decision of cases is a matter of lesbian rule, of equity and its flexible measure. Suffering is particular and its measure is specific to the time and occasion of the plea. It is transitive and the dolorific calculus is similarly instantaneous and subject to change.

Such contingent factors and the flexible rule that they engender are much to the fore in a case brought before the Court of Queen Fiammetta as reported in Boccaccio's *Questioni d'amore*. Two women, two sisters, debate which of them suffers the most. The first sister, rather late in her youth, fell in love with a young gentleman. Coming to love late, she was mightily struck and decided to consummate her desire. She seduced the young man and the two then became greatly enamored of each other. The flames burned, their vehemence increased, their love was all consuming.

Misfortune struck when the young man was found guilty of a crime and was exiled for life from the city. Dreading death he left without any prospect of returning. The woman was left alone and inconsolable, doleful and desperate.

The second sister had also fallen in love and sought likewise to consummate her desire. Unfortunately for her she was unable to fulfill her ambition. Circumstances got in the way and she suffered mightily the pangs of thwarted passion. Queen Fiammetta was then asked to decide which woman was suffering the most?

She responds that the suffering of each of the women was great, "but considering adversity to be most grievous to her that has tasted prosperity, we deem that the woman who has lost her lover suffers most." This decision was challenged. It was argued that the second sister who had to live with the continued presence of the man she desired but could not enjoy suffered most. Her sister who had irretrievably lost her enamorata was at least free of his presence and could in time move on. Fiammetta responded by saying that this objection might become true—if the loss was an old one—but as between the two sisters at the time of the debate, the greater grief was that of the sister who had loved and lost. She who loves well never forgets. The other sister, by way of contrast, might still hope to fulfill her desires with another: she could hope to love again, and hope is a great diminisher of grief.

The point is made again in a reprise of the judgment in slightly different circumstances. The issue in the next case is that of whether a lover who is shunned by their enamorata suffers more than a lover whose partner is unfaithful. Is frustration more painful than jealousy? The case is again brought before the Court of Queen Fiammetta.

The first lover had for long resisted what he calls the "snares of love." Eventually, however, he succumbs and falls for a woman he has recently met. He is pierced by Cupid's golden arrow. She however is shot with an arrow of lead. She sees his love but shuns it. She is cold, cruel, and indifferent. Nothing would change her behavior and the frustrated lover was left with "infinite sighs and many tears."

The second lover pleaded an ever greater grief. He had a lover with whom he had enjoyed all the gifts of love. He was wholly enamored of her and was uncompromisingly loyal. She, however, did not believe his protestations of infinite love and expressed interest in another lover. He was furious and hurt. Over time he became obsessed with her infidelity and not an hour would go by without his thinking of her indifference toward him and her interest in others. With those thoughts came great unhappiness. A sorrow he believed to be quite beyond that of the merely unsuccessful lover.

Queen Fiammetta hears the pleas and pronounces judgment for the jealous lover. Her reasoning is as follows. The unsuccessful lover can still hope that his grief will later be eased but the jealous lover will always suffer doubt—once suspicion enters the relationship nothing can draw it away. His sorrow is the greater.

The unloved lover challenged the decision. He argues that at least the jealous lover has tasted love and continues to enjoy the intimacies that he desires: the suspicious lover can still delight in holding his lover whereas the unloved lover can only experience the pain of separation. Queen Fiammetta responds by acknowledging that the frustrations must be great and the pain intolerable but nonetheless we have to believe that no love is in vain. The jilted lover has to hope that he will eventually succeed in his desires. The solution to his grief, in other words, is simple and singular; it is that of gaining the affection of the woman he loves. It may hurt to have to wait but it may well be that the waiting ends happily: "The inconstancy of her heart may well at some point make her attainable." She may simply have been waiting for proof of his love. This and other thoughts must serve to comfort him in his admittedly serious sorrow.

The jealous lover suffers more. The greater the love, the greater the grief caused by the fear of infidelity: "His mind is full of infinite terrors, which neither hope nor any other pleasure can ease." Every act of his beloved will bring suspicion: her feet, her hands, her eyes will seem to wander. Every word she speaks will appear to be full of double meanings. And by the same token, if he finds a reason for jealousy he is compelled to pretend that he has not seen it. Filled with such doubt he cannot enjoy her embraces, intimacy just brings the thought of the others that she will hold and "infects his mind's ease" like a virulent virus. He is plagued by imaginations of her deceit. If she by chance acts with love toward him, he will suspect that it is simply so as to dispel his doubts; if she acts indifferently toward him then he immediately believes that she is in love with another. Fiammetta concludes by noting that the jealous person harbors an infinite number of suspicions and such a life is much more grievous than that of the suitor who can still hope that his love will come to fruition.

It is an interesting determination and a graphic depiction of the confusion and suffering of one who is jealous. It suggests that jealousy is much harder to cure than almost any of the other wounds of love. This was indeed recognized from early on in the tradition. The *Code of Love* states as much, by Rule 28: "The slightest suspicion forces a lover to think sinister thoughts," and in Fiammetta's terms it potentially leads to immeasurable pain. Jealousy will destroy love and this doctrine is confirmed nicely by the *Treatise on Perfect Love* which begins with the question: "Can jealousy play any role in love?" The answer is straightforwardly no. Jealousy is no more than the expression of suspicion, fear, and unjust accusation. Love must exclude fear and in doing so it banishes jealousy forever. That is the principle but it also has to be acknowledged, as Fiammetta's decision does, that not all love is perfect and those that suffer jealous thoughts suffer terribly.

Jealousy, however, is consistently deemed to be the paradoxical enemy of true love. Jealousy certainly marks a passion. Rule 21 of the *Code of Love* dictates that "true jealousy makes love grow." True jealousy—*vera zelotypia*—refers primarily to the lovers' fears that they cannot give enough to their beloved. It is a birthing pain, a contraction prior to expression and in later amorous doctrine will be translated as zeal rather than as jealousy. In its dolorific meaning, jealousy is an impulse toward possession, it illustrates well Nietzsche's aphoristic notion of love as "lust for property," but it isolates, limits, and separates the lover from the communicative space of relationship, the in between of desire. The early rhetoricians used the image of a clenched fist as opposed to an open hand to depict the difference between jealousy and love, the proprietary practices of law strictly so called and *lex amatoria* or poetic justice. Jealousy, a proprietary emotion, breeds distance, confusion, and tentative love. It tends to cause the afflicted to vacate the domain of image and affection for a phantasmagoria of sinister specters. Ardour is turned to fever; zeal becomes sickness. Thus the second rule of the *Code of Love*, often mistranslated, is that "a lover is always ardent," or more literally "he who is not zealous cannot be in love." The verb *zelo* means to love with zeal, with ardour, passionately, and by the time that Capellanus was writing that was its primary and more or less only meaning. Love must wax or it will wane.

Whatever the philological details of that particular rule, the *Code of Love* enacts generosity and, no doubt, liberality not suspicion as the principle of proper passion. Thus, Rule 10: "Love will always flee an avaricious house." Miserliness, caution, tentativeness and withholding all act as obstacles to love. The very first *Precept of Love* is to the same and compelling effect: "Miserliness is a terrible disease, embrace its opposite." At one level we can take that to mean don't hoard, possess, control or otherwise attempt to own a lover. They are not property or at least to the extent that they belong to each other it is *animus gratia*, a gift of the spirit and not a matter of mercantile or mundane exchange. That, however, is too literal a meaning of the precept. The gift economy of love is predicated upon generosity for sure but this is not a matter of things but rather an emotional exchange. The roots of generosity are affective and altruistic: lovers, to coin a phrase, hold all things in common. Within the gift economy of emotional exchange, jealousy thus lies at the furthest extreme of the dolorific calculus while the gift freely given is felicity itself. At one pole, insidious doubt, at the other free expression, fluid exchange if not necessarily exchange of fluids. The point is lucidly expanded in two cases reported by Poirier.

The first, Judgment 29, was a complaint brought by a Knight who had publicly and vocally declared his love for the defendant woman. He had tirelessly paraded his desire and had frequently told his closest friend how his lover was to be honored and admired. Strong stuff. But the friend had betrayed these confidences and had become the woman's lover. This, the complainant argued, was mortal treason; it was the felony of theft, and contrary to every rule of the art of love.

The Bailiff of Love summoned the woman and the friend and requested an explanation. The friend said that while he greatly regretted the consequences of his passion, he had been powerless to prevent it. He had fallen in love with the woman and had yielded, helpless before his desire. He had done nothing that could be construed as dishonorable and there his defense rested. And it is true that the *Code of Love*,

Rule 4, does dictate that "love is always either waxing or waning", and by Rule 17 it is confirmed that "a new love forces out the old." Such can be acknowledged but does not resolve the issue.

The co-defendant woman was brought forward and asked why she had transferred her affections from the plaintiff to his friend. She replied that for a while the Knight had loved her loyally and generously and she had returned that love without any thought of taking any other lover. Time, however, changed the relationship. The Knight became infected with jealousy. He began to doubt her. His doubts led to awkwardness, to obsession, to fear and inappropriateness. He became melancholic and started acting bizarrely. He would whisper disconcerting questions in her ear when he met her. And all this despite the fact that she had been constant, true, and loyal. Eventually his phantasms became self-fulfilling. She hated his jealousy, she despised his possessiveness, and started to mock his hallucinations. She said that he had gone mad and she had fled his madness. It was his jealousy that pushed her away and she eventually turned to another lover who was zealous, generous, and free of jealousy.

The Bailiff of Love heard the arguments and pronounced judgment for the defendants. The plaintiff must lose his plea because jealousy clouds the heart; it is a species of madness and is unworthy of a lover. He was ordered to seek his own peace, free of jealousy and open once again to love. The lovers thus were entitled to enjoy their love. It was happy and it was free of jealousy.

It is a strong determination but one that is exemplary of the later law. Judgment 15 before the Bailiff of Love offers a discursive confirmation of the principle. Here the Bailiff is asked to resolve a question of love: Can there be jealousy in love? His answer is a vehement negative: "once a lover has freely chosen the object of their love, then they must believe in their loyalty and assume nothing but good-will in their beloved." The amorous logic that underpins this decision is simply that love must conquer jealousy, and generosity overcome avarice. The reasons are set out in terms of the dolorific effects of jealousy. Where jealousy is seen and spoken, it causes harm to lovers. More than that, jealousy is so powerful and tyrannical a force that when it takes hold, it captures the heart and drives out all love. At a more pragmatic relational level, jealousy engenders confusion, dispute, and noise. On one translation that would mean that jealousy leads to violence, to blows. Which is not inaccurate, particularly if one takes account of the theory of jealousy that the Bailiff subsequently elaborates.

Jealousy is expressly contrary to amorous law. It leads to bad love, the wasting of relationship, to emotional avarice. The Bailiff is quite direct about it. The jealous lover is insatiably greedy, avaricious of the emotions and time of their lover because jealousy demands everything, it covets, it hides, it seeks to take everything back. Thus jealousy turns generosity into property, love into accountancy. Jealousy doesn't sleep; it doesn't stop. It is deaf to good counsel. And finally, "jealousy desires to purloin the goods of others." Which is to say that jealousy is theft. It steals emotions. It is the larceny of love.

The crime of the jealous lover is in the end that of seeking to sequestrate or hide the enamorata from the world, from friends, society, and happiness. Jealousy isolates, it removes the lover from the domain of love and hides them in a secret and asocial sphere. Specters prompt suspicion, suspicion leads to isolation, and with isolation comes suffering, even unto madness or at least off the scale of the dolorific calculus. A last judgment, this time from the High Court of Love, can serve to illustrate the attempt of the doctors and procurators of love to draw jealous or miserly lovers away from their suffering and back into the hecatombs, which is to say into the pleasure of play, and the domain of desire.

Judgment 49 before the High Court of Love concerned the ratification of a mandate of grace obtained by the defendant from the Chancellery of Love. The complainant woman accused the defendant of delinquency She said that she had long and happily given all of her heart to the defendant. She had given him as much pleasure as she possibly could. She could not, however, always welcome, acknowledge or please him as much as she would like because her husband was suspicious and ever watchful over her. Thus she would often ignore him in public and certainly could not welcome him as she would have wished. Even if marriage was not love, a wife still had a duty to fear her husband—*uxores maritos timeo debent* as Symphorianus notes. Thus on the day of the events complained of the plaintiff woman had felt obliged to walk past the defendant without acknowledging him at all. She knew her husband was watching her from a distance and so when she had seen him, her lover, she had turned her face away and pretended not to hear the words he whispered as he passed. Patience, she argued, is an essential virtue in love affairs, and so too was the sharing of suffering that separation will bring.

Despite the desideratum of equanimity, of taking time and remaining calm, the thwarted lover had become enraged. The woman's complaint continues that taking offence at her apparent nonchalance, he lost his patience and devised an infelicitous and malevolent scheme for revenge. That night he came to the woman's house and to attract her attention threw three or four large snowballs at the window. When she failed to appear below to talk with him he took a large rock and threw it at the window. The result was that several panes of glass were shattered. Shards of glass flew everywhere and one landed on the woman's nose causing a nasty cut and much loss of blood. More disagreeable still, not content with the damage he had caused, the defendant then ritualistically tore up and stamped on a pretty ribbon that she had earlier given him. He had further attempted to harm her by speaking ill of her. All of which amounted to a considerable amorous delinquency and he should be ordered by the Court to make honorable amends. He should walk bareheaded and barefoot, dressed only in a shirt, through the town and publicly and loudly declare that he had "falsely and malevolently wounded and defamed his lover, and that he now repented and begged for her forgiveness."

The defendant argued in reply that the woman was irrationally and unreasonably fearful of her husband. No wife had ever been as tyrannized as she by her spouse. She seemed incapable of taking a single step without her husband knowing it. She did not seem able to leave her house without a guardian one step behind her. No lover in human memory had ever had to suffer as he had. He could not approach her by day or by night. The only time he seemed able to visit her was in the very depths of winter, when the guardians were driven indoors by the cold, and even then he could not talk with her at any length. On the night in question, it had been unbelievably cold and he had waited outside her house for several hours in the hope that she would come out and play. He had waited and waited. His feet began to freeze. He started to cough and then banged on her door but nothing emerged. Partly to warm himself up and partly to attract her attention, and then in desperation he had thrown some snowballs at her window. One of the snowballs was quite heavy and had broken the glass but he could not have known that it would, he was far too cold and numb by then, nor could he possibly dream that she was under the window and would be hurt by the falling shards of the shattered panes. He continued by saying that he bore her no malice and wished her no harm. He never had and never would. And as for the ribbon he had thrown it to the ground and was dancing on it for joy. He had a beautiful lover and he wanted the world to know.

For the above reasons, the defendant had sought and obtained letters of pardon from the Chancellery of Love and he now asked that they be ratified by the High Court. The High Court complied with his request. Love will often lead to injuries—*causa bellandi est amor*—and here they were unintentional and quite excusable. A slip or chance infraction should not be punished and so pardon was affirmed and granted.

Reformulate this conclusion in terms of the dolorific calculus. As the *New Laws* put it, sighs are the mainstay of the Chancellery of Love. This means that suffering is both the subject matter and the object of the amatory lawyers' writs. Suffering prompts intervention, injunctions, or because here the jurisdiction is that of the *lex amatoria*, letters, correspondence. Suffering is to be weighed; sighs counted; tears noted. So here is the list of reasons to be dolorous, Part I: Jealousy, loss, fear, rejection, distance, separation, uncertainty, misunderstanding, coldness, are in roughly that lexical order of weight, the points on the scale of the dolorific calculus.

Someone who is shut out from love by the jealousy of a husband, a lover lost in the cold, suffering, numb and unattended, can be excused some minor modes of self expression or lightheaded calls for attention. Here the classic principle of pain requiring relief gains legal expression. The purpose of the laws of love is to end suffering, relieve pain, and promote joy. They are part of the gay science and as such take poetry and play, pain and pleasure, lightly and lengthily. They seek to indulge in the classical meaning of the term, which is to say that they endeavor to give time to love. In that context the lovers' exile, their distance from each other was a cause of considerable suffering and of the instant misunderstanding. She was under a duty to be more inventive in escaping the unnecessary jealousy of her husband. He was to be excused for the excess and the wound that frustration had led him unintentionally to inflict.

Statues have always tended to lose their noses. It was one of the oldest of forms of defacement and in the late Middle Ages, around the time of the decision in this case. "Cutting off the nose" was a recognized if rarely exercised punishment for sexual infidelity. It was a visible species of castration in that it rendered the face ugly and deformed. Records also indicate that it signified an erotic mode of vengeance and this fits with the classical practice of removing the nose, *denasatus*, as a symbolically extreme sign of humiliation and of exclusion. It was a measure used, as Valentin Groebner has well elucidated, against heretics, pagan idols, prostitutes, Jews, and occasionally an adulterer too would lose their nasal member.

The link between nose and genitalia was frequently explicit and allows us a further concluding observation. The cut that the complainant woman suffered to the nose admirably signified the frustration and separation that the defendant lover suffers. In this economy of signs the cut to the nose indicates an absence of intimacy, a lack of play, the opposite of sex. The loss of blood and the cut are both signs of amorous deflation, of premature loss of fluid, of thwarted desire. By a further token, in the secular or non-amorous economy of marital law it also probably represents the risk that the wife is taking. She could lose her nose if her husband catches her *in flagrante delicto*—red handed could easily become red nosed. In any event, concluding words, these are graphic figures of pain, examples of the inborn suffering of love, and the laws are correctly interpreted as precluding any further punishment being meted upon the suffering defendant lover. The Chancellery of Love cannot alter the social situation but it can write letters of comfort, it can correspond and recommend, intimate and offer uplifting words, and in doing so it may ever so slightly lessen the scale of suffering upon the dolorific calculus of unfulfilled desire.

Figure 10 *Bona fide* (good faith/contract)—Whither, *A Collection of Emblemes Anciente and Moderne* (1635).

9
Fidelity and Faithlessness

The laws of love are predicated upon the precedence of the rhetorical over the economic or merely mercantile. The emotional economy, libidinal exchange has priority over the realm of mere things, the stuff of mundane circulation, of contract and legal rule. Recollect, for example, that according to the High Court of Love, one kiss freely given is worth more than all the goods in the world. Rhetoric teaches faith in amorous words, in the persuasion of love, in the value of emotion and the economy of relationship. Nowhere is this more evident than in the case law on fidelity and on truth in matters of the heart.

The roots of the word fidelity lie in the Latin *fides* and can provide important clues. The original meaning of the word was not faith in the sense of following, obeying, or being constrained by, but rather emotional credit, something given and circulated between lovers. Thus the primary meaning of faith in another was trust in the sense of giving credit to, as well as enduring, waiting for, attending. According to Benveniste it even had the meaning of being persuaded of and so attentive to the credit offered by another. Faithfulness meant patience and the persuasion that what was given would return.

Case 14, heard before the Court of the Countess of Champagne, concerned precisely such a question of waiting and belief, and specifically the effect of absence upon a lover's faith. The facts were that the defendant woman had a lover who had been called away on the Crusades. He had left the country to serve the King and had been away for a very considerable period of time. So long, in fact, that even his friends despaired of his return. The woman sought a new amour. This came to the attention of a close friend of the absent lover. He took it upon himself to object to this infidelity and came before the Court to oppose her new love.

The woman defended her decision on the principle that amorous desertion should be a legitimate basis for taking a new lover. Under the *Code of Love*, Rule 7, if a lover dies then the survivor should wait two years before taking another lover. Following that guideline, the absence of her lover, whether alive or dead, she didn't know, for considerably more than two years should be adequate ground for taking a new lover. More than that, she argued that her lover had not only been absent but had also utterly failed to communicate: she had received no letter, no message, no messenger since he had gone. In her view, he had let her down. She interpreted the failure to write as a sign of insouciance and argued that it too should justify termination of the relationship.

The Court heard the arguments on both sides at length. Judgment was given for the complainant. The Countess of Champagne determined that an amour cannot be abandoned simply on the basis of a lover's absence. It was not an adequate reason. First because the absence was not of the lover's choice, but of necessity and for good and honorable reasons. Political duty or worldly engagements sometimes necessitate separation. Second, mere length of absence was no justification, the lover had to be given credit, trusted, his absence endured. That was the proper meaning of amorous good faith, the root meaning of fidelity. It meant precisely that the lover be trusted, and on the flip side it allowed that if she had reason not to trust him, if she had obtained clear evidence that her lover had been derelict in his affections or had been unfaithful then she could leave the relationship. Here the defendant had not presented any such grounds. The absent lover's failure to send letters or messengers was quite possibly a sign of great intelligence or radical caution rather than dereliction: letters can go astray and reveal the secrets of love to the wrong parties, messengers can betray their assignment or can die or be taken captive on the way. Then again, for these and other reasons, the secrets of love entrusted to couriers may well fall into the wrong hands. The defendant was therefore wrong to seek a new lover and should instead have waited either for the return of her lover or for proof positive of infidelity.

Trust should be accumulated. It is the credit of the amorous economy, the banking system of desire. It depends upon belief in the other as well as belief in oneself. Most particularly it depends upon faith in the persuasion of the other during their absence, namely that they will be true to a desire that for long periods of time has no physical expression. Such faith had to be disproved; it could not just be given up. In an epoch when time, distance, and social circumstance—age, status, class, and marriage—were a constant source of melancholy and separation, trust was at a premium, at the root of all relationships, the very sign of an amour that would seldom gain physical fulfillment. As Boethius put it, *maior lex amor est*, love is the greater law and one which exceeds both the obstacles imposed by social decorum and the privations occasioned by separation or distance. Certainly it seems evident from the cases that love is first an interior commitment, a spiritual passion, an intensity that persists through correspondence, tokens and messengers, through memory and images when presence fails. If the pleasures of love belong in the end within the domain of poetics, if physical expressions of intimacy are alike best understood as part of the elaborate rhetoric of love, then corporeal presence can never be more than one factor in the elaboration of relationship. Consummation is the complement of intimacy, it intimates—it generates credit, faith, belief in the form of physical inscription but it is still simply a mode of communication, an avenue to conversation. That is the theory, from the earliest case law to the aesthetic strictures and linguistic constraints of the *précieuses* for whom eloquent conversation, *bel esprit*, and the "air galant" were of the very essence of the political realm of love.

A case heard before the Court of Narbonne can help reinforce the point in a graphic if somewhat distressing way. While fighting in the King's cause, a lover lost an eye. On returning home, his partner rejected him because of his mutilation. She no longer wanted anything to do with him. He complained to the Court and judgment was given for him. The disfigurements occasioned by war are both predictable and unavoidable. They are suffered in a good cause and should not be punished. To this the Queen added that the vivacity of spirit and the heedlessness of harm that led a man to war and subsequent disfigurement were likely also the qualities that had attracted love in the first place. Character underpinned physique and so it would be a dilatory and immoral lover who left her beloved because of the mere incident of a wound. The defendant had offered no legitimate ground for ending the relationship. Of course she could have, she could have cited simple loss of desire, but she didn't. And so she was held to be breaching her trust, acting unfaithfully and the Court ordered her to reconsider.

The principle of fidelity is an interior principle, a question as much of the logic of love as of its exterior expression. To trust is to remain true to desire, to enflame, to yearn, to lust by whatever means are available, when the beloved is absent, as also when present, when whole, when mutilated, as the body ages. That is because in the final analysis, fidelity understood as trust and as communication is a question of art and not of mundane pragmatics, mere bodies, things. To focus on the roots of desire itself was a means of attending to the erotic health of a relationship, to the intimacy rather than to the surface or appearance, the skin or physique of the lover. These indeed were generally described in formulaic terms: red lips, round cheeks, long legs, golden hair and so on, the detail didn't matter. That was because the poetic cause of love was a lexicon of reasons, a tabulation of the logic of amorous commitments and of the means of maintaining them. Within this lexicon the surface, the body, the organ was simply a text, the peculiar sign—*signa propria*—of transition into another space of amorous conversation. Consider the following debate from the *trobairitz*.

The question posed is: Which of two lovers behaves better in the following circumstances? A woman has two suitors and has to decide which to choose. She comes up with the idea of a test (*assag*) which will prove who loves her most and so who in turn she should take as her lover. The test is time honored and trusted. She will sleep one night with each of the men. Before she does so, they each have to promise and swear that while lying together they will go no further than kissing and hugging. Each man so promises. One keeps his word, the other disregards it and goes all the way.

The judgment of the woman troubadour, known only as Lady H., is radically in favor of the suitor who kept his word and ventured no further than kissing. He had succeeded in passing the test, in honoring his lover's words, and was worthy of her trust. The other was not. He had gone beyond her words and thereby irrevocably lost any right or hope he might have had to her heart and to future joy.

What is striking here, apart from the interesting amorous cartography of the test set, is the language of the opinion. The disobedient lover is described not as having broken his own promise nor as going beyond his own words but rather and specifically his offence is that of having "gone beyond the words of his lover"—*los ditz de son Dòmna passer*. He didn't break his word, he broke hers. And on the other side of the test, the faithful lover had shown much greater amorous erudition: "he believes her every word"—*e cre de tot quant ditz*. Behind which judgment lies a concept of love as fidelity and of fidelity as credit, trust or belief in the other. The words of the beloved become the criterion of faith because it is our trust in the other, our belief in the power of their words, which marks the emotional credo, the affective economy of amity or love. Trust in the other's language is in this sense a transitive notion, a crossing of boundaries, a constitution of the space between the lovers in which all that matters in the end is the truth of their words, their eloquence, their ability to believe in what the other says, the flames that their words inspire. In that same vein the test acts out the terms of any future relationship. Language becomes a shared phenomenon, an intimate dialect, a matter of rhetorical jurisdiction insofar as the words shared between the lovers become their own persuasion in the court of the heart. The function of lovers' language, according to Callières in *The Lovers' Logic*, to borrow from a later disquisition, is to transform both lover and beloved. Love unites and changes through "an ardent desire to join, to convert oneself into the object that gave birth to love."

The trial that Lady H. made up for her suitors was in essence a test of their fidelity. She wanted to know if they would give her credit, believe in her words, take a potential lover's discourse seriously. The question was whether they would indulge her, give her time, honor a space outside of themselves, a space between, a language that would mark the beginning of a commitment. Madeleine de Scudéry makes a similar point in discussing the laws of love in the Sapphic kingdom of the Sauromates. Fidelity is unto death; it is the first law of the kingdom, its most ancient and important custom. Those that are "married in love" are bound forever to respect the speech of the beloved. She goes on to depict norms of love (*galanterie*) which require a constant conversation, an ethic of speech: "a lover cannot end a relationship without setting forth the causes of their inconstancy ... nor without declaring the subject of their infidelity." The law of love is a law of language. It is primary in the simple sense that it transforms an infant and speechless, physical and wordless desire into an art, a cause, a territory, a home.

The bond of love is its own law. Sticking with Madeleine de Scudéry, it is love that should define marriage and not marriage love. Indeed marriage was famously depicted by her as slavery whereas for the Sauromates love was marriage, an indelible bond, a passionate attachment. In that context, it is unsurprising that fidelity, rather than convention or property, is the measure of relationship. Fidelity in this context refers to amorous credit, a loving trust in the words of the other, in the space that is shared. And this, as Scudéry also acknowledges, is old law, ancient custom within the domain of love. The reference is probably to the gay science and to the troubadour courts.

There is no shortage of amorous law on the question of marriage and its non-relation to love. Amorous fidelity paradoxically entailed legal infidelity or at least suspension of marital commitments. At the beginning of our era of amorous laws, that was simply because marriage was a property relation, a servitude of the feminine, an arrangement between fathers and not necessarily based upon any kind of affective relationship between the couple. The context and definitions, however, change over time and quite dramatically so it is best to follow a chronological order. Thus the *Code of Love* starts with Rule 1: "Marriage does not constitute a valid reason for not loving." An interesting illustration of the rule, and of the faith that should be placed in a lover's words, can be taken from the Court of Queen Eleanor of France. A man, a potential lover, seeks the love of a woman who is already bound in love to another. She rejects his importuning and declares her fidelity to her beloved. Under pressure from the new suitor she does, however, offer a glimmer of hope. She says that if she ever loses her present lover, she will take the suitor in his place. A while later, she marries her lover, and the suitor demands that she keep her promise. The woman denies the claim on the basis that she has not lost her lover but merely married him.

It is an unusual case but it was succinctly settled by reference to well established precedent: "We do not presume to oppose the judgment of the Countess of Champagne" in which it was held that the lover's dominion did not extend into marriage. For that reason the Queen took the view that the woman ought to keep her promise. As for the precedent judgment of the Countess of Champagne, it is a written opinion that judges a dispute as to whether love can play any role in marriage. Her judgment, after extended argument, was: "We state and affirm unambiguously that love cannot extend its sway over a married couple. Lovers bestow all that they have on each other freely, without compulsion or any consideration of necessity, whereas married couples are bound to comply with each other's desires as an obligation." They are faced by offers that they cannot refuse. The consolations of love give nothing more than what was already possessed as of right.

The judgment ends by maintaining unequivocally that the domain of love is indelibly outside of the pact or diplomatic alliance of marriage. They belong to separate spheres and are judged by different laws. That is how it was. So much so that marriage was deemed to preclude love, even after the married couple was separated, as sometimes happened. The Court of Lady Ermengarde was petitioned by a man with the following question. A woman was married but is now divorced. Her former husband now presses her to become his lover. The Court pronounced judgment against any such liaison. If a couple have been joined in marriage, whatever its nature, and then later are separated, it is quite wrong for them to become lovers. It would mix the amicable and the material, the spiritual and the mundane, and in confusing those separate causes and spheres was deemed unethical because ambiguous, confusing and ill defined.

Fidelity, the faith or credit that passes between lovers was generally thought to precede and exceed any venal or imposed marital arrangement. A disputed question of love from the *trobairitz* offers a brief glimpse of the reasoning. The question debated by two women, Iselda and

Carenza, is that of whether it is better to remain single, a virgin, or to marry and have children. The answer given by Carenza is that Iselda is one of the most beautiful, erudite, and worthy of women. She should choose a husband who is intelligent and wise, a gay scientist, perhaps a troubadour and so likely at least to produce distinguished children. Iselda for her part expresses pleasure at the thought of an eminent husband but distress at what she terms the penitence of giving birth to a child. The breasts will sag, the stomach droop, the body decay. That, she opposes. But that is sadly the technology, the medical science of her day. And at least her choice of a learned husband would potentially allay some of those fears.

Mahieu le Poirier reports a similar judgment in the *Court of Love*. The parents of two deaf children petitioned the Bailiff that their children, who were clearly in love, be ordered to marry. The children resisted the petition on the basis that their hearts were united in love and they wished to live this love without changing their lives—marriage, in their view, often stole the unity and accord of lovers. The greatest joy lay in a love that was its own authority. The Bailiff concurred: if marriage did not please them, then let them live their days as lovers. That is the greater wisdom and the dictate of amatory law. It offers a glimpse of a shift in position, a historic change toward recognizing that it is the choice of the lovers and not the social arrangement or symbols contingently attached to the relationship that matters. The children had expressed themselves well enough and their choice should stand.

The same principle underpins the next case that the Bailiff heard. A man complained that his lover was somewhat too demanding. She wants him to love her exclusively, and demands that he wear a ribbon of hers at all jousts and tournaments that he attends. He pleads that he loves his wife, that he married her for love, and she greatly pleases him. He held the defendant woman in the highest esteem but argued that his inclination had led him back to his wife. The Bailiff heard the arguments and determined that loyalty requires that we are bound to a lover and cannot leave without good reason. It is wrong to abandon love and so here the plaintiff should return to his love for his wife. He was longer and more greatly bound to her and it is she that he should honor and enjoy, her ribbons or armor that he should wear at tournaments, her coat of arms that should accompany him in public.

The Bailiff's two decisions represent a subtle shift in the focus of amatory law and indeed an expansion of its *nomos* into the domain of marriage. Fidelity as trust was not predicated upon social circumstance, nor much impeded by political or legal designations. In a sense this has to have been true precisely because love was outside of marriage and against both ecclesiastical and secular law. Don't forget that the laws of love were for long deemed heretical. If that was true, if love was pursued in the face of marital commitments entered without any real subjective consent then by the same token why should marriage preclude love. The two belong to different orders of commitment but marriage as a diplomatic alliance can as well be subverted by the interior cause of love as by its exterior pursuit. If the spouses become lovers then let it be.

The larger picture may well be that of the constraints, both physical and legal, upon feminine choice. Put it like this, marriage was predicated upon the legal inferiority of the woman. So all the secular legal doctrine holds. Marriage was at best a necessary evil, at worst a form of involuntary servitude. Against that, the principle of love argued a fidelity to a spiritual and amorous equality, to the cause of keeping the flame of freely given love alight. That twin axis reflects the shifting border and changing conceptions of marriage and of love that we glimpse first in Poirier. It marks the beginning of an epic shift toward the modern conception of love as passion, and marriage as the free choice of amour. On one side, marriage is deemed deadly, according to Madeleine de Scudéry it was "l'amour finy," love liquidated, an abyss of the soul, the opposite of the "sweet freedom of affection" for which lovers seek. Start with that, and a cautionary determination from the High Court of Love.

The action was brought by the heirs of a deceased lover against his former enamorata. They claimed that she should be held responsible for his death. The amorous principles involved in the case were of such importance that the Procurator General of Love attached himself to the complaint. The deceased had been passionately in love with the defendant, a married woman. So much so that his health suffered: if he could not see her, he would stop eating and drinking for days on end. He would become ill from desiring her. As to the particular case, the deceased, already weakened by the ardor of his desire, sought to seduce the defendant. For a long time she ignored his advances. Over time, however, she softened, and well-calculated gifts persuaded her to take him as her lover. It so happened that a friend of hers who lived close by was on vacation and she suggested that the deceased move into her apartment so as to be close at hand should the night offer chances of encounter. He was insatiably present. He employed minstrels to play from midnight to dawn outside her house. He would wait all night if needs be to see her.

On the night in question, the husband had gone to sleep early and the deceased had slipped quietly into her room. After that, things had not gone well. The lovers were naked together in bed when the minstrels struck up and on this particular night started off with some raucous dance tunes. They woke the husband. He was not in the mood for dancing. Dazed and confused by sleep he had no idea what was going on. Thinking that there were burglars in the house, the husband sprang up, seized a weapon, and went furiously in search of them. The defendant pretending to be lighting candles, ran to intercept her enraged husband while the lover fled stark naked into the house. He had no idea where to hide. All seemed lost when he ran into an elderly servant who took pity on him. She knew the house inside out and told the vulnerable lover that the only safe hiding place was the old hen house in the courtyard of the building. She took him there and locked and barred the doors. She then went and hid his clothes She managed to conceal them but inadvertently left one of the lover's shoes by the side of the wife's bed.

The husband found the lover's shoe. It enraged him even further and he spent the next several hours searching the house from top to bottom. While he searched, for two long hours, the naked lover trembled like a leaf in the hen coup. Already weak from fasting and pining, the cold, the pecking of the cocks and the capons, caused him considerable pain and anguish. A hundred peck marks pierced his skin. When the husband finally retired the maid came and let him out. She gave him one of her dresses, which was far too small for him, and he left barefoot and scantily dressed, in a perilously feverish condition. He staggered home, but by morning he was dangerously sick. There was nothing the doctors could do. His fever increased and he died without seeing his beloved again.

The deceased's heirs argued that this was a despicable and dishonorable death. The defendant should have tended to her distraught lover, she should have visited and ministered to him. She was to blame for his death. She could not revive the deceased and so they asked instead for honorable amends to be made. She should go barefoot, bearing a bright torch, and declare publicly that she had "falsely and wickedly been the cause of the deceased's demise, she repented, she begged for their mercy and forgiveness." Having done this, she was then to make a cross and build a memorial by the grave of the deceased. At the base of his tomb she was to carve the following: "Here lies the body of a brave and always attentive lover who was pitifully abandoned by his amour. Her parting gift to him killed him fifteen days later. God tends his soul." In the alternative, it was argued that she should build a chapel and dedicate it to the memory of the deceased.

The defendant replied that the aspersions made were quite false. She had loved the deceased wholeheartedly and with a singular passion. His death hurt her horribly. She had lost a wholly admirable enamorata who, had he lived, would have gone on to great things and given her great happiness. She suffered doubly because she had lost him and because she could only mourn that loss secretly in her heart, not openly as she would wish. As for not coming to the aid of her lover in his time of need, she had tried many times to bring him a blanket, a sheet, a flag, anything to cover and warm him, but her husband's constant presence had prevented her from doing so.

After duplications, replications, and reduplications the parties rested. The Court pronounced judgment for the defendant woman. She was to be absolved. She was not responsible for what had happened to the deceased and could not be faulted for her behavior. Costs were to be shared between the parties.

Obviously enough there are great risks to secret liaisons; there are dangers to love affairs and things can as here easily enough end up badly. Juvenal's "secret adulterer" is a timid and ambivalent figure, a fearful paramour who has by the time of the case just reported, the mid-fifteenth century, run up against an emergent marriage. Start, however, with the figure of the adulterer. He is weak, sickly, penitent, and very easily put to flight. He is an almost incorporeal being, so thin as to be virtually all spirit. As the case depicts him in his moment of flight, "he sprang from the bed, as he had to, without hesitation or thought, naked as if emerging from his mother's womb." In other words an infant, a child, not yet part of the Hegelian rationality of the social, a victim sacrificed in this case to the greater ends of an emergent institution of emotionally invested marriage. And he died from cold and from henpecks, from the wounds inflicted by the most timorous of birds.

The husband by contrast may not be a sympathetic figure. He is full of rage, he is violent, he is dismissive of his wife. He sleeps in a separate room, he is by implication neglectful of his spouse. But for all these defects he is still at least minimally justified in his rage, he has been hurt, he suffers even if his suffering measures pretty low on the dolorific calculus of lovers. In any event the suffering husband is a marginally ambivalent figure, a fissure in the old law, the intimation of a new state of relationships. Where for the earlier laws of the troubadours, the husband was always depicted negatively, as "tedious," "jealous," "villainous," "cowardly," or "dull-witted" it is now as much the lover as the husband who attracts these epithets. The change is subtle but clear. The henpecked lover precedes the henpecked husband one might fairly say.

Two observations. The first is that the old law required that all amorous acts have their reasons. It was thus held, as we saw, consistently and vehemently that no amorous arguments could be extracted from the artificial reason of secular law, which concerned property and not subjects, duty and not desire. Marriage as an exclusively proprietary relation would thus be wholly irrelevant to the logic of love. The second point is that this had obviously begun to change, a glimmer, a bit, but nonetheless it had moved. If the spouses were lovers it would in theory at least be wrong for them to go outside their relationship to find other affairs of the heart.

The *New Laws* make this very point. The disputed question is whether a woman whose spouse is unfaithful can herself take lovers. The answer is unequivocal. The law holds that where one party has taken a lover, the other can equally do so: "*dolus cum dolo* se compence"—one sorrow will be rewarded by another. Which is also to say that where the spouses are lovers then marriage turns into an amorous adventure, an affair of the heart and subject to the various codes and laws of love. To stray from the spouse was to belie the heart and break the code of love. It was a wrong, an indifference, even nonchalance, and expressly prohibited by the later *Edicts of Love*.

The *Edicts of Love* derive from the late 1660s, the end of our era. It is the brief epoch of our last example, at the beginning of the modern. The *précieuses* of the mid-seventeenth century had a horror of traditional marriage. For Madeleine de Scudéry, ever the radical, marriage was simply not a part of her feminine "justice and truth." In her vocabulary a woman was not married "to" someone, but "against" someone, and throughout her work, a woman married was a woman enslaved. The other reporters of the doctrines and principles of the *précieuses* make that same point. Antoine Baudeau de Somaize, author of the *Great Dictionary of the* Prétieuses, records that marriage was termed the finish or ending of love, and marked the absolute loss of feminine freedom.

According to Michel de Pure, author of *The* Prétieuse *or the Mystery of the* Ruelles, there were two options open to women. One was to "move beyond marriage" by transcending it. That meant ignoring its requirements, its unjust uses and dull-witted interactions, in favor of the more refined pursuits of feminine society. Aesthetics would replace domesticity. The more radical view was that marriage should be avoided altogether in favor of short-term agreements by which the parties would commit themselves to staying together for a period of a year and then either renew the agreement or end it. An alternative version of this was that the couple would stay together until the first child was born at which point the woman was entitled to a portion of the man's wealth and was free to leave the relationship. The man would raise the child.

Underlying this attention to the detailed mechanics of relationship was a desire to keep the spiritual affairs of the heart free from the imposition of domestic duties and property relations. Women too should have emotional rights, symbolic and real recognition. It is these rights that are spelled out in the laws of love set out to govern the new Sauromates in the novel *Clélie*. Love is in this realm coincident with the art of life. To live well was to love with taste and discrimination. It was an aesthetic enterprise, a fashioning of a new language and the elaboration of an aesthetics of conversation. Taste displaced duty, discrimination took place of veneration, and desire became the law. Here, just to conclude proleptically, love as passion became the principle of social life and love as the greatest bond engulfed all other commitments. Thus, for the Sauromates, fidelity was the primary virtue, the founding ethic, the great promise or spiritual gift. In her own words—and why not?—the *précieuse* Madeleine, the latter day Sappho, says "amongst us fidelity is held in such great esteem that we believe in keeping faith unto death. Those who marry for love, are not free to remarry." Or at least not without compelling reasons. And there it stands. Full circle. Love outside marriage becomes marriage as love.

PRINCEPS. 157

In Senatum boni principis.

DIALOGISMVS.

Effigies manibus truncæ ante altaria diuûm
Hic resident: quarum lumine capta prior.
Signa Potestatis summæ, Sanctiq; Senatus
Thebanis fuerant ista reperta viris.
Cur resident? Quia mēte graues: decet esse quieta
Iuridicos: animo nec variare leui.
Cur sine sunt manibus? Capiant ne xenia: nec se
Pollicitis flecti muneribúsue sinant.
Cæcus at est princeps. quòd solis auribus, absq;
Affectu, constans iussa Senatus agit.

Figure 11 *In senatum boni principis* (On the senate of a good prince) Andreas Alciatus, *Emblematum libellus* (1531).

10
Intimate Violence

Intimacy and violence are curiously closely connected. In medieval French, just to get etymological with you for a moment, "violence" and "viol" or rape were treated as synonyms. In fact violence is composed of "viol," rape, and the Latin suffix *entia*, meaning thing, and can be translated loosely as the act of rape, and by extension any physical or later verbal intrusion by force. It would seem from these roots that there is something inherently sexual in violence, in potential at least, and this must have to do with the sudden shift from speech to force, from conversation to the body, from words to things. The classical lawyers captured this unintentionally well in defining violence as a failure of words, or more precisely as something that cannot be spoken—*nulla esse dicere*, nothing to be said, meaning that the recourse to brute force both exceeds words and defies verbal description. Coquillart in the *New Laws* incorporates this point by describing the fall from words to blows as a descent into mere noise (*bruit*). Noise is the mode of transition from language to force; it is the phonic expression of an absence of speech, the articulation of inarticulacy. By this definition, violence is the failure of communication, the moment when words run out and, to borrow a phrase, the body speaks.

If violence is the expression of a lack of language, an aphasic expression of a linguistic wound, then we can also posit that the remedy for violence must logically incorporate a restoration of words, a return to communication and to speech. It is an obvious point but it is one that gets lost in the passion of noise or in the excitation of blows. Staying with the *New Laws* the reference cited comes in the course of a case of a disputed question of love: "How should a woman respond when her lover hits or beats her?" According to the old law, the report relays, the woman must remain silent and endure the beating. The new law is to the contrary: where one lover abuses the other verbally, the abused partner is entitled to reply in kind and more. A positive incontinence is permissible: "for each word delivered, she can respond with seven or eight." If the dispute becomes noisy, meaning, as we saw, that it comes to blows, then blows can be traded. Man or woman, the party attacked can reply in kind and seek to reconcile their differences, express their inarticulate anger and maybe even dissipate their antinomies in a strangulated yet strangely desiring way. Say for the moment that it is a fine line that the *New Laws* here draw. It is one that recognizes quite radically that intimate violence is a mode of communication, an exchange without words but nonetheless an expression of an extremity of affect, a mute yet forceful release of desire.

Intimate violence, being intimate, is a two way street, and it is essential to acknowledge that as a mode of intimacy it is also an expression of relationship, albeit a failed communication taking the place of words. It does happen and it will happen and the laws of love would be much less relevant if they denied it or sought in the modern manner simply to liquidate the violence by ending the relationship. There are elements of noise, of violence, in all intimacies. They may be greater or lesser in degree and frequency but the notion of an end to relational violence is certainly not plausible—any more than is an end to terror or to drugs—and it is probably not desirable. Passion is a species of violence, a noisy negotiation, something human and hermeneutic, to be understood rather than denied or repressed into other and less fertile forms. So the laws of love have always acknowledged that violence will occur and will have at some point to be judged. Initially, however, the parties are the best judges, they can negotiate, fight, endeavor to understand, keep the space of communication open even if bruited and bruised. And if the weaker party, man or woman, feels threatened then he or she should seek sanctuary. That is the decision according to the *New Laws* though Coquillart does also make reference to violent partners being exposed to ridicule, and specifically refers to a tradition in which the violent spouse was tied to the back of an ass and paraded in public on non-law days (*dies non*) or what we would term holidays. The more violent spouse, often the husband but also quite frequently the wife, was to be ridiculed publicly during the course of festivities. The public eye, the immediate community, the kin, neighbors and friends of the cohabitant combatant would thus formally participate in disapproving of their behavior and in drawing them back into communality and communication.

It hardly needs to be pointed out that language is social, it exists only in the form of dialogue as Volosinov pointed out a century or so ago. The recognition that intimate violence is negatively yet also necessarily a linguistic phenomenon places it firmly in the social, and before the law. Especially so if law is defined as poetic rule, as a grammar or order of speech, of amity, of being together. Violence is here a problem of the absence of speech. The non-relation between violence and language marks a lack which the *New Laws* seek to remedy with the affirmation of speech and the permission to engage in passionate discourse, in argument and invective. It is curiously practical advice and it gets taken up much later, just by way of digression, in the anonymous early seventeenth-century feministic treatise *The Law's Resolutions of Women's Rights*, which at one point, in addressing intimate violence between spouses also indicates that the wife is neither without powers of persuasion nor without implication in the intimate argument. The author of the treatise cites to an amorous logic which dictates that if the husband can beat the wife, as the common law allows, then "the sex feminine is at no great disadvantage," because what the husband can do, the wife can do: "I pray why may not the wife beat the husband again, what action can he name if she do ..." She can surprise him in many ways both obvious and subtle and she should not imagine that she does not have those powers. Even Bracton in his twelfth-century treatise on the laws and customs of England, *De legibus*, noted a certain equality in intimate relationships: he quite seriously declaimed that while the man could withhold money, the woman could withdraw from sex, and while she might starve, he would likely go mad. Nor do the laws of love, an eminently realistic body of regulations, ignore that truth of relationship. That said, the point of the digression is that both the earlier and the later statements of amorous law address the intimate dimension of intimate violence, they acknowledge that it occurs in a space between lovers, that it is relational, connective, and even if it is a failed form of communication, it is nonetheless an attempt to communicate, a strangulated speech, noise bruited to the other. Certainly it is not indifference, it is not insouciance, and it is close to being the opposite of what the *Edicts of Love* vilified as nonchalance.

Intimate violence starts in dialogue, in speech, in relationship, and even if language at some points cedes to blows the function of the laws of love in addressing this key and still contemporary issue is explicitly that of understanding the linguistic dimension of the violence and of returning the parties where possible to speech and even to intimacy. The latter term also bears a momentary consideration. The intimacy that qualifies amorous conflict is a term drawn again from the Latin, *intimus*, and refers precisely to a relationship, to an intimate, to a proximity that entails not one but two. At the same time we can note that the verb *intimo* refers to the transitive state of being intimate and means to bring into, to flow into, to draw in. It even has a secondary and more public meaning still which is to publish or make known, as in the English to intimate. The intimate may be, as Cicero put it, the finest and deepest and most exacting space of care but it equally only exists through intimations, through the proximate space of speech. It is the boundary point where body and speech merge, where the body most visibly comes to communication, where person and face are in some measure one and the same. The point being, that all of these connotations suggest what we still only dimly acknowledge, namely that the intimate is also social and public, a question of speech, of conversation, of serious reflection and here of amorous law.

For all that it is social, the intimate also draws in and invents the proximate and unique language of leisure, of the off hours, of the hecatombs where hedonists and heretics play. In this sense the person is constituted through playfulness, through humor as well as depth, lightness as well as profundity. The cases of love are very clearly addressed to both the levity and the excess that mark the distinctive boundaries of the intimate and the possibilities of its rupture. Take some examples of cases where amorous play takes a turn toward confusion, conflict or worse. Judgment 4 from the *Judgments of Love* was a case heard before the Court of the Mayor of the Green Woods. The complaint, brought by a woman, was that her lover had surprised her and upended her in public, causing her, to use the Rabelesian terminology, to land bare assed—*sans culottes*—on the ground. The details are interesting. The lover had approached her and decided to engage in the then common ritual of kissing her dress.♥ In the event, he had accosted her so enthusiastically and so roughly that she had been knocked down and her skirts had ridden up over her waist for all the world to see. She was displeased and asked the Court to order him to desist from such games or at least only to engage in them with her permission. She asked that he be ordered to show her respect, to make honorable amends, to atone for the wrong done by waiting in future for her to ask him to tryst or to play. Only after he had been given license could he in future participate in any amorous engagements. The Court so ordered and the defendant appealed unsuccessfully to the High Court of Love.

The Court treats the ludic lightly. It is a case that belongs *in rem levem* or among the better humored sources of law but as Renaissance legal

♥*Quod autem amantes vestem amicorum deosculantur*: lovers will frequently kiss the clothes of their beloved, according to the gloss to this case. Which I didn't know although we do still hear of suitors who are unworthy to kiss the hem of a dress. Or some such. And while on a footnote I will also just briefly add for the interest of the jocularly inclined that the harm described in the complaint is "une cotte verte" which translates in that period as "a green butt."

antiquary Henry Spelman pointed out, these are nonetheless matters of custom, of amity and law and hence the need for deliberation and determination. The use of force in this case had been largely accidental and relatively minor. But there had been an element of violence, a rudeness and roughness that the Court sought to address, as our glossator Symphorianus puts it, not so as to punish iniquity but so as to protect an innocent. What is at issue is explicitly the concern of a minor jurisdiction—*ab audientia minoris iudicis*—and yet out of little things grave consequences, happy truths, plural knowledges, can flow. The second point of fascination is that the issue is expressly one of honor and of atonement, which can be translated here by saying that the key to the case lies in the symbolism of the infraction and the properly symbolic manner of its reparation. Here the resolution was that of instituting a less boisterous avenue of communication but the point is of more general significance. Affairs of the heart are governed by rhetorical rules, by norms of oratory, and by an intrinsically poetic justice. Both the norm and the infraction are to be understood according to the rules of their genre. This means treating love according to its proper symbolism—exposure, blushes, requests, rebuffs, kisses, tickling, gifts, trysts, all have their customs and norms, their poetry, their erudition and eloquence. The function of the court of love is precisely to address the symbolic dimensions of the love affair, including those that lead to conflict and to its reparation or, in the language of the courts, and more nicely, to its satisfaction. What will it take to return the parties to communication, to rhetorical health? The question is raised in several further cases concerned with the causes and the incidents of the intimate use of force. This indeed, because nearly all of the following cases come from the *Judgments of Love* is probably to be accounted the lawyer Martial d'Auvergne's most signal contribution to the development of the laws.

Judgment 11 again concerns rough play. Here the complainant was invited at dusk on a hot day to join her lover and some of his friends and neighbors in going swimming. The party walked to a local lake where they decided to go fishing. The men were to hold a long net across the water and the women were to approach from the other side of the lake and chase fish into the nets. The complainant happily joined in chasing the fish but her lover, so the complaint goes, was much less concerned with catching fish than with trapping her. He manipulated the net in her direction and then, although there was plenty of room to go around her, he jumped sideways and tripped her up. She fell headlong into the water, her clothes were soaked, her dress ruined—or more exactly, *gastée dedans la riviere*. The verb *gaster* is medieval French and has the primary meanings of to ravage or to rape. She was raped—violated—by the water, which is a strong way of putting it or at least indicative of a vehement reaction. Then, to compound matters, the lover, still not content, pretended to offer his hand to help her up but instead grabbed her and, taking advantage of her discomposure, started to fondle her breasts and feel her up. This went on for some time until she recovered and pushed him away.

The complainant, greatly upset, demanded that the Court punish the defendant severely and publicly. A wrong committed so publicly, she argued, must be punished appropriately visibly, and the defendant should therefore be made an example. The defendant replied that he had done nothing wrong. He claimed not to have intended to touch her breast, and if he had, that was a chance encounter, a slip of the hand occasioned by his concern and his attempt to warm her. She responded by saying that her fall had been too heavy not to be deliberate and that if his subsequent attentions had not been outrageously indiscreet she would never have bothered to mention them at all. With which sentiments the Court largely agreed. Judgment was for the complainant. The miscreant man was to present the aggrieved woman with a new dress. He was to kneel before her, raise his hat, and recite: "My Lady, by order of the justice of love I am bound here before you to beg your forgiveness and to throw myself on your mercy and good grace. I pray that you accept this dress which is offered in good faith and recompense for my deeds. As to my indiscretions, pay no further mind to them, I solemnly swear that I had no desire to injure or to anger you. I would rather die than hurt you."

The Court here ordered a public conversation. A talking cure, a symbolic redress. The lovers had to intimate their reconciliation before the very friends and neighbors in front of whom the events occurred. The defendant had clearly stepped across the line, gone beyond the pale, and the symbolic function of the judgment was to bring him back, to recover his words and to restore the couple to conversation. There is an interestingly Pascalian character to the decision. The couple are in effect ordered to make symbolic amends, to enact a theater of love, to act "as if" their love is mended. And as if by way of proof they are ordered to converse intimately before others. The most proximate and secret of feelings are intimated or aired so that all those affected, those that know the lovers, participated in the events, or saw the aquatic attack, could now take part in restoration and resolution. As for the out of hand prank, the insult, the forcible fondling of breasts, the indignity and slight of the carefully engineered fall, the decision implies that it was again the recourse to the non-verbal, the failure of conversation, the nonchalance or lack of amorous care that is most troubling. The offence is not simply against the plaintiff, but it is rather an inelegant and ineloquent act that offends the laws of love, that goes against every principle of amorous good conduct and the desiderata of any and all maps of the heart. He had acted in an untutored and ignorant manner and needed a decision that would teach him as well as reform him. It is lack of communicative connection, the intrusion of things, the sudden and unannounced manipulation of the other's body that constitutes the amorous wrong, the intimation of violence.

The careful delineation of the space between the lovers, the cartography of the affair as acted out in the public sphere gains considerable further attention in a floridly semiotic case that involves accidental harm to a lover. Judgment 21 came on appeal before the High Court of Love. The petitioner, a young woman, said that for some time she had been undergoing medical treatment which, among other things, involved blood letting. Every afternoon blood was drained from her foot into a bowl of warm water. The bowl of blood was then, according to the prevalent medical fashions, placed on her window ledge to dry. After the procedure was completed the woman's doctor recommended that she sleep and recover her strength. She found sleeping difficult and so asked her lover if he could find some musicians and have them come and play outside her house and so help her pass the time and maybe sleep a little.

Her lover dropped everything so as to comply as quickly as he could. He found the requisite minstrels and they came the following afternoon with their instruments and began to play. On hearing the music, excited and light headed from the loss of blood, the petitioner sprung from her bed and seeking to hear the players better, threw open the shutters on her window. In taking a pot of violets or maybe marjoram from the window ledge she knocked off the bowl of blood. It landed on the appellee and drenched him in blood. His shirt and doublet were spoiled and there was blood all over. But he continued to play with the musicians and thought little of it because night had fallen and the damage and gore was likely not so visible. The downpour even smelled quite good, of violets or herbs. He remained blissfully unaware, happy in his musical task and confident that whatever she had done had been done out of love for him.

Eventually the minstrels tired and the time to take his leave arrived. He left with happy steps and made his way rapidly across town. Unfortunately a short cut on the way home took him past a late night bar where a fight had broken out. The mêlée had spread down the street and by chance, in making his way past the combatants, the blood soaked lover was stopped and questioned by a member of the Night Watch, an early apparition of the Paris police. He was questioned as to his business being abroad so late: Where was he coming from and why was he there? He replied somewhat evasively that he had been repotting marjoram. This was scarcely convincing and the night guard raised his lantern to the man so as to see his face more clearly. In doing so, he saw that the complainant was covered in blood and immediately concluded that he must be one of the combatants in the brawl. As Aristotle long ago pointed out, spilled blood is generally not a good sign. And Cicero supports that point in viewing blood as most likely a mark of enmity, of cutting or slaughter. In any event, unable, for reasons of discretion and loyalty, to reveal where he had actually been, the lover was arrested and held overnight in the cells.

He hardly slept at all. It was uncomfortable, cold, and undignified in the prison. His complaint to the Court was that this misfortune and harm came to him by virtue of the appellant's lack of care. He demanded that she make amends for the damage done, pay for the ruined clothes and at the very least reward him with six or eight lengthy embraces, with kisses and hugs.

The appellant woman responded that she had done no wrong. It was her chambermaid who had dislodged the palettes of blood, not her. More than that, all she had done was to throw violets to him as a gesture of warmth and affection. That he was arrested was hardly her fault, and not of her volition. And finally, he was himself to blame. It was his choice to go home by the back streets. Had he taken his normal route he would never have run into the Night Watch in the first place. So she owed him nothing, neither financial nor honorable amends, but if he wanted kisses she would happily give him those and more. She even offered to launder his shirt or give him another and even better one, so long as he promised to love her more than all others.

The High Court reviewed all of the arguments and evidence. Judgment was for the appellee in the form of ordering the woman to compensate her lover with kisses. Specifically, with a half-dozen well-placed and tender kisses, each one of which was to last the length that it takes to recite the *De Profundis* and *Fidelium*, two of the longer Latin prayers that Catholics used to recite during worship and in the original and rather slower tongue. By this means, the Court signs off, the lovers can return to their own good graces, and the future becomes sweeter.

The case involves unintentional projectiles, the intercession of chance and other distant causes. It also entails the passage of fluid, here blood, and its unwanted intrusion upon the enamorata. There is a covert violence done to the recipient. The dowsing of the partner with blood results in his feeling emotionally slighted, linguistically excluded, and in a minor way violated. It was an accidental emission, accompanied by silence, without warning or cause, but the drenched lover ends up by treating it as being also a form of interpretative violence—the violence of the absence of words—and one that has to be recuperated through speech and restored by the return of words to the parties themselves. Consider the case then as raising certain intricate questions of interpretation or as the marker of a move from a diurnal to a nocturnal law, from the mercantile and its black letters to the amatory and its more fluid emissions. A shift in jurisdiction means a mutation of meaning.

Start with the fact that the case takes place on the street, in public, outside the beloved's house, at night. First, nighttime, as we have seen, is the domain of love and under the special protection of the laws of love. The *Treatise on Perfect Love* addresses this question directly: Why do lovers burn more fiercely and suffer more intensely during the night than the day? The answer is that during the day the spirit is dissipated in exterior realities and does not turn toward love; "but at night, all the occasions for erring having evaporated, they can enter the secret chamber of the heart and there find love, and with love comes both ardour and sighs." The Renaissance common lawyer John Selden—in a treatise entitled *The English Janus or Other Face of Common Law*—later affirmed what amorous doctrine had already ruled and expressly acknowledges that night is subject to special rules. It belongs to the feminine, to the Furies, and has its own measure of time and of meaning. Hence, for example, the English "fortnight" which signals a nocturnal measure of time and stands for a feminine embrace of temporality.

The cover of darkness allows, so the High Court dictates, for amorous intrigue, for clandestine affairs, for the fragile and fraught enactment of lovers' trysts. That said, defined by reference to the feminine and to the amorous purposes that femininity governs and that the *carte de tendre* later mapped, the safety of lovers was in the keeping of the *nomos* of the night. The figure of such security, the night guard of love is the "Oublier," a figure drawn from spiritual law and who comes into the city at night and, according to the redoubtable Symphorianus, personifies the safety of all lovers. Any incident that infracts amorous "securitas" is a slight to the "Oublier," a spiritual crime, *laesae maiestatis amoris* or treason of the heart as common lawyers would doubtless call it.

The figure of the "Oublier" as the amorous night watch also raises explicitly the fascinating point that the laws of love are a nocturnal jurisdiction predicated upon the forgetting of the secular and its municipal decrees. In their place, with darkness, come the laws of love and the hedonism of the hecatombs, the pursuit of pleasure, the sloughing off of mundane laws and cares. Night figures according to another law, it is subject to an older *nomos*, it is a different jurisdiction. More than that, and more practical as well, the cases indicate that when the domain of love is entered, when night has fallen and the other cartography of the heart has descended then a special care is owed to all matters of amatory passage and communication. To throw water on a lover and then to laugh, for example, is not simply a wrong done to the enamorata but a crime against the dignity and well being of the "Oublier," of love. Everyone is affected and as the amatory maxim goes, *ignorantia culpa est*, ignorance in matters of love is a wrong. By an even stronger token, the dousing of a lover with blood signifies a matter of interpretation beyond any diurnal or merely positive law. Perhaps it could even be intimated that at night water turns to blood and that the suddenly sanguine lover simply wears outside what all amorous tykes bear coursing within.

The principle that all incidents of intimate dispute, of conflict or here of projectiles thrown impact not simply the lovers but the domain of love and its denizens as well also helps explain the character of the judgments. Decorum, which we here have to take in its root meaning of both honor and dream, and so the good dream, the uncanny forgetting that the "Oublier" represents has to be restored. The future of the lovers is a collective concern, the space of intimacy a complex and essentially shared space, its language a common endeavor, its future a concern of all. Thus the intimate and intrinsically appropriate character of the judgments. In one case the appellants are summoned to the High Court to be engaged in an interrogation of the circumstances and the tones in which the incident unfolded. And in the latter case it is the *osculum amoris*, a kiss that promises satisfaction, that is ordained for the health of the lovers rather than for mundane reasons of compensation or retribution.

Another instance, Judgment 51, the very last of the cases reported in the original edition of Auvergne's *Arresta amoris*, takes up this very point of amatory restoration as opposed to judgment or isolation and blame. The case is brought by a young woman, joined in the action by the Procurator General of Love, against the defendant, one of her former lovers.

Her argument begins from the principle that in matters of love all foibles, surprises and shocks should be forgiven—*amici vitia ferenda*, friends should tolerate each other's faults. In this particular instance, the plaintiff had been playing in an open courtyard with some friends when she saw the defendant walking gloomily across the sward. She spontaneously decided to surprise him and grabbing a handful of dirt she ran up behind him and put it down the back of his shirt. The defendant had reacted quite incontinently. He smacked her fiercely on the behind and not content with that he knocked her down and then dragged her along the ground by her hair for all the world to see. His actions were in disturbance and infraction of the safekeeping of lovers and constituted a crime against love. Committed in public, the offence is doubly reprehensible.

The plaintiff asked that the defendant be ordered by the Court to make public honorable amends for the wrong he had done to her. She asked that he be ordered to return to the very same spot where the events had occurred. There he was to appear bare headed and dressed only in a shirt. He was to carry a torch and publicly declare, before all of the women who had witnessed these events, that he had done wrong. He was to repent for the harm he had done, for having hurt her and for having spoiled her coiffure. Next, because this had been an extreme case and one which touched upon the very core of her honor and name, she also asked that the defendant be condemned to corporal punishment. She asked that he be tied naked to a post and that all of the women who had witnessed the events were to be allowed to come at their leisure and beat him until he was raw. He was to be made an example for others. And in addition she asked that he also pay damages.

The defendant argued that he had done no wrong. Men did not have to put up with everything that women threw at them. Women should serve men and they most certainly should not put dirt down their backs. Whether in jest or otherwise this act had been most unwelcome. More than that, the dirt had been full of red ants, which had bitten him and caused him extreme discomfort. It had been torture and it should be no surprise that in these adverse circumstances he had responded heatedly. He had subsequently sought the remission of the Chancellery of Love and had obtained letters condoning his actions.[♥♥] He asked that the letters be confirmed.

The Procurator General of Love intervened to the effect that the defendant had clearly admitted the acts complained of. This was a great outrage and offence against the laws of love and required the most severe possible of punishments. Anyone who hit another lover was guilty of treason, of the crime of *leze Majesté* as the text puts it, and he should be sentenced to death by public execution. He was now, Symphorianus notes, an enemy of Cupid and a living threat to the safety of all lovers.

[♥♥]A recognized procedure in the courts of love whereby letters were obtained by way of what we would now term declaratory judgment permitting or remitting wrongs done.

The plaintiff reprised her argument and added that the letters of remission were surreptitiously and falsely obtained and should be withdrawn. The defendant replied that his offence had been greatly exaggerated. He had lost his temper and, granted the provocation, with reason.

The Court heard the arguments at length and pronounced that the letters of remission were improperly granted. It was ordered that the defendant be stripped naked and beaten by four elderly washerwomen. Next he was to be tossed in a lice-ridden and filthy prison blanket and then thrown naked into a bed of nettles and thistles. As if that were not enough, he was to be banished thenceforth from the realm of love.

Decision published, the original edition of the *Judgments of Love* then concludes. The last case clearly symbolizes an extreme instance, a grievous infraction of the safety of lovers, and a breach of the conditions of possibility of love. Whatever the occasion and however justified, amorous violence, whether public or private, was deemed the most extreme of threats to the realm of love. It threatened the very medium of amour, the oratorical organization of the dialogue of lovers, the eloquence of exchange. It was for these reasons, because of the breach that it made in the rhetorical space of love, because it entered a domain deprived of language and so also of spirit and soul, that extreme condemnation was required. Where the other cases covered less serious infractions, lesser forms of treason, Judgment 51 serves as a final reminder that to enter the domain of love requires sweet words, rhetorical skill and refinement, love letters, poetry, communication. Without "high forms of speaking," "euphuism," "preciosity" there would be neither poetry nor possibility of relationship. Without the means of intimacy and intimation that the laws of love inculcate, there would only be artless lust, possession but no culture, property but not love. Eloquence and love are the dual and inseparable subjects of amatory law whose art is coined as *Philomusus* in a seventeenth-century amorous rhetoric, loosely meaning love of the muses, a linguistic rite, a medium of ceremonial self-expression. "Letters," *Philomusus* informs us, "are Cupid's bellows" and allow a meeting "in soul. But in a dream …" or as Auvergne has it, in the other space of love, at night and protected by all of the sureties that the laws of love can portend.

The symbolic character of the final judgment thus plays on the fragile and voluntary quality of all love affairs. It provides a striking and strikingly early instance of an attempt to address the incursion of the non-verbal into the domain of rhetoric, and so too into the realm of love. The judgment is remarkable for the heavily symbolic character of the punishment meted out. There is always something erotic, a dimension of the sexual in the physical manifestations of intimate violence. Lost for words, the assailant violates and takes from the body of the other. It is a mode of marking the skin, of inscribing an inarticulate message and that symbolism or writing, that hermeneutic of pain, also needs attention and account. Thus the symbolic quality of the remedy awarded. The skin of the defendant was to be put on view and marked, inscribed, pricked, and stung. The community of those affected was to be engaged in a ritual of denigration, a public shaming that mirrored almost perfectly the crime committed.

The defendant had slapped, knocked down, and dragged the plaintiff along the ground by her hair. He had soiled, hurt, and humiliated her. He had refused to talk and adamantly resisted apologizing. The High Court in its determination reproduced these offences in reverse. The defendant was now to be ritually soiled, hurt, and humiliated. The violence he had perpetrated publicly was now to be enacted equally publicly on him. Those who witnessed the original violence would now witness its symbolic re-enactment. A theater of amorous cruelty or at least a dramatic instance of justice being seen to be done.

And because the past is always contemporary, and because in many respects, as Stendal put it, they were happier and more amorous and erudite then than now, there is the point that the couple were former lovers, ex-amours, rather than being in relationship. The defendant had proved by his behavior and by his subsequent unrepentant attempts to justify it, that he no longer really belonged in the domain of love. He had stopped communicating. He was refusing by his own argument and admission to enter dialogue, to apologize, show flexible or reengage. He was excommunicated, banished from the rhetorical realm of lovers for acting contrary to its spirit, ineloquently and out of all proportion to the prankish tickling he had received. In short, he had failed rhetorically and spiritually and was no longer a fitting subject of amorous conversation. Nothing more and nothing less than that. He was not subjected to anything more than a symbolic correction, he was neither imprisoned nor exiled except in the sense that those who adhered to the rules of amorous eloquence were warned against talking to him.

The flip side of the last point is the observation with which I began. Intimate violence, being intimate and relational, requires the attention of experts in relationship, in intimacy. They alone have the language within which to address the travails of affection, the narratives of amity and enmity, the transitions from speech to noise. Secular lawyers tend not to be competent in that regard. Historically the canon and common lawyers recommended silence and subordination as the roles of women. Their more contemporary propensity, their default is to lurch rapidly into the agonistic symbolic violence of trial. They incarcerate, separate, and repudiate relationship. They have tended to conduct a war on violence, as if violent means can somehow end intimate violence once and for all. And that is symptomatic of a deep-rooted misunderstanding, and a reflection of the limits of the juridical. Intimate violence intimates violently. It seeks to express, it is a strangulated mode of communication, and as a general rule, far more often than not, this inarticulacy is an attempt to stay in relationship, to find a place, a role and a voice in an unfamiliar terrain. The erudition *in eroticis* that the gay science teaches endeavors precisely to lead amorous subjects from violence to intimation, from noise to speech, and so back into expression and into relationship.

Figure 12 *Venus and Cupid—Emblemata amatoria* (1620).

11
Suicide

It was Hegel I think who remarked that either we love or we die. A stark option, one might well think, a mortal wager, high stakes for the most mundane or corporeally driven of enterprises. Hegel's reference was to spiritual love and the potential it offers to redeem the soul through *caritas* or pure desire. We don't, however, have to agree with Wilhelm Friedrich von H. on the immortal end of love. There is also a more immediate and physical sense in which love promises life in quite literal terms. Consummation is an act of reproduction. It gives birth, it continues, it passes on. At the very least consummation offers the possibility of future life while the failure of love, the defeat of desire, logically entails the opposite of life, the specter of not living on, emptiness, nothingness, death. The old term for the pursuit of love, *fin amor* or end of love is appropriately ambivalent. It refers to the goal of love, erotic pleasure, fulfillment of desire, but also suggests a terminus, an end, both the "little death" of consummation and the more enduring ending, the demise that stalks, the self-inflicted death that haunts the unrequited lover, the practitioner of distant love and its impossible phantasms of fulfillment.

It is perhaps simplest to say that passion has its risks and that violent love will often meet with violent ends. The courts of love were full of such questions of the suffering, the harm, the conflict and death that the pursuit of desire will sometimes bring. The doctors of love treated the effects of amorous failure, the malady of erotic melancholy in imaginative and often fertile ways. The best cure of course was fulfillment of the thwarted desire; Casanova's observation that once enjoyed the fury of love wanes was long recognized as medically sound. But enjoyment was often not possible, the love affair in its purest courtly form being the poetic expression of a long distant love for an absent and unattainable object of desire. Epistolary poems were forever addressed to an elsewhere of affect, to a mystical space of absence which Bernard de Ventadorn famously dubbed "there, where my love is." Or maybe the beloved was simply not interested. Whatever the cause, where consummation was unattainable then both the doctors and the lawyers of love recognized that broken heart or no, frustrated lovers had to acknowledge their failure and come to terms with their fate. The *Code of Love*, Rule 5, is adamant: "love cannot be lawfully extracted from an unwilling partner." No means no. The High Court of Love was perfectly consistent: forced love is a crime even if in a particular case the freedom of one party threatens the solitary and inconsolable demise of the other.

Suicide, the threat of taking one's life by way of revenge upon an uncaring partner or as a symbolic retribution in the face of unrequited desire was from early in the tradition contrary to amorous law. Significantly enough, because historically women were most usually the explicit objects of *amour lointain*, of unrequited desire, the earliest intimations of the refusal to allow the threat of suicide as a proper argument for love come from the women troubadours. A bare fragment from a mid-twelfth-century dialogue between Lady Almuc and Lady Iseut involves a plea by the latter on behalf of a jilted lover. Lady Almuc has set her heart against her former lover who had displeased her by dint of being inattentive to her desires. She refuses to see him, and returns his letters unopened and unread. He is distraught, so much so according to Iseut that he is slowly dieing a painful and lamentable death. In light of his plight Iseut asks her friend either to see him and make up or, failing that, to pardon him so as to release him to love again. Lady Almuc refuses. She will not take him back unless he makes amends for the wrongs he has done her. She is adamant. Until he repairs the error of his manners he must suffer whatever fate holds in store for him, including the languishing death that he seems currently intent on meting out to himself. For her part, she is done with him, and according to the law, quite properly so. Death is no argument; it has no place in the logic of love, no role in the dialogue that constitutes desire.

It is a common theme, *à la mode* in the thirteenth century, and it establishes a customary norm of amatory law. Love takes precedence over death. This is not simply a matter of love conquering all, although it certainly could be. It is rather that the fate of the rejected suitor or discarded lover is a matter for open analysis, for free discussion, for the logic of love's laws. A relationship is a rhetorical enterprise, a question of eloquence to which acts of violence, arguments extracted from the threat of death cannot contribute in any constructive manner. Love has its reasons and while they may be at times obscured by fever, fury, fear, or despair they are not intrinsically mystical nor wholly without definition and cause. Next rule then, was that desire can neither be constrained nor cowed by the fury of the lover—*furore amoris* as it was called by the Latin lawyers. The threat of self-immolation was absolutely excluded as an unfair ruse or illegal trap. Being a spiritual thing, love is freely given, *animus gratia* as the commentators say, or not at all.

Another and this time anonymous dialogue makes the same point. One friend, say Amie, pleads with another, here Amile, to relent and so spare the life of a jilted lover: "it would be foul and ignoble to let him die." More than that and quite persuasively she continues by pointing out that her client is defenseless in the face of his spurned desire: Amile could have him burned or hanged or drawn and quartered and he could not resist, could not lift a finger, but "one kiss would restart his heart and send blood through his veins like the flames of a wild fire. And if he dies anyway, you will no longer have to worry about forgiving him" the wrongs he has done. That may seem a pretty powerful argument, a mere kiss freely given to save a life, but it was quite alien to the law of love which holds very much to the contrary. First, desire cannot be forced and so succumbing to threats of suicide would defeat the very logic of love by denying the relationship between the lovers as it devolves or dissolves according to the dictates of authentic desire. Second, a kiss is never simply a kiss. It is variously a sign of belonging to the realm of love (*osculum amoris*), or a promise of consummation and an indication of love to come (*osculum ab ore*), and in neither case can the labile encounter properly be divorced from the desire and the hope it arouses. If the heart does not accompany the lips, the kiss is insidious, and doctrine terms it either that of the spider or the kiss of Judas. It isn't worth it.

The theme recurs throughout the judgments of love. Poirier reports a case in which the Bailiffs of Love, petitioned by friends of a deceased woman, were asked who was at fault for her demise. Her lover, with her agreement, had asked her parents for permission to marry. Her parents denied him and he then fled, telling her that he would never come back. She took her own life. Who was to blame? Here of course suicide was not a threat but a fact. The Bailiffs could no longer influence the disappointed lovers and so came to the only logical decision, that the parents were at fault and should bear the blame. Love should only be denied for valid reasons and they had not offered any. They had controverted a fundamental amatory axiom, Rule 8 of the *Code*: "no-one should be deprived of love except for the most compelling of reasons." The rule was all over the case law as well. The Court of the Countess of

Champagne, to take an earlier example, had made great play that marriage was not a reason for abandoning love, and by the same logic parental decision could not legitimately block the path of desire. Take away the particular circumstances and we can probably agree a more general norm. It is often the parents who are to blame. Parents need to have reasons and they should certainly account for their acts and decisions. Freud in accord. By and large. But that is a separate point. There may be reasons for amorous suicide but they are never enough, they take the subject out of the realm of love, they diminish desire and end all possibility of relationship. Hence the need to account and to render judgment on suicide, even when the deceased can no longer either hear or benefit from the wisdom of the judges. You can't be bitter when you're dead.

So important is this theme, so crucial to the very existence and continuance of the realm of love that it is the subject matter of the very first case reported in Auvergne's *Judgments of Love*. It is perhaps also worthy of note that the author of the *Judgments*, Martial himself, was reputed in his youth to have attempted suicide after only three weeks of unsuccessful marriage. At nine o'clock in the morning on St. John's day, he jumped out of his window. He broke his leg and all but died. Perhaps that near miss gave him a stronger sense of the pointlessness of suicide as also of the possibility of mending all of the wounds that the heart can suffer. Be that as it may, the anecdote is described as scandalous and is probably apocryphal, the general point that suicide defeats every purpose of love stands true. The denunciation of all suicidal pretensions is indeed the threshold requirement, the rule of entry, the principle of membership of the voluntary jurisdiction of the laws of love. To choose life over death is axiomatic and emblematic. Any act or intimation to the contrary is not simply an infraction but explicitly treason according to the High Court of Love. The first case reported comes before the Provost of Mourning and is of sufficient importance to be pleaded by the Procurator of Love joined in suit with the aggrieved young woman. She pleaded that while she had acted in all respects properly in difficult circumstances, the defendant had deceived her and used her by pretending to kill himself.

The young woman was attractive, happy, well kempt, gay, and of good reputation. She had always been honest and open in the service of love. The defendant met and became infatuated with her. He started calling on her and after several encounters asked her to become his lover. He presented her with various gifts and a ring. She gently refused the gifts on the grounds that she did not plan on becoming his lover and did not wish to profit from his importuning. According to the old law it is amorous simony—sale of something spiritual—to profit from a love that should be freely given. She therefore refused the gifts and politely and graciously turned him down whenever he again asked for her affections. She did, however, and perhaps unwisely, acknowledge his persistence and his loyalty. She told him that she could see much that was good in him, that she liked him well enough, and that she foresaw that he would enjoy much love in his future.

The young man misinterpreted her kind words and took them to be markers of her reticence. In his view she was being coy. With coaxing she would come to express her true feelings, her desire for him. He became greatly excited, nervous, volatile, and increasingly demanding. A while later he arrived at her house and baldly stated that if she did not give in to his desires he would be dead within three days. She was astonished by this declaration and curtly told him that while previously she had liked him she would soon hate him if he talked like this. He ignored her and suddenly started kissing her. She slapped him and pushed him away but he persisted and feigned great agonies of disappointment. He pretended to wail and weep in pain, he ran from the room and then returned with briny water dispersed over his face in an attempt to make himself appear more pitiable. And tears will often do it—*lachrymae in amantibus artes sunt*, tears are of the essence of the art of love the jurisconsult Benoit de Court notes in his commentary—and the complainant briefly gave way. Hoping to cure his despair, she sought to comfort him with hugs and kisses. He interpreted her sympathy as a sign of passion and immediately his hands and his lips began to wander. He grabbed her breasts. Bad move. She was outraged and lost her temper. She ordered him to leave and never return.

His desire unabated, the defendant returned to her house the following day. He was well dressed, a dagger in his belt, and pretended to be happy. They talked for a while and then he suddenly embarked upon a set speech: "My love I rue the day that I was born. I have never in all my life suffered so much and so horribly as I have suffered for you. It seems, however, that my grief leaves you unmoved, that you have no interest in curing my pangs. I have no choice, you leave me no option, I will kill myself here and now in front of you rather than languish a second longer in unrequited love. I am staying here for good. The only way I will leave is stone cold, carried out feet first." Saying this he stood up and taking the dagger from his belt began to cut his arm and then, dramatically, pretended to stab himself in the heart. Blood that he had secreted in a bag in his doublet flew everywhere. Fearing that he would kill himself or even her, she grabbed the handle of his dagger but he continued to swear and to declaim that he would kill himself, no matter how, within the hour.

Alone, terrified, fearful for herself as much as for him, uncertain of whether in seizing hold of his dagger she had further wounded him, confused and emotional she yielded to him. She lay back in empathy and let him consummate his desire. He had his way. Story over except that in the following days he told several people that he had seduced her by subtle and secret means. He boasted that where others had failed, he had succeeded in enjoying her. He dragged her name through the mud. He defamed her.

The Procurator of Love ended the pleading by asking the Court to punish this deceitful and treasonous behavior to the full extent possible under the law. Specifically, he should make reparation for her wounded honor and for the harm he had done to her amorous reputation. Thus the Court was asked to order that he pay penance in the form of walking barefoot, head uncovered, handicapped by lead weights and holding a burning torch across the town. While walking he was to repent and loudly cry out that he had falsely and maliciously deceived and betrayed his lover. As for his defamation of her character, the harm he had done her amorous prospects was to be recompensed by means of paying her a substantial sum of money and then never speaking to or of her again. If the Court was not willing to order such recompense then the Procurator offered in the alternative the suggestion of public corporal punishment so as to deter others from contemplating similar deceits. He should be dragged through the mud, beaten with young willow branches, demeaned and denounced in the most visible way. And finally, crowning touch, as a traitor to the cause he was to be banished from the realm of love, he was never to be loved again. This, the Procurator concluded was the least that the Court could order in the face of such manifest treason, such insouciant and easy deceit.

The defendant did not deny the facts pleaded but claimed rather that his actions had been justifiable. He had long been in love with the plaintiff. He had served her well and loyally. He had done everything that an amorous suitor should do to persuade his enamorata of the truth of his desire. She, however, had responded in the strangest of manners. She had promised to love him dearly and to hold him in the highest of good graces and yet on meeting him she would often act as if she did not know him, on occasion she would snub him, turn away, or ignore him completely. He had no idea where he stood with her. Much as he might have wished to end this sorry dalliance he simply could not. The more belligerent he felt toward her the more he loved her, indeed to the point that he could neither eat nor sleep. Night and day he thought constantly of her. He trembled randomly, he felt as if a thousand thorns were pricking his throat. In short he was lovesick. He confessed his illness to his lover. He begged her to take pity on his condition and to save him. He pleaded for the salvation of her love, the remedy of *jouissance*. She ignored him.

As a final resort, last pitch persuasion, to show her the full extent of his agonies he devised the idea of pretending to kill himself. The death might have been feigned but the argument that he made was perfectly truthful. If he could not win her good graces then there was nothing left for him to live for, and he did plan to commit suicide. As for the charge of defaming her name, that was an invention. He had told no one of his success. She had dreamed this up as a way of tarnishing his good name and he asked the Court for damages to compensate this wrong.

The Provost of Mourning heard the arguments and took time to consider the complexities of the case. Judgment was for the plaintiff. In light of the defendant's confession of the facts he was to make immediate and full amends for the deceit that he had practiced on the plaintiff. Specifically, he was ordered to go barefoot, head uncovered, kneel before the plaintiff and declare loudly: "My Lady, I know and confess here, before God and the world, that I have wickedly and falsely betrayed you. I beg you and the justice of Love for mercy." With that he was to be banished from the domain of love and in addition was to pay her substantial damages. The judgment was upheld but the terms varied on appeal. The defendant, barefoot, loaded down with heavy weights, was to make a pilgrimage to the statue of 'Monseigneur Sainct Valentin' and report back to the court with proof of his journey within the month. After that he was to swear to the plaintiff that he and his heirs for the next three generations would leave her entirely alone. So great was the crime, the treason and the fraud on love, that he was to be an outlaw from love, shunned from then on by all of the denizens of the domain of desire.

The first case in the *Judgments of Love* is evidently emblematic. To love is to live and to live is to love. Such is axiomatic and indisputable. The domain of desire is constituted by hope, by the drive of lack, by the imagination of future fulfillment. It is in essence a sphere of creativity, of epistolary skill and rhetorical eloquence. The Statute of 1400 is quite explicit—and no better source could be used—that every act relating to the jurisdiction of love be motivated to augment and expand the domains of affection and desire and to promote relationship rather than to diminish it. In this vein the Court belongs explicitly within the troubadour tradition of the gay science, and of the Gay Consistory of Toulouse. Love was a species of celebration, a poetic enhancement of life and a source of pleasure. The entire social enterprise of love and its voluntary laws was playful and pleasurable, to which end the Statute ordains emblematically, line 181, that on the day of "Monseigneur Saint Valentin," all of the members of the Court of Love are to gather to dine together "in joyful recreation and amorous conversation." Their task, as judges, officials, clerks, or members of the Court is expressly to honor and augment love while simultaneously subjecting anyone who dishonors, reproaches or blames love to effacement from the register of love and erasure of their name from the records of the Court. If a poet who spoke against love was subject to such radical censure, it is clearly the case that someone who feigned to kill himself because of an unrequited desire could expect the most severe of reprimands, exile, friendlessness, indeed to become *homo inamabilis* and even *indoctus* or unlearned in love.

If love is conceived as joyful and conversational, light and communicative, a form of gay eloquence, then it is understandable that the threat of suicide would be deemed the most egregious of infractions of the laws of love. The Latin sources confirm the point. The law of nature itself affirms life and proscribes the self-infliction of death: *mors voluntaria detestanda*—a voluntary death is to be avoided at all costs. Or, as Cicero might have put it, such loss of eloquence is the opposite of urbanity, alien, uncivilized per se. It is the dark side, the erased face of a desire and can never be recouped or revived. It makes sense then that the first case concerns precisely the most virulent and dire of threats to the cause and the comedy, the life and manners of love. And yet it may also be that there is here an element of excessive protestation. The pain and suffering, the dejection and despair that lovers frequently experience requires its own modes of expression, its forum of conversation, its dialogues and determinations. It is a repeated theme in the case law and we find it again in some of the last of the judgments of love. Two cases heard by the Council of Love are reported in an early seventeenth-century text authored by Honoré d'Urfé. Both cases are petitions for permission to commit suicide.

The first petition is that of one Ursace. He claims that he wishes to die because his life has become unpleasant, useless, and shameful. Unpleasant because he has for a while loved and been loved by a beautiful and virtuous woman. She was recently captured and forcibly carried off to a foreign country and there made a slave to her captor. His life was useless because her abductor was infinitely more powerful than he and so immune to any attempt that Ursace might make to rescue her. And shameful because he had a thousand times sworn that so long as he lived his lover would not suffer and now that was a lie. To live while she was enslaved was dishonorable. Life being a gift for the good it seemed logical that if life led only to ill then it should be abandoned. That was the relief he requested and confidently expected to be granted.

The second petition is that of a woman, Olymbre, who has been left by her lover. She felt that she owed everything to this "virtuous and good friend." Having given herself to him, she could not now nor ever undo their ties, she could not cease to love him and therefore requested the relief of the Council as the justice of love required.

Judgment of the two cases follows a single principle. The laws of love long held, Rule 24 of the *Code*, that all amatory acts must be bounded by thoughts of the beloved. The paramour is paramount. Thus the Council ordered that if Ursace was to take his own life it could only be after he had sought and received the permission of his lover. This he had not obtained and so could not act to bring about his end. He was pleased by this conclusion. Most attempting suicide are. As for Olymbre, she too had failed to obtain the consent of her friend to her death. In the absence of such consent her request had to be turned down. She claimed to live not for herself but for her lover and in consequence she could not dispose of her life without the permission of him for whom she claimed that she lived. A poetic conclusion and yet also a very pragmatic one. In both instances the petition was denied but the point of interest is not the substance so much as the manner in which the decision is reached. It can form the basis of a conclusion.

What is evident is that in matters of love the most pressing issues concern the space between the subjects and not the subjects themselves alone. What is at issue is not the solitary and singular but the shared and traversed space of communication and articulation of various desires and plaints. More than that, the shared spaced between the lovers is also a species of intimate public sphere, a space or avenue of passage whose terms and boundaries are the subject matter not simply of the lovers' discourse, but also of the laws of love. The discipline of *rectorica*, of the rules of amorous eloquence set down as the justice of love, are concerned precisely with the maintenance and expansion of the spaces within which desire can be augmented and relationships—correspondences, imaginations, friendships, and other affairs of the heart—can flourish. The key lies in the concept of the shared space of amatory encounter. How are these sites of affective exchange—historically the alcove, the *ruelle*, the salon, as also the avenues of *billets doux*, of the salaam, the gift, the postcard—to be protected? How can affective acts and expressions be made safe in the institution, in the intimacy of what is nonetheless a public sphere, a space of counter publics, of resistance and affection. How is such a radical and uninhibited space to be maintained?

The cases illustrate that these questions of rhetorical expression, of the safety of conversation and correspondence, are answered at least in part by recognizing the priority of discourse, the necessity of holding the sites of amatory dialogue open as a social space, as a subject of thought, as a jurisdiction that is intimate and public, both visceral and juridical. Recollect that the laws of love were rules of rhetorical felicity, grammatical norms of eloquent expression worked out over the *longue durée* of amatory practice. They offer a serious introspection—a knowledge of rules of intimate encounter and of their affective expressions. The erudition of love is truly a matter of bonding. To know is to come to know over time, a transitive venture, a patient and curiously collective engagement. Nowhere is this more evident than in the last two cases of requests for the judicial relief of death. The pleas were taken seriously, at face value, with a certain degree of compassion even for the sufferings engendered by the failure and more specifically still the ending of love. If love is extinguished then according to the Hegelian logic cited at the outset, life too must in a sense also come to an end. Sure enough there is an intimation of mortification, of the negation of the body that comes with the loss of a loved one. But the solitary individual, *haec imago*, this face and flesh is never all that there is to the affair. The great goal of love is the face to face and so there is already and always necessarily a further face, a principle of plurality that accompanies the amatory adventure. To kill oneself is in this sense necessarily also to kill another, to excise and destroy an entity within a collective space, to detract from the in between of amatory engagement, to diminish a shared argot and enterprise. And in all of those senses the suicidal urge has to be brought to language, to conversation, and finally into the intimate routines and erudition of amorous law.

Ursace and Olymbre were not the first lovers to think of killing themselves when love went wrong. Their singular petitions required the corrective of a more broadly shared conversation, the purposiveness and playfulness of the laws of love. Martial d'Auvergne recovered from his attempt at suicide and went on to record the judgments of the High Court of Love in Paris, beginning of course with the case of a feigned suicide and its expansive and heavily symbolic retribution. No room for the pursuit of death, no tolerance for a narcissistic and necrophilic desire in the annals and laws of love. In the place of such affective self-implosion we find rather a move to dialogue, a pressure toward conversation, the healing of renewed correspondence because it is in the interests of all to engage the suicidal lover, to listen, to coax, to reconnect the amorously unreconciled with the community and the relationships from which desire originally sprang. That, and for the more epistemologically minded it is a primary principle of amatory law that grief eventually engenders understanding—*vexatio dat intellectum* as they used to say. The art of love is long; death will come soon enough to erase it. The *fin amor* is not gauged to helping death but rather to prolonging love.

Figure 13 *Imaginem eius mecum gesto* (I carry her picture with me)—*Emblemata amatoria* (1620).

12
Gifts

A wealthy man who gives a young and beautiful model an expensive ring on their engagement has a reasonable chance of suing to get it back when she breaks her word. It is a legal anomaly and exists in a state of doctrinal exception. He cannot recover any other gifts that he has given her, however expensive, whatever their burden of promise, or conditions of hope. For her part, the woman recipient of the ring cannot sue in law for the time and effort she has given to her amour in care and attention, she cannot enforce his promises to see that she is financially secure, that he will make good the lease she gave up or the mortgage she abandoned. Nor can she claim the loss incurred through jobs turned down or career paths left unattended. That's how it goes in courts of law.

For modern lawyers the donative and the legal, gifts and contracts, are opposites. What is given is freely donated and becomes the property of the beneficiary by virtue of possession. Title passes with the thing. The promise of a gift, however, is unenforceable. It is mere words, a naked pact, and not worth the paper on which it isn't written. When friends or cohabiting lovers make promises they are legally just so many airy words. These, the law intones, are merely private expressions, bare intimations one might say that no court of law would dare engage, police or enforce. What is given rests with the recipient. What was promised remains in the hands of the promisor. The law anxiously keeps out. There is the possibility of sex in the exchanges, there are strong emotions behind the promises or gifts and law neither has the competence nor the skill to address such things. The losses that lovers suffer must lie where they fall. That is the secular legislative sentiment, the laconic legal wisdom, the abiding rule.

Some have challenged the seeming insouciance of the learned lawyers. There are minor and telling exceptions. As noted, if a ring or band is given with the exchange of promises to marry, then upon breach of the promise many jurisdictions will allow for an action to reclaim the ring. It is a species of heart balm they say, a matter of emotional replevin or return. Similarly, though usually in equity rather than in strict law, where someone in an amicable or amatory relationship promises to give something to their friend, lover or spouse, then if that results in justifiable reliance upon the promise and a significant change of financial position results, there may be a precarious chance of recovery in equity, at the discretion of the court. In both those examples, however, it is not the promise; it is precisely not the amorous purpose nor the generosity of intent that triggers legal intervention, but rather the commodity or the market price of the gift or service that prompts a reluctant legal intervention. So the question remains both moot and mooted. What should be done with amorous gifts when the lovers fight or part? Should gifts be returned? Or in terms of the more subtle questions of doctrine, what erotic norms govern the rights of lovers whose gifts are refused? Those who want their gifts returned? Even those who wish not to be given things, or who deem certain gifts insulting or demeaning or inappropriate?

According to the *lex amatoria*, to love is to give. It involves an exchange, a correspondence, *facio ut des*, both doing and giving, performance and promise. Coquillart in the *New Laws* goes so far as to formulate the maxim that "without gifts one would never love." The intention or act of loving is indeed held to be synonymous with doing and giving. The *Statutes of Love* makes the same point. By Law 13: "Devise something, and take it for thine ease, And send it her, that may her soul appease: Some heart, or ring, or letter, or device, or precious stone: but spare not the price." Go back to the earlier law and it is an unbending axiom that love itself is a gift and that one of the cardinal virtues of amorous practice is *largueza* or generosity. The *Precepts* and the *Code* both stipulate that avarice is contrary to love, and by Rule 26 and elsewhere in the *Treatise on Love*, Capellanus treats *largitas*, an open and abundant generosity, as being intrinsic to the ethics of loving. The women's courts were in accord.

We have seen already that love is in amorous law treated as *animus gratia* as a spiritual thing and so freely given. To accept payment for love was classically deemed simony, a trafficking in spiritual things. Thus, to use the most common example from the cases of love, kisses cannot be sold, but must be freely bestowed, and freely given are said to be worth more than incalculable quantities of gold. The significance of the kiss can be taken further. Kissing, the gift of insufflation, together with tears of joy, is the express sign of entry into love. The *osculum amoris* or kiss on the mouth seals the *alliance d'amours,* the formal love affair, and is the pre-eminent of gifts. It is the precursor and emblem of amorous intent. It indeed marks entry into the voluntary jurisdiction of the courts of love. Here everything is by consent, by word and opinion, by correspondence and dialogue, through rhetoric and the eloquence of persuasion. And in this domain of voluntary jurisdiction, of poetic justice in amatory practice, kisses are precatory. They intercede, they entreat, they promise. They are exemplary amorous gifts and they well illustrate the principle of grace, of amorous favor, that constitutes the libidinal economy to which all amorous gifts belong.

The general rule expressed in the judgments of love is that the amorous economy of gifts depends upon a dual generosity: a desire to give and a desire to receive. Both must be present for the gift to be genuinely expressive of the intent or act of loving. In Judgment 19, heard before the Court of Queen Eleanor, a man had given numerous small gifts to his enamorata. She accepted the gifts readily enough, they were appropriate tokens and evidently they pleased her, but she utterly refused to love him. He complained to the Court. Queen Eleanor decided in his favor: "Either she should refuse these little gifts, these obviously amorous tokens, or she should respond in kind, with the gift of love." The libidinal economy has its own norms of reciprocity. Their measure, however, is neither venal nor mercantile. It is not a question of the value of things but rather a matter of generosity of spirit, of the desire to augment and to be augmented, to ornament and to please, a matter of doing and giving, promising and making.

Case 21 heard before the Court of the Countess of Champagne provides further insight into the doctrine of the gift. The Court was petitioned to provide an opinion—we would say declaratory judgment—on what gifts a lover may properly accept from their partner. She replied that a lover is permitted to receive these gifts: "a napkin, hair-bands, gold or silver tiara, brooch, picture, bowl, vessels, plates, a pendant for remembrance." More generally, small gifts were appropriate so long as they complied with one or other of the following principles. The first and primary role of the gift is to adorn the beloved, adding to her beauty or his elegance, honing her wit or expanding his appeal. A gift that adorned in such manner was one that added to the eloquence and cultivation of the relationship, and such gifts were increasingly to include poems, *billets doux*, letters and conversation. The primary role of the gift is thus to eroticize, to charge and advance the relation, to act as Rousseau would put it, as a token, a salaam, a coinage of passage into the domain of desire.

The second proper role of the gift is as a memento of an absent lover. The object or image that served as a reminder had a special significance in an era where both geography and social codes of conduct served to distance lovers and acted as obstacles to communication. The image of the beloved was to be loved in its own right, but it was also a secret sign, a mark of an amorous affair that existed in defiance of convention, social cost, and Church doctrine. The amorous token was to be treasured and hidden: a ring for instance given by a lover was to be worn on the little finger of the left hand and with the stone turned inward to the palm of the hand to keep it from view. The left hand, in a slightly Eastern turn, because this hand is unsullied by dishonorable gestures or "base acts of touch." The little finger because it contains the coda of life and death, "more than any other finger." And turned inward so as to keep the love affair from being exposed or "noised" abroad.

The Court clearly dictates that the gift satisfy criteria of appropriateness to love, and these included attention to the practicalities of entering and maintaining a nocturnal domain or secret economy of libidinal passage. The gift was thus concrete evidence of faithfulness to the interior cause and unique jurisdiction of desire. The gift, given and received, marked an inseverable entry into the logic of love, and the law of its codes and courts. And to this, as its inverse, the Countess added the much repeated principle that the material value of the gift, the weight of gold or silver, the cost of cloth or finery, the risk involved in conveying it or wearing it, were irrelevant to the amorous acts of giving and receiving. Questions of venal cost belong to the mercantile world and its secular courts. Where love is concerned, gifts play their role within an amatory economy which is subject to laws of love that address desire and not duty, the movement of the free spirit and not the constraints of mundane calculation.

Judgment 30, reported by Martial d'Auvergne, is concerned directly with the transition between the mercantile and the amorous, between the mundane market and the libidinal economy, between spirit and greed. The complaint is brought by a man who had for a long time showered gifts upon the defendant woman. When he first met her he had been financially comfortable and at ease with the world. Without care, unclouded by anxiety he had devoted himself to his amour and to pleasing her every whim. When she asked for something, he would immediately give it to her. He refused her nothing. He gave her everything with an open heart, countless gifts, endless tokens of affection. His worldly wealth was entirely at her disposal. She accepted his gifts and as long as they kept coming she entertained him and gave him hope. Eventually, however, her demands reduced him to poverty. He had spent all he had and she now turned away from him. Worse than that, when she saw him in public she would point him out to her friends and mock him. Her outstretched finger was a dagger to his heart. He asked the Court to condemn her behavior. He had been her first and longest serving suitor. She should honor him for the services and gifts that he had given her in the past; she should save her devotion for him alone.

The defendant argued in reply that those who sought love should not come empty handed. Gifts given in the past were of no relevance now. While his wealth had lasted, the two had enjoyed themselves but that time was over and he was greatly deceiving himself if he thought her amorous interest in him would survive the demise of his coffers. Poverty brings sorrow not joy and she wished no part of that.

The defendant, joined in argument now by officials of the Order of Love, dismissed her arguments as wholly unworthy of the domain of love. Her argument implied that we love only for money. In effect she had confessed to selling her love. In doing this, she had wickedly used the plaintiff and wasted his energy and time. Even worse, she had a reputation for entertaining several suitors at the same time, for bleeding them dry and then more cruel still, mocking them in public. They asked the Court that she be ordered to make honorable amends and return everything that he had given her. To this the sorrowful plaintiff lover added that as far as he was concerned he wanted nothing back from her but only that she return to her former affections and love him again.

She replied that what he requested was impossible. Love could hardly be enjoined by an injunction. Where love was obtained by force it would bring only bad luck and pain. More than that, the impoverished plaintiff was like someone ill, a sickly and indisposed being far removed from the joy and happiness that love should portend. To give her affections to him could be nothing more than a duty dutifully observed.

Held by the Court that this rebel woman be condemned to make good, to restore and return every item that the plaintiff had given her. The fact that the plaintiff wanted none of his gifts back did not alter the determination. A plaintiff lover is seldom the best judge of what is right. She was to give full restitution or all her goods and possessions would be impounded by the officials of the Court.

Subsequent case law supports this decision as the founding or threshold requirement that love be freely given, that the libidinal economy is predicated upon giving and receiving according to norms of desire rather than lust for property. It is the intention of the giver, the desire of the recipient, and not any more diurnal or worldly desire for wealth that dictates the circulation and symbolism of gifts according to the rules of amatory law. A subsequent and curious case, again heard before the High Court of Love in Paris illustrates this point very well.

A desolate and upset suitor brought an action against his enamorata complaining that she had improperly and unkindly rejected a gift he had made her. More than anything else in the world, he claimed, he wished to be in her good graces. He longed for her to remember him, and that she think fondly of him was his greatest desire. To further that end, he decided to have a keepsake and memento of his love made for her as a gift. He ordered skilled craftsmen to make the most beautiful and expensive handkerchief possible. An ornate and expressive gift for her. It was to be woven from the very finest silk and on it his name and a small heart were to be embroidered in gold letters. The rim of the handkerchief was to be fringed with pansies. The handkerchief, a common and proper symbol in the various genres of libidinal economy, was made and then presented by the plaintiff to the defendant woman. She looked away and refused the gift with the words "I will never take it." Worse still, since refusing his gift, she no longer greeted him when they met in public, and her demeanor toward him had soured when they met alone. He felt this was wrong. The gift had been improperly refused, and her subsequent rejection of him was equally to be faulted.

She responded that her actions should not have come as a surprise to him. He was not her lover and she had never held out any false hope to him. The gift was not only inappropriate—too intimate and too expensive—but it was also a covert way of mocking her. He knew that she could not accept so fine a gift. If she took it she would in effect be confessing to loving him. And then again, however fine, it was only a handkerchief, something to wipe the nose with. All told, she was right to refuse.

To this the unhappy lover replied that in matters of amorous gifts, it was not the thing but the intention of the giver that was to be attended to and intimately accepted. He had fashioned a soft and beautiful handkerchief out of love for her. He hoped thus that every time she put her hands in her pocket to pull out her keys she would see his handkerchief, and whenever she wiped her nose she would equally remember him. If he had in some way offended her, that was the furthest thing from his intentions and he begged God to forgive him. He had never intended to displease her and if his gift was unsatisfactory he offered to give her something else, anything indeed that she requested.

She replied that he was deluding himself if he thought that she would accept something else from him. For the very same reason that the handkerchief had been rejected, other gifts would similarly be turned back. She did not wish to mislead him. By the same token she did not want to set a false example for other suitors. To accept the gift without entertaining the love that prompted it would be wrong and misleading.

The High Court heard the arguments and deliberated at length. Judgment was eventually given in favor of the woman. She acted properly; she was right to refuse the gift, which in the end, or in terms of the economy of love, was neither acceptable nor valuable. If you neither love nor intend to love, you cannot accept the benefit of amorous gifts because they are the harbingers of increased desire. To this the Court added the argument that a gift that seeks to override or seduce the will of another, a gift that changes someone's intentions is improper. The gift should follow the intention and not override it. A gift should express but not interfere with choice.

Underlying the decision is a principle of the sanctity of gifts in matters of love. The economy of gifts is not based upon mundane values. The gift is without measure; it is a sign of exuberance, a mode of indicating affect, and in all a firmly spiritual expression. It is a mode of manifesting desire in the space between lovers and so is irreducible. It is not property, it is not a secular thing but instead a spiritual signal, an erotic indicator, a token within a hedonistic design. Taken as such, as our commentator the eruditely amorous Symphorianus puts it in his gloss to the text, *donum non accipere beata res est*: to refuse a gift is a beautiful thing. It shows spiritual inclination, strength of purpose, and a willingness to submit mundane demands and desires to an interior drive, to an ethics of love.

More generally, the refusal of gifts shows insight into the interpretation of the signs of desire. The gift that is rejected is refused because however valuable or enticing, acceptance would confuse amorous intent with venal designs. If the giver is not loved, the gift must be returned. This is also because of the danger that such gifts will confuse their recipients; they are likely to deprive them of foresight and to turn emotional truths upside down. If a gift will blind insight and alter the truth of the recipient's affections, it should not be accepted. The spirit should lead and the gift should follow. It should express a prior or prescient amorous state. Accepting the gift similarly marks openness to love. It should not be forgotten in this context that the gift is also a promise, a sign of love to come; indeed it is a species of kiss or anticipatory marker of more to be given. The law is clear that gifts should not be used to achieve unethical or untoward ends. The gift signals the intent of the giver, and it is to be interpreted according to the qualities of the person who gives. If accepted, and here is the clincher, the last line of the gloss, the gift signals and will lead to the pair becoming concubines, meaning that they will likely "lie down together." Such an end should not be signaled unless intended, unless anticipated and fully and faithfully meant.

The amorous gift signals much more than the thing given, the simple material good or equivalent monetary amount. It indicates future pleasures, greater gratifications, the emotional openness and longer term of intimacy. It is the gift that more than anything else permits entry into love in a spirit of generosity and abundance. Giving and receiving, donation and acceptance in mutual desire are central to the constitution of the space between lovers, to the existence of the intimate public domain, the nightly realm in which lovers pass their messages and keep their trysts. The amorous importance of the gift lies in the complexity of what it signals. It is coded and nuanced, a properly hermeneutic marker that will communicate intimately and uniquely. It will send a message about the lover who gives and about the lover who receives. These require interpretation, erotic erudition even as well as the spirit of the gay science and its eloquence of love.

Return briefly to a case discussed earlier in terms of contracts of love.♥ Heard before the Court of the Marquis of Flowers. The complaint can be recapitulated in terms of gifts. The couple had recently become lovers and in the manner of the *alliance d'amours* they had sworn to unite their hearts as one, to love each other perfectly and eternally. She had promised, among other things, that she would never have any other lover but him until the day she died. She promised also that insofar as it lay in her power she would never do anything that displeased him. The plaintiff man complained that his beloved had failed to keep these promises. Specifically, soon after their union she seemed to become less enamored of him, distracted even. Worse still, she entertained other men, listened with pleasure to their conversation, laughed at their pleasantries and badinage. She even accepted small gifts and bouquets of flowers. He argued that she should accept gifts and flowers only from him. That is what she had promised or so he claimed.

The point of interest here is not the interpretation of the contract of love, which point has been covered, but rather the status and meaning of small gifts and flirtatious conversations. The Court of Flowers did not uphold the man's complaint. It took a much more generous and spiritual view. Small gifts convey a hedonistic message. Little tokens, flowers

♥Chapter 4, "Contracts of Love," p. 74.

even, and any accompanying "air gallant" or poetic conversation is part of the everyday ethos of the domain of love, of aesthetic exchange, of precious or precocious interaction. If minor gifts, petite donations, help pass the time, amuse, incite to dialogue, then these are goods that the generous and open should positively wish for the pleasure of their amour. Not all gifts are equivalent and part of the skill of the lover lies in the ability to interpret the different types or levels of gift and to distinguish between those that are playful, minor, and to be trusted when given between non-amorous friends, and those that are properly portents of love and to be accepted or refused according to the amorous desire of the recipient.

If the law of love properly belongs to gay science it is healthy to recollect also a little of what that meant both as knowledge and as practice. The early Occitan term was *gaiessa*. It embodied a hedonistic spirit; it implied a degree of judgment (*sens*), an ability to trust, a shared space of eloquence between lovers. If love improves life, if it energizes, transforms, and transcends the realm of mundane needs, that is in large measure because of the risks and pleasures, the excitement and danger of giving oneself to a shared space, to an in-between domain where pleasure can flow and enjoyment expend itself. In this view, small gifts, such as bouquets of flowers are just part of a more general excitation, they are innocent aspects of shared ecstasies or of what Derrida briefly termed the "no more one/more than one." The domain of love is here conceived as open, generous, gregarious, and communicative. Love should be expressed, spread, disseminated as much as possible and as hedonistically as possible. If it is not a question of enjoyment, of living well, then what is love worth? The answer of the Court of Flowers is clearly that amorous law supports an intimate public sphere replete with laughter, conversation, admiration, privilege and pleasure, small gifts and flowers freely exchanged.

On the other side of this hedonistic perception is an ethical norm or principle of trust that the parties giving and receiving small gifts do not abuse the alliances or relationships that preexist such exchanges. Trust must flow three ways for the intimate public space of gallantry, of amicable pleasures, to be possible. The lovers have to trust each other and they have to trust their friends and confidants to respect their commitments. The *Precepts of Love* are to that effect. Precept 3: "When a woman is joined to another in love, do not knowingly try to seduce her." Which is perfectly plain, not hard to observe but still requires both attention to extant emotional ties and an honest assessment of the border between gay play and amatory importuning. Hence the extraordinary importance in amorous law of being able to read and interpret gifts—as also tokens, symbols, words and conversations—accurately and precisely.

On the other side of the line from amicable interactions, small gifts, little tokens, and amicably gallant conversation lies the impropriety of dissolute donation. The inverse of the previous decision of the Court of Flowers comes in Judgment 16, a case which at first instance came before the Auditors of Love's Causes, a body of amorous actuaries expert in addressing the intensity of emotions and the justice of affective exchange. The petition was made by an impoverished lover who sought relief from certain amorously occasioned debts and most specifically from a debt owing to the defendant woman.

The petitioner claimed that he had been unlucky in love. He had been bled dry by the voracious appetite of women for gifts. Attempting to please various women, and so find a lover, he had expended his fortune on grand gestures, excessive gifts, and extravagant entertainments. He had also spent vast amounts on his own adornment, again, so he claimed, to please the women he sought to seduce. The result was impoverishment. He could not pay his creditors without taking back what he had given away. For this reason he had petitioned the Chancellery of Love for a writ of relief, for letters that would release him from his debts. He now asked the Auditors of Love's Causes to confirm the letters of release.

The defendant woman, one of his creditors, contested the release. She argued that she was not wealthy but she had nevertheless loaned money to the petitioner out of compassion and concern for love. He had come to her in a state of disarray and had begged her to help him. He needed six crowns to pay for a velvet doublet he had ordered to be made. At first she refused this unlikely request but then she was moved by his expression of his parlous state, by his tearful expressions, and so finally lent him the money. He promised profusely to repay the debt in a short time. He never did. She requested the Auditors to order the money he owed be returned to her, and this for two reasons.

The first was simply that debts occasioned by borrowing money from women were privileged and could and should not be expunged. Second and much more to our point, the expenditure and gifts had been occasioned not by loving well but by profligacy. By his own confession, the petitioner had given excessively and he had given to many women in many different locations. Thus his impoverishment was not attributable to love, but rather to his idiocy, his ignorance of amorous law, to his philandering, his obsession with seducing large numbers of women. He devoted so much time to pursuing different women that he left himself no time to work or earn. The real cause of his indebtedness was his addiction to gallant and empty gestures, to excessive and unnecessary giving. His impecuniousness was his fault and not hers. It was certainly no reason to release him from his debt to her. He was untrustworthy. He was an inept lover, and he should be ordered to make good his promises to repay.

The petitioner replied that he did not have the means to repay the debt. Nor, he argued, had the loan come to term—he had borrowed the money so far for somewhat under a year. She was not indigent. She could wait.

The Auditors held in favor of the defendant woman. The petitioner was ordered to repay. The amorous logic underpinning the decision is twofold. First, there is a question of interpretation. Giving and receiving, the gift relationship, is to be interpreted according to the amorous intentions of both the parties. There has to be an intention to give, an amorous animus, and a desire to receive, a willingness to entertain the possibility of love or the promise of relationship as the case may be. As regards the spirit of love, the *animus gratia* of giving, this had not been present in the more restricted act of making a loan. His ineptitude was not grounds for turning a benevolent act of monetary aid into an amorous gift.

The second ground of the judgment devolves from the first. It takes us back to founding principles of amatory law. The twelfth-century *Cort d'amor* states very clearly that the first condition of love is good faith—*bona fes*. That is the inaugural Judgment of Love and it is well received. It means that expressions of love should be made in good faith and received as intended. Gifts being one such expression are subject to that same principle of good faith as trust in the amorous intention of the giver. In the case in question, however, the petitioner had given excessively and to many. He could not be trusted. It is indeed an axiom of gay science, as Symphorianus notes: *qui plures amat, minus amat*—meaning that someone who loves many, loves each one less. Dividing love between several lovers distracts and detracts from the space between, from the intimacy and the intensity of desire. The force of love is sapped and drained by the many tributaries down which it flows. And in such circumstances the petitioner was again at fault. His protestations were false, his profligacy distracting, while his philandering was patently the cause of his undoing. His was an untrustworthy adventurism, narcissism and not love. Hence the loan was to be repaid because even if it was given out of a species of love—women will often save men—it was not received in an amorous spirit but rather for more venal ends.

The laws of love treat amorous gifts as *sui generis*, as unique and subject to their own norms of free exchange. If we return to our starting point, to the contemporary rules governing promises, gifts and other exchanges between lovers, then amorous law seemingly provides new resolutions. The ring given with the exchange of promises to marry is a symbol of love. It is one of the oldest of all indicators of attachment and if given with amorous intent then, according to the *Cort d'amor* the annealed gold ring is the seal of love, the mark of a bond, a spiritual sign. Judged according to the norms of amorous giving and receiving the engagement ring should stay with the recipient. It cannot be sued on as a contract because an amorous gift is a special kind of promise. It obeys its own voluntary law. It can be returned out of free will or generosity of spirit but there are no mundane rights attached to a gift willingly given and freely and honestly received. It would be like asking for the return of the kisses and the tears with which a relationship began. Can't be done. The ring stays with its recipient. And if it is over, melt it down, make a pin, a globe, a heart. Love often ends in tears. Move on. Go start anew.

By contrast the various promises that lovers make late at night, the oaths that declare "I will always care for you," "if you give up your life, your world, your degree, your job, your apartment and come live with me and be my love then what I have is also yours," or "I will pay you for your kindness, or your work, or your help, I will make it up to you," these promises and their kind are subject to the norms of good faith spelled out above. It is always and everywhere a matter of interpretation. As Coquillart points out in the *New Laws*, these promises are not to be interpreted "stricti iuris" or according to the letter of the law, but rather according to the norms of love that require generosity of spirit and honesty in promising. Under these norms, there is no reason that the promise to care, or to compensate, should not be kept. It is a spiritual thing. A matter of faith and of keeping faith. Promises made between lovers in the domain of love will be enforced in amatory law. They will be enforced because they were promised in amity, because of their amorous intention, and not because of what was promised, not because of any amount or thing or merely mundane content of exchange. Give and the heart alone can grieve or make amends. Promise and the amatory concept of good faith will hold that the words are true, that a lover's words cannot be broken.

Figure 14 *Certus amor morum est* (love of law is a secure thing) Richard Brathwaite, *The English Gentleman* (1630).

13 Conclusion: Does Love Have Standing?

The modern history of the laws of love has been that of a sorry misplacement. The laws have been discounted, marginalized, mislaid, confined to peripheral spaces. They have formed at most a very minor jurisdiction. Their paradoxical competence has been that of a forgotten erudition, their momentary and generally esoteric manifestations have been in the curious form of very obscure, highly serious and worthily scholarly recollections of a paradoxically dour gay science and an extremely technical art of speaking justly in civil matters. Where we encounter the laws of love today, it is as an anthropological relic or as an amusing curiosity. As if love were simply a curiosity, a marginal aspect of social life. As if the hidden intimacies of the public sphere were no more than bizarre distractions from what is really taking place, the main event, politics or institutional action as usual. And as if working life were free of love and hate, libido and lust. No fun in that, neither erotics nor pleasure. So take another example. Yet one more marginal text. A genuinely minor contribution. A little symptom in the form of a lawyer's spoof of the laws of love that appeared toward the end of the last century, just a few years back, in the halcyon days of late 1994. First, however, a little context.

This was the era of political correctness on U.S. campuses. Sexual orientations proliferated, and the fin de siècle excesses of the sex wars hit both the legislatures and the courts with novel claims, both rights and wrongs that needed new determinations. Legislatures throughout the common law world were busy criminalizing sex and penalizing erotic enjoyment. Even as staid a figure as Lord Ordinary of Appeal, Justice Ward acknowledged the incoming tide. Asked to decide whether a same sex couple could be "spouses" for the purposes of the Rent Act he bravely dissented and concluded that they could: a gay couple could have "family qualities." To this he adds: "I have not reached this decision lightly.

In truth, it has caused me a great deal of anxiety. I have worried that I have gone too far ... but to conclude otherwise would be to stand like King Canute, ordering the tide to recede." When this same question later reached the House of Lords, the last instance of juridical certitude, the arbiter of things divine and human, even further anxiety was engendered. Follow the theme upward, and Lord Millett in a dissenting judgment—the majority sided with Lord Justice Ward—acknowledges: "I have given long and anxious consideration to the question whether in the interests of unanimity, I should suppress my dissent, but I have come to the conclusion that I should not." It is, if I might be so bold, a remarkable glimpse of the phenomenology of judging and what in Justice Ward's terms could be deemed the Canutist complex.

Judges, let alone law lords, do not in general publicly acknowledge actively contemplating suppressing the law or the proper meaning of the rule. Most unusual, so much so that the author of the majority opinion, and I will make nothing of his name on this occasion, Lord Rodger of Earlsferry, soothed the dissent by citing the gay scholar and poet A. E. Housman on how to deal with "corrupt texts." This is already a tantalizing breach of what Stanley Fish in his Oxford lectures on "professional correctness" regards as the limits of the legal form. He deems it an improper stepping out of bounds, a traveling beyond disciplinary competence, where judging correctly requires "forgetting" other disciplines and modes of thought, and just doing law. Deciding a case, for Fish, is like hitting a baseball. You just do it. But here Lord Rodger recognized the signs of the times and sought around for textual help. The theoretically incorrect answer that he gave, and with considerable and admirable flair, was that the judicial interpreter should address not the words but "the writer's thought." Even or especially for a lawyer this must be recognised as a pure fiction, a rhetorical invention, the stuff of what a philologist and poet might suggest to beautify a text and render an interpretation elegant, touching, and effective. Lord Rodger's suggestion, though Housman would doubtless have put it more poetically, being as he was a touch gayer, more of a poet, is that the judges become intimate with the author, that they scour his interior, read her soul.

The text is in this reading a face. It is *index animi*, a poetic reference to the spirit that moves, to the breath that reveals. And this in turn refers us briefly and elliptically to an antique historical role of common law. English law is classically defined, among other things, as a "nursing father." This is according to no less an authority than Sir Roger Coke in his mid-seventeenth-century legal treatise on *Justice Vindicated* from the "*false fucus*" put on it by Mr Thomas Hobbes and various other maniacal legalists. Nothing worse than a false "fucus." For this and other reasons the law has to watch over the souls of its citizens, it has to guard life from errancy and texts from corruption and misinterpretation. And this requires going below the surface, getting under the "fucus" (from the Greek *phûkos*—cosmetic) and dealing directly with the question of justice, the cause of law. This is a method familiar to the gay science and to the lawyers of love. They were poets, trained as orators, steeped in the *Song of Songs*, in the eros of verse, in the spirit of love.

The recourse to the eloquence of justice required interpretative attention be paid to the drive, to what the amorous judiciary called the *intentio*, the amorous intention, the textual desire, the tenderness of authorship. All of which is to say that in 1994 love was in crisis and the judges turned not to Professor Fish and his protestations of the purity of law, but to the maverick and miscreant literary figure of A. E. Housman for their necessarily and pleasurably corrupt interpretation of a statute's authorial intention. English law lords, after all, do not as a rule express anxiety of decision nor do they generally reveal the intimate "truth" of the life of a determination. Even less do they admit to prolonged doubt or stronger still, thoughts of suppressing the true meaning of law. They do not generally go outside their discipline to determine a case on the strength of a gay philologist's view of how to cure textual corruptions. These are all bold and radical sentiments, rare words, and they provide lucent recognition that new forms of love, new sexual mores, had swept through the public spheres of the Anglophone legal world. Eros, one might hypothesize, had galvanized *nomos* into motion, into new appropriations and novel opinions as to the meaning of law.

If the English law lords were anxiously recognizing these changes, the United States legal community was blazing an even bolder trail, all the way from grammatical and lexical codes of good conduct to a legislative war on "patriarchy" and the mooting and making of sexual and racial hate crimes. The marginal was becoming central; the hidden injuries of amorous conduct were rising to the social surface. Questions of intimacy were appearing in public. The Queen of America was going to Washington. Through all of this, against its will, one could say, law was falling into history. But lawyers don't know any history, haven't read the laws of love, don't understand the gay science. How then are they to deal with amorous intensities, with lust or the outskirts of intimacy as it shifts from the domestic to the political, from the night to the day, as too from the erotic to the erogenous, from abstinence to consummation? Would they dare recognize their incompetence, the need for a different jurisdiction and a distinct personnel? Only very indirectly. Probably not at all. Which takes us, and not without a slight whiff of the Morellian method—the truth lies in the incidental and overlooked—to the marginal text, the minor contribution, authored by students as it happens, that takes up again the notion of the law of love.

It is in answer to the questions and anxieties raised by the gender troubles, by new sexual orientations, different modes of identity performance, and the other outcries of the sex wars, that the prestigious *Yale Law Journal* published a tentative draft of a *Restatement of Love*. It is a very quiet and quite unnoticed little epistle. Note straight off that in the formal terms of law publishing the piece is a very marginal one. It is buried in the essays section of the *Journal*, after the articles, just before the notes. It is extremely short and distinctly slight on the case-based illustrations and other details that generally make common law productions prolix, plentiful, and textually prolonged. Note that the usual length of an article in American law reviews in the 1990s is around one hundred pages or upward. Articles are short books, only much less readable and much less read. The lead article in the same issue of the *Yale Law Journal*, Volume 104 (December 1994), under the somber title of "The President's Power to Execute Laws" is a characteristic 115-pages long with over 550 scholarly footnotes. The essay that immediately precedes the *Restatement of Love* is just short of 40 pages in length with 170 footnotes. After such a wealth of scholarly substance the *Restatement* is genuinely a squib, a little piece of a mere 23 pages in length, authored by two students and with a risible 58 footnotes, most of which simply continue the main text in variant, even Derridean forms. But length, especially in matters of love, is surely not everything. The curiosity of the piece deserves further attention.

A *Restatement* is a peculiarly American legal form of text. It is a collectively drafted, highly respected synoptic statement of the common law, the case law, in a given domain. Thus there are Restatements of Contracts, Torts, Agency, Restitution, Products Liability, Family Law, Foreign Relations Law, of Judgments even. These encyclopedic efforts are drafted painstakingly by academic leaders and practitioners in the specified field. They are used fairly extensively in teaching law; they get updated from time to time except where legislation or indifference supersedes them. They provide a systematic restatement of the relevant body of case law, together with comments, explanatory texts, and illustrations taken from the precedents. Although not authoritative in a technical legal sense—they do not bind the judges—they are accepted as very relevant guides to the law and are cited frequently by the courts. It is this form that the *Restatement of Love* mimics, plays with, and reproduces.

In the context of a plethora of campus codes of speech and conduct, new sex crimes, administrative offences—sexual harassment, domestic violence, date rape, hate speech, the suggested reinvention of the tort of seduction and much more—the reporters of the *Restatement of Love* pose the question of what a law governing amorous relationships would look like. They start from a familiar lacuna: "Romantic relationships have been presumed unsusceptible to a structure of rules." Love is passion, a force or mania that knows few limits and offers few explanations. François Callières in *The Lover's Logic* notes that when love intervenes, when "ingenious sonnets and impassioned stanzas" start to flow, "the search for rhyme likely chases reason away." And Blaise Pascal too famously intoned that the heart has its reasons of which reason knows nothing. If love is madness, a species of frenzy or erotic sickness, then law is perhaps neither the best means of guiding discussions of it nor an adequate salve for remedying its wounds. But non-marital love relationships, office affairs, intimate amours in the workplace, love and hate in the factory bureaucracy, in the appointments committee or in the classroom keep emerging.

The intimate goes public, and the unwritten norms, the customs and oral uses that traditionally kept these contretemps hidden from general view, swept under the carpet, but mainly just ignored, no longer seem to be doing their work. Lawyers have stepped in to arbitrate, mediate, and judge, but these lawyers, schooled in the rationalism of secular positive law have neither training nor even any remaining intuitive inkling of how to address the intimately erotic, the emotionally charged, the sexually explicit. It most often produces anxiety, moments of Canutism, aphasia or blanket censure in the form of prohibitive codes of practice, civil and criminal offenses that would outlaw public expressions of desire. A new and unthought Puritanism without erotic principle or emotional acumen. A law without law. Injustice. And so the reporters, Gretchen Craft Rubin and Jamie Heller, seek to draft a code of customary norms and applicable rules that will "specify the parties' rights and obligations."

What follows is amusing enough. I will summarize it shortly. But first observe the contradiction that stems from the initial definition of project and flows through the results that follow. If love has its own laws, if intimacy is genuinely different—idiosyncratic and emotive, particular and passionate—then it makes little rhetorical sense to subject love to a law, to rules, to rights and obligations that are identical in form to the public norms that govern mercantile relations. Love needs its own law and that means that in rethinking love we must also rethink law. It is not enough to apply the methods and manners of secular municipal regulation to the passionate, the amorous, the imaginative spaces of love affairs, of lust, longing and the fulfillment of desire. These need a different treatment, an erotic *nomos*, a law that suspends judgment, a code that attends to the emotive, that is not afraid to address the spiritual dimensions of passion and its excesses. Just to get a little technical, a touch medieval with their asses, and as has been repeated frequently by way of reference to our amorous glossator Symphorianus, questions of love are a matter, obviously enough, for a spiritual jurisdiction. Even Etienne Forcadel, the famous sixteenth-century constitutional reformer, in his *Cupido iurisperitus* or *Erotic Jurisprudence*, published in 1553, makes the same point. Love transcends mere secular law, it is joined he says immediately to a spiritual *nomos*, a higher and less obvious law, a more subtle and amorous casuistry, and it is this that needs to be addressed.

What our reporters Gretchen and Jamie come up with has much value. I am not concerned to belittle or discount it again. So I will move to a positive accounting of its virtues, the table of constructive contributions. It is first of all pretty funny. They offer a cross sectional diagram of romantic relationship. It starts with courtship and ends with dissolution. The relationships that go wrong do anyway. And that is what lawyers are mainly concerned with. Breached contracts, severed alliances, broken love. So they start with dating, and in light of recent history they begin with blind dating. They provide a boilerplate, a standard form, for blind dates. Helpful guidelines are set out. So, for example, arrangements for a Saturday date should be made on Wednesday. That is the custom and practice, and even if it does not go back to time immemorial, it does have its reasons in the tacit and illiterate uses of men. "Calling on Tuesday is too eager; Thursday is arrogant; and Friday implies a belief that the invitee is available on demand." Thus the Wednesday night caller acts reasonably. Among the other rules that the boilerplate stipulates is the requirement that parties "screen before the blind date." A telephone call at the very least is recommended. A blind date need not be mute. No need to be deaf either, even though "telephone evidence is often of limited reliability"—exaggeration or selling, legally called "puffing" is difficult to strain out.

I could go on and describe the structure of the *Restatement* further, but it is not very long and the general tenor has been adequately and sympathetically relayed. As to substance, there are several nice moments. There is a concept of acquiring an easement during the course of a relationship, meaning that where one party, for example, continually wears a favorite T-shirt belonging to the other party, then he or she may take it with them upon dissolution of the relationship. Or, in the rather more technical example that they give: "C continually uses Q's walkman without Q's permission. The use is known to many of their friends, and Q could have learned of it early in the relationship through reasonable investigation. After a certain period of time, C has an easement by prescription, and Q cannot regain sole use of the item." To this are added numerous Latin phrases, legal maxims, and carefully mimicked items of legalese. The principle of "res judicata" (it has already been litigated) is applied to annual holidays, corporate opportunity doctrine is applied to friends who seek relationships with an other's ex amour, the principle of the "eggshell plaintiff" is extended to the wounds of love—meaning that you take the susceptibilities of the beloved as they are. Couples splitting up face a "constitutional moment" and have a duty to give reasons, "outlier cases"—obscure decisions that favor your case, are to be discounted. Leveraged buyouts of failing relationships are frowned upon but recognized. And so on.

On the face of it the *Restatement* is a pretty minor intervention, rather slight, small even in the face of amorous conflict and changes in sexual mores. It takes some common sense insights about youthful love and overlays them with a legal structure and commercial jargon drawn from a wide and disparate array of doctrinal domains. It refuses to think differently about law, it fails to think the difference of amorous law, and in doing so it avoids the difficult issues, the questions of living together, of living on in relationship, of ongoing needs, of wounds and indiscretions. That said, the virtues of the piece also need to be acknowledged, expanded and extolled. It is light. Gay, even, in its attention to topics that generally pass by indefinition or censure. If it takes humor, as it undoubtedly does, to address questions of amorous practice, of libido and lust, passion and rage, then humor should be weighed carefully and interpreted closely. It takes lightness to discuss the seriousness of the emotions and that lightness should not be a bar to understanding or to further contemplation.

Here then we have a humorous statement of some snippets of a former and remodeled law of love. Customary practices, oral norms, hearsay refashioned to fit incongruous contemporary forms of congress. In its way it is a fragment of a gay jurisprudence, a playful or poetic justice, a funny and only partially comprehended recollection of earlier unwritten traditions, of an amorous *nomos* that was always above and more than mere secular law. That is our starting point, the humor of the unfamiliar, the comedy of manners revealed, the uncanny or simply funny sense in which we covertly know that affinities and affairs are rampant in our institutional corridors, our public domains, and yet we have neither name nor *nomos*, neither erotic erudition nor amorous law by which to converse and comprehend, advance or remedy, extend or extinguish them.

The *Restatement of Love* makes a beginning, both by being humorous and by expressly addressing a number of the antique and continuing questions of love. The very act of opening up discussion, the project of lightly yet persistently raising the *quaestiones disputatae amoris* or disputed questions of love in the public sphere is a major event, an important achievement, an interestingly proleptic sign of work yet to be done, and a marker of an erotic knowledge still to be acquired. If we move to the case illustrations, they take up a number of issues that the courts of love had long dealt with and that the laws had variously codified during the long term of amorous law. The questions are pertinent but the responses are problematic. Take an example.

The illustration to section 3.1 (2) (c) concerns the doctrine of standing. Standing refers to the legal requirement that only someone with a legitimate stake in a controversy is entitled to sue. The illustration proceeds as follows: "X and Y are in a long-term relationship. X is unhappy because Y gained fifteen pounds in the last year. When X tactfully tries to express a grievance to Y, Y retorts that X has no business complaining, because X is not materially injured. Of course, Y's weight may 'hurt' X in numerous ways. X might be less attracted to Y, or may worry about Y's health. X certainly has an injury in fact. Yet under the newly proposed merits-based analysis, X has no claim to relief against Y. This conclusion follows not because X is uninjured, but because regardless of injury to another, a person's weight is his or hers to control without interference."

The immediate problem with the illustration lies not in its substance; it is a perfectly legitimate question of love, but rather with the language and specifically the legalism of its statement and resolution. Doctrines of standing, universal rights, absolute autonomy are all mercantile juridical concepts, attributes of commodities rather than intimate aspects of relationship. The language doesn't work, it doesn't address the affective issue. Just to get a touch risky for a moment, if there is a question of standing then it is not a matter of stakeholding, but of standing or falling, erection or dilation in their erotic guises. Does love have standing? It is first of all a question of tumescence and detumescence. A matter of excitation, of eloquence and its poetic effects. What matters is the desire that flows through the relationship, the pleasure of being in the space in between, the prolonging of attraction, the force of desire, the physical conduction in being together. In amorous law, there are no absolute rights and there is certainly no individual autonomy that can wholly exclude a lover from speech or comment upon any aspect of intimacy or desire. Mood swings, the process of aging, physical changes, illnesses all impact relationships, and if they cannot be discussed, if "X has no claim to relief against Y," then in this already belligerently legalistic formulation, in this paradigm of "X against Y" the repression of the subject of physical pleasure or of the desires or pains that prompted the changes goes unanalyzed and untreated. The legal is agonistic, combative, military in its movement, whereas the laws of love have always tended wherever possible to suspend judgment in favor of an erotics of conversation. Law curses. Poetry gives standing.

It is the merit of the *Restatement of Love* that it offers a space, a humorous and marginal space, yet nonetheless a public location, a discursive forum within which to speak to questions of love, to the critical intimacies, the amorous and violent issues that bring us together and push us apart. That is a start. It raises the question. It opens a door. The space however, and the law of love that our *Restatement* reporters deem fit to govern it are both historically and theoretically a touch errant. They are predicated too closely upon positive law. They miss the emotional point, the *nomos* of eros, the justice of love. The laws of love demand another kind of space, a different law, an eloquence that fosters desire and furthers the possibility of recognizing the erotics of relationship in what is often simply and superficially viewed as a coldly competitive and callously indifferent public realm. So the next question is that of how to reconfigure and advance the gay science and its laws of love in contemporary terms, in a world of rapidly changing yet equally uncertain sex roles, gender preferences, sexual orientations, and subcultural styles of eros and blame.

Start with the question of standing. It is really a matter of jurisdiction. Not only does desire engender competence, standing within the space of love, but it also generates discourse. The *Restatement* illustration cited denies this. No standing. So no claim, and no need for response. Caesura. And if I cannot ask the question, then you cannot judge it. There is neither speech nor *nomos*. From our point of view that means that there is neither forum nor even language for discussing the amorously disputed issue. No safe space, no amorous venue or erotic erudition to call upon. No *nomos* or advice. To this we have to counterpose a law of love that was concerned precisely with constituting an intimate public sphere, historically a space of secret signs, hidden missives, women's courts with their jurisdiction over the nocturnal adventures of lovers.

It became the architectural space of the salon, the *ruelle*, the dressing room, the alcove. These all have their mark as spaces and conversations that are both intimate and public, secluded yet visible, to the side of the mercantile or administrative and yet subtly also within them, part of them, indeed key to their lines of power. I will say a bit more.

The libidinal economy refers to the drives, to Eros and Thanatos, desire and death. Obviously enough the laws of love privilege the erotic, they seek to foster pleasure and revive the movement of the free spirit. In doing so they are forced to address the drives, to look to the hidden triggers of volition, the motors of motive, the sources of what the subject desires and so likely does, directly or indirectly, within both intimate and public realms. That is the theory and in Freud's terms the libido is largely unconscious, invisible, only indirectly available to scrutiny. The laws of love make a similar point. The Court of the Countess of Champagne was quite explicit, Judgment 21, envoi, that where lovers come to the courts of love to air their disputes, they should come anonymously, their names should never be submitted to the judges, and the trial was to be conducted wholly "in camera" as we say, secretly, according to its own order and law. Later, the Statute of Love of 1400 stipulated that litigants be identified by colors and not names and later still, in the *Judgments of Love* reported by Martial d'Auvergne, we learn that the night watch of love, the nocturnal guards of the safe passage of lovers were called "Oubliers" or those who forget. All of which can provide an initial sense of the hidden and lateral quality of this intimate public sphere, this minor jurisdiction of love. It is depicted in terms of the avenue of the night, its trysts and encounters are covered and protected by twilight or darkness, it facilitates the expression of desire in the safety of the half seen.

Night and its nocturnal jurisdictions, its feminine laws, its amorous furies, can provide an initial sense of how the laws of love have been obscured, protected from the diurnal legalisms of the commercial realm, lost as esoteric knowledge or faith. The reference to night and forgetting, however, is also to be understood more theoretically. The *Treatise on Perfect Love* puts it well in answering the classical amorous question: "Why do the intensities and inquietudes of love strike more fiercely at night than during the day?" The answer is that the day distracts and projects desires into a mercantile world, into the domains of necessity and greed, and in doing so withholds attention from love. The *Treatise* actually puts it rather better than that: "day disperses the spirit in exterior realities ... whereas at night all avenues of errance and of wandering from desire disappear and the secret chamber of the heart can be opened to the consolations of love." Which means most immediately that night allows for passion, facilitates intensity, opens up a safe space for the pursuit of desire. Intensity, physical desire, lust, suggest both vulnerability and with it forgetting, a loss of the diurnal or commodified self.

Jean-Francois Lyotard, recanting author of the book *Libidinal Economy*, takes the point further and talks of *"a theatrics of masks without faces."* His theory is that of the libidinal band, a body generating intensities, a stretched out skin that spans from you to me: "these masks mask no lost origin, they become conductors of one another ... without a law of concatenation, and therefore according to anonymous singularities." Anonymity, forgetting, merging of intensities, "conducting bodies, pulsional connections ... libidinal fragments," all suggest a movement away from diurnal law, from rights and claims and "actions against," toward shared spaces, reach, touch, conduction at the level of drives, in the disorder of domains of desire kept for far too long from speech and its variable forms of social recognition.

While Lyotard focuses on drives, their effects and excitations, he also maps a libidinal economy that intertwines and pervades the social, the market, the political economy: "there is as much libidinal intensity in capitalist exchange as in the alleged symbolic exchange." The gay science and its laws of love understand that erotic investment in social goods, in property and power, as a partially concealed, not quite acknowledged, slightly dirty social form of sublimating desire. The stuff of advertising and of puritanical censure. To which the answer is that love should also be in love. Sex in sex. There is standing in desire. Or at least that is not a bad place to start and it requires a shift, a transition, a conceptual movement from the prosaic world of a secular law and its mercantile concerns to this variously marginal, minor, and partially hidden zone of amorous affairs and their *nomos*, meaning their erotic eloquence, their erudition and their justice.

Returning to our example of the *Restatement of Love* and the illustration to section 3.1. (2) (c), X is held to have no claim against Y. This treats X and Y as separate yet equivalent individuals and further addresses X's relationship to Y in terms of property in a claim. Most importantly, the focus on the individual of itself effectively refuses a forum, denies a language and resists furtherance or facilitation of the relationship. It is purportedly a *Restatement of Love* and yet it is here busy discounting love in favor of property, the autonomy of a claim right and here its denial. But the grievance is a common one. This is not a rare or unusual or unknown complaint. It is a familiar emotional inquietude, one frequently experienced by lovers. If the law of love has no role to play, nothing indeed to say to as obvious and everyday a rupture as complaints about the fluctuating weight of the beloved, then the laws of love are substantively pretty worthless. The law formulated by the *Restatement* here rejects the lovers and precludes them from any conversation or forum in which to work their differences through, in which to find or refind their erotic drive, their fantasies, their desires. So in this instance, as formulated by the Yale Law School doctoral student reporters, the law of love has little to offer. It is not of much use. And that of course is because the reporters have not done their research, haven't got beyond the joke, haven't found the *seria in nugia*, the truth that really makes the satire funny. There are very good reasons, strong, comprehensible, pragmatic and well functioning reasons to eroticize law. The lesson of the gay science, however, is also that in recognizing the role of desire in relation to law we have equally explicitly to acknowledge that this is not exactly the law we came with, not the formal system of rules with which we started. Forget. Go by night. Think law in a feminine key. A pleasing law, a law of pleasure. In short, think again.

A blush, a tremor, a tingle, a gaze, a sigh, a tear, a rush of blood. These intensities are the signs of transition from one law to the other. They mark an erotic investment, what Lyotard terms a physical conduction, a bodily presence and with it the emotional charge and indeed sensual disorder of immanent desire. Something is happening, a libidinal politics is opening up, a substrate of energy and drive is taking hold. These physical signs are also the marks of an amorous *nomos* for here the passions take hold, assert their jurisdiction, and with this transition also comes—if only we knew it—the *lex amatoria*, the law and justice of love. The erotic basis of action, the role of desire in doing, lust in speech, longing in performance pervades the social realm. According to the fondly remembered Madeleine de Scudéry, amorous relations are the most important thing in public life. They are life and death. Love is a grace and not a duty; it is a passion that is lifelong and unconstrained. It deserves a language, a law of its own. Take another example. The *Amorous Edict*, reported in 1669 by Jean Donneau de Visé, establishing a women's Court of Love in Paphos, Cyprus. The *Edict* charges the Court with debating and deciding differences between lovers. Specifically, the women judges, selected for their amorous and poetic skill, were to decide on all issues relating to "infidelity, negligence, coldness, mistrust, cruelty, jealousy, injustice, and indiscreet gossiping, contempt, scorn, false rumours, hurtful remarks, and secrets exposed, whether justified or not." That is a pretty fair range of application, a generous jurisdiction over the emotional intensities and dysfunctions that are forever appearing coyly or but dimly glimpsed in public life. Love or hate, consume or kill, is pretty much the bottom line, the coda of business, the manners of politics.

Return then to the lover who has gone to seed, grown melancholic, or put on weight. The *Restatment of Love* dismisses the complaint. It will not be heard. It lacks substance or ground. Which is odd, all things considered. And quite contrary to amorous law. Return to what Sir Henry Wotton, in his *Courtlie Controversie of Cupids Cautels*, calls "the discourses registered in the Library of eternall memory, to President, or rather perpetual Relicke, unto all future posterities." A very common law sentiment but unusual in being in praise of love and in pursuit of pleasure. Amorous precedents, cases of love, are seldom cited these days. Wotton was one of the last in England at least. Where he tells his stories and relays his amorous cautions by way of narratives of cases, we can return to the case law of love itself and ask how such an issue of love would be addressed.

Love is plural. Even Narcissus fell in love with an exterior image of himself. The more usual course of non-narcissistic love affairs is dyadic. I love to you, as Irigaray puts it, meaning that desire extends beyond the singular subject, it stretches into a space in between the lovers, it is its own domain, a third space, not mine, not yours but ours. It is therefore also a shared space, intimate and public, emotive and social. And capable of being addressed either ill or eloquently, justly or unjustly. That is the principle at least that underpins the laws of love whose purpose was classically and consistently to foster desire, to eroticize relationships, to remedy and augment the space of attraction, the channels and flows of amorous intentions in the public sphere. As Du Tronchet puts it in his discursive collection of *Love Letters*: "The law and majesty of love cannot be contradicted. You can see from that law just how heretical and stubborn it would be never to want to love and never to suffer someone to love you, and to refuse to be converted by services, gifts, prayers, pleas, admonitions, or by the impositions of the justice of love. I fear greatly that you will suffer worse punishment than Narcissus, that you will be lost amidst the multitude of graces that nature has given you, and that you will drown in your own beauty." The cases come down to much the same effect. Those who refuse to love are banished from the domain of love. Lovers must shun them, the amorous chefs of erotic concoctions must turn them away from their tables, couturiers refuse their orders, hairdressers ignore them and so on as occasion and epoch require.

The object of love's laws far exceeds the individuals who dispute or debate. The goal is that amorous desire, drive and pleasure gain acknowledgment and even recognition in the public sphere and as part of who we are and what we do in public life. Love has standing. This is because the lawyers of love well recognize that there is an intimacy to the political, there are emotions within the institutional, both drive and desire in business projects, in an advocate's practice, in a pedagogue's scholarly life. Amorous speech, the sign systems of the pursuit of pleasure should not be feared but rather attended to and given expression. The courts of love provide a forum for such expression, as well as elaborating the erudition of its eloquence and often also the answer to the questions that lovers bring. In the case in hand, that of the lover who puts on weight, the precedents are unanimous in recommending that a space be created within which the lovers can safely address the issues of attraction and physical appearance, disquiet and comfort, food and love. A circle needs to be formed.

The earliest case law from the Court of the Countess of Champagne is very clear that amorous commitment is a spiritual adventure first and a physical consummation second. That is the definition of mixed love (*amor mixtus*) and it gains confirmation in cases that variously espouse the cause of fidelity across time, space, and change of circumstances. Thus, as reported earlier, where a lover has traveled abroad and has not been in communication for a long period of time, the absence of the lover is not grounds for terminating the relationship. Similarly where a lover falls ill or is mutilated in war, is blinded as happened in one case, or loses an arm as occurred in another; the beloved cannot use this as grounds for terminating the relationship. The first principle in this situation is thus that the physical presence and indeed the appearance of the beloved is secondary to their virtues, their intellect, their spirit, conversation and correspondence. Indeed there are many cases from the later era of the *précieuses* in which it is the epistolary skill of the lover, her Latin, her philological acumen, her poetic ability that is the trigger of desire, the cause of the fall into love, long before the enamored actually meet. The underlying doctrinal reason for this is that the letters give access to the spirit; the correspondence is a better guide to the other than their face. The face, the body or image is itself just another letter, another sign of the spirit or intimation of the soul—the often repeated maxim being that the face is simply an index, a sign: *vultus est index animi*. So too the body is but a carapace, a skin, a signifier.

That the general amorous principle supports fidelity to a desire that passes through the body but is not confined to it, that it supports a radical attachment to images, does not resolve the feelings nor reduce the conflict that changes in weight can occasion. Age sediments. Love, according to the *Code of Love* and other sources, disrupts patterns of eating and sleeping. If someone in love finds it hard to eat, if they likewise don't sleep much, and if their waking time is full of palpitations and anxieties, then it is likely that they will lose weight. When the relationship stabilizes then it is almost predictable that some will gain weight. Those who are in love simply with the body of the other, with their external appearance, will find the change troubling and perhaps regard it as a breach of an implied promise—I will love you so long as your body pleases me. It may also be viewed as a change of personality. The lover is anxious, melancholic, self-obsessed or simply exuberantly oral but whichever it is, the disputed pattern occasions a disturbance in the flow of desire. The amorous doctors would have to decide on the causes of the weight gain and the Court must rely upon their expert opinion: *ut in arte peritis credendum est*, that in matters of art the expert is to be believed, as Symphorianus would say and indeed did.

The next point to raise is that the issue of weight gain does not require judgment. The relationship in the illustration is ongoing; the space between the lovers has not been severed. All that has happened is that one of them has expressed a doubt, which the other has had difficulty in hearing or addressing. This might end the relationship. It might preclude some other friend or colleague from appointing or promoting, preferring or publishing this somewhat more engorged subject. These things are happening all the time. We blow hot and cold and those winds of affect are rooted in our perceptions of who is desirable and who is not. They have many sources. This is incontestably one of them. The function of a court of love is to recognize this. Weight is given standing. The law of love treats every dimension of desire as important and its task here is to draw the disaffected couple as much as they can back into the erotic space that has grown cold between them.

It is not a matter for legislation, it is not a case that requires judicial determination, but rather it calls for a certain tenderness of attention, a willingness to listen and provide a space within which the full range and possibilities of mutual desire can be explored by the couple. With help they can figure it out. They can dance, hike, cook for each other, embellish their skins, tattoo or pierce, paint or write erotic verse, converse in Latin, or Russian, speak to the causes of their inquietude and mutually arouse their dormant amour. That said, the key point is that it is the space of conversation and correspondence that the laws of love have constantly and vigilantly to address and hold open. Can the lovers speak safely here? Can their speech be facilitated, their desire rekindled or inflamed?

The laws of love provide a language, rhetorical rules, principles of eloquence, a poetics of desire. Their justice resides in the length of their attention. They are amorously merciful which means they indulge love, they give love time, they provide a space and language within which to address what law cannot resolve but can help give time, space, and voice. There is a principled refusal to judge that is predicated upon facility, upon a radical patience in the face of the juridical rush to determination. That was the lesson of Christine de Pisan's *Book of Three Judgments* which in fact reported only debate and no determinations. Suspension of speed, amorous indulgence, was the principal meaning of a book of judgments that had no judgment, that waived rule, application and outcome. And the same is true of Poirier's Bailiff of Love who refuses many times to actually determine. Love is as lovers do in good faith. And again in the Court of Queen Fiammetta, reported by Boccaccio, each judgment is debated by its auditors and in an almost Homeric style it is changed where the reasons of those who doubt it are found to be persuasive. The amorous court, we jurists might say, can always be found *per incuriam*—which is to say that it omitted some relevant reason or ancient relic, a precedent or narrative that might have led to a better or more poetic justice, to a longer conversation, to an augmented desire.

Cupid is blind because Cupid and the forces of love that this figure represents are historically deemed to be divine and not human, spiritual and not temporal. Put it like this. Cupid is a God and we mortals cannot look directly upon God without bursting into flames. The blindfold on Cupid's eyes thus spares mortals from the death that would ensue from being looked at directly by one as powerful as the son of Venus, of the first law of love. The pseudonymous Philomusus, author of *The Academy of Complements* of 1638, a treatise on amorous rhetoric, makes a similar doctrinal point. Love is painted blind, because love cannot be dissembled. Love is as it is. Love spills as it flows. It is a drive, a pulse, an unconscious force, a cause of radical anxiety to judges, something professionally unknown to lawyers, the subject matter of the lost art of the laws of love.

Which takes me back to my starting point and the various expressions of anxiety, the fear of Canutism, and other symptoms that attached to judges forced to address whether homosexuals can be spouses for the purposes of a statutory provision. Anxiety is, of course, a symptom and here most probably a mark of blindness, an expression of not knowing, a manifestation of a peculiarly juridical unconscious. Blindness, however, is also a path to insight. The unconscious can be addressed, the figure or image that generates fear can be rendered visible, exposed to speech, invested with energy and rendered eloquent by poetics. By poet A. E. Housman's poetics in the earlier example, by the laws of love in my present and more general argument. No harm, at least, in trying. We can learn and learn again. If such knowledge of the laws of love leads to eloquence, anxiety turned into rhyme, then it also likely addresses the accidents of intimacy, amorous conflicts, public emotion much better, more justly, than does the law of commodities, the censorship of prosaic jurists or the idle and uninformed daydreams of lawyers as currently trained.

Turn then to the specific anxiety. Can same sex lovers be spouses? That was the question, and like most of the questions that turn on the roots and limits of marriage it causes a considerable degree of emotional disquiet in the presiding judges. What would the laws of love have to say? What would the gay scientists make of these rare expressions of prolonged inquietude? The judge who refused to suppress his dissent was quite direct. To include a homosexual couple within the scope of wife or husband would be "to read 'black' as 'white'" and could not be done. To do so would be "self-contradictory nonsense." That was the dissent. The majority opinion showed a touch more interpretative imagination and made an inspired stab at an appropriately literary source: "When Housman addressed the meeting of the Classical Association in Cambridge in 1921, he reminded them that the key to the sound emendation of a corrupt text does not lie in altering the text by changing one letter rather than half a dozen words. The key is that the emendation must start from careful consideration of the writer's thought." That is a pretty good start. It introduces literary history, both philology and poetics, into the interpretation of a legal text, and one as prosaic as the Rent Act at that. But the Rent Act doesn't have an author, there is no "writer's thought" to consider carefully or otherwise. And if there were we can be pretty certain that at the time that the statutory drafters were putting the Act together they were not thinking of gay couples as being included in the ambit of husband and wife. So something else has to be going on here.

What is going on is almost Joycean in its beauty. The Court is trying to say—prompted mind you by the European Convention—something that James Joyce put rather well: "a man or a woman, who cares?" It is not a question of what the writer thought. It is not a matter of emending a textual corruption. Not literally at least—erotic, exciting, and perverse though that textual exercise might well be. It is really and simply a question of an amorous principle and of issues long debated and addressed by the laws of love. To be a spouse, to be espoused simply means to embrace, to join in love. The first principle is obvious enough upon retrospection. What is at issue is affective alliance, commitment or espousal. When lovers come to court their amorous self-determination, the sanctity of the space in between the lovers is what the court will initially recognize. The space between, as the early courts were wont to phrase and frame it, is not an individual space but rather an extensive connection, a libidinal pulse, a site of symbolic trajectories, missives, of destinerrance and destination. It is a shared space and so neither male nor female. It is transgendered or, as the feminist author Irigaray puts it, this *entre nous* or between us is the exemplary site of difference, of the masculine and the feminine and of the third possibility of their diverse combinations.

The *trobairitz*, the women troubadours were not afraid to sing of their love of similars, of their Sapphic desires. The *précieuses* were equally unrestrained. Even more radical arguments have been made by more recent commentators who like to view all of the practices of the gay science as implicitly homosexual. Gay meant gay even back then. Take the example of the Lacanian medievalist Jean-Charles Huchet who has argued extensively that the laws of love were simply the means by which men communicated with men across the body and desires of women. He also wrote a paper that claimed convincingly enough that the women troubadours were simply anagrams of male names and part of an elaborate theater of male-to-male amorous communication. All of which makes our case rather stronger. The gender of lovers is an attribute of the theater of justice and love. It is a question of masks and according to an *Ordinance of Love* published in 1555 by Gilles d'Aurigny the mask is one of the first and most visible signs of entry into the domain of love. Here is how it goes: "Item. In that putting on a mask is the first and best means of exciting youth into the feats and adventures of love it is hereby ordered and expressly enjoined that anyone who wishes to aid, comfort, facilitate or promote love should open their doors and their hearts to masked lovers. No questions will be asked because the masked are amorously special, and must be treated with good grace and honour." Masked lovers were given the freedom of the amorous city, freedom of the night, and the liberty to remain anonymous and welcome in the carnivalesque atmosphere of amatory play.

Times have changed but the performance of gender identity and sexual orientation has if anything become even more complex than the theater of masks initially indicates. Serious sociologists, psychoanalysts, cultural theorists, lawyers even can accurately point to a trajectory in terms of gender difference and gender roles that has led back to a theater not dissimilar to the early modern dance of masks. The sexual revolution and feminism in particular changed the nature of the difference between the sexes. Gender roles became conflated, confused, redefined, and somewhat indeterminate. The sexes now share many of the public and institutional roles that were previously the domain of one or other. Men now work in the *gynaeceum*, as primary caretakers of children, women run corporations, gay men are governors, lesbians adopt children, the late Queen Mother's hip surgeon was a trans-sexual. Gender and sexual orientation decreasingly define life plan, social presence and public role. It is far from clear, as the admirably named Michel Tort propounds it in his excellent analysis of the *Fin du dogme paternel* (End of the Paternal Dogma), what the roles of the sexes are, what it means to be a man or a woman, or indeed, as Joyce would have it, why we should care. The mask is the thing. Go with the game, the dance, the play.

The case law supports a similar conclusion. The trials of love were tests of the spirit. The spirit of love existed between lovers, it was amorous intensity, shared extension, the "more than one/no more one" to which the late Jacques Derrida sometimes referred. Here we are in uncertain legal territory, we need a different *nomos*. That is what the laws of love variously provide. As for our latter day gay lovers and the dispositions of the Rent Act, consider this. First, the theater of justice and love was a play of masks. The performances of amorous identity were plural, often cross-dressing, and indeterminate of gender. Not so much a case of gender trouble as of trans-gendered play. A gay respite from otherwise very rigid sex roles, the gender norms of the Christian *longue durée*. Second, the principle governing the case law is one which gives expression to the desire between the lovers and not to any exterior claim or cause. Thus Poirier reports a curious case heard before the Bailiff of Love. The complainants were the parents, respectively, of a mute (*muel*) man and a mute woman. The mute children loved each other but did not wish to get married. The parents asked the Court to order them to marry.

The children responded by arguing that their hearts were as one, united in love, bound to each other, and that they neither wanted nor could ask for anything more. They wanted thus to live on as they were, as friends, as lovers bound by the ties of their own desire and joy. They were happy and felt that marriage, Christian ceremony and property law, would only sow discord and anxiety. They wished rather to live amorously as they were doing, in their own accord and by their own authority. For these reasons they urged the Court to allow them to remain lovers by their own lights. The Bailiff concurred, holding that where love is honest and joyful, it should act as its own measure and write its own laws. The couple were happy, in love, bound by their own mutual declarations, by their own alliance and the other and various symbols of love. It would be quite wrong for the Court to intervene, and it was equally inappropriate for the parents to endeavor to impose marriage upon them.

The decision espouses the cause and protects the space between the lovers. It is one of innumerable examples of the amatory courts treating love as its own law. More than that, the decision recognizes the facilitative role of the courts of love. What matters is the conduction of desire between the lovers. What governs is the paramount interest of the domain of love itself. A court that intervened, destabilized, undermined, or redefined the intimacy between the lovers would be acting outside of its competence and contrary to the erotic *nomos* that presides in all matters of desire. The law would be reverting to its secular type and stealing from the lovers rather than helping promote their intensity and cause. It would be yet another case of purloined love letters. Another example of a heavy footed legally authorized theft or interdiction of desire. And by these principles, just to state the obvious, the gay lovers should equally be able to choose and the courts should recognize the desirability of that choice. That is what it means to give love standing, and that is how to give space to a law of desire.

The example of mute lovers and then of gay lovers and marriage can allow for some suitably terminal observations. The case reported by Poirier involved mutes. Such a figure is highly suggestive. An interpretative cornucopia one might say. It signifies, by accident or coincidence, the very foundation of law in a silent desire. Law, the early and better-spoken jurists were wont to say, is a mute magistrate: *lex est mutus magistratus*. Muteness is here most obviously a latency, a potential or power. It is the auditory equivalent of a blank page, an empty tableau, the potency of silence, of an inanimate justice—for *lex est Iustitia inanimata* as well. Muteness here indicates source and scripture. It signifies the oracular originary site of legality. The law pre-exists speech. The divinity, the oracle, the absent source is recorded in the tablets, the scriptures, the texts of law. Writing comes before voice. A thoroughly grammatological point, I know, but nonetheless of amorous significance. Those who love books, texts, laws, love what is mute. And by the same token the mute *lex scripta*, the textual tradition, is both conceptually and historically prior to *ius non scriptum* or customary and unwritten law. As the language implies, Roman law comes to England. And muteness thus signals also a history, a precedent jurisdiction, another standing, and most importantly a plural and different genre of law. The mute is as the past to the present, infant to the adult, desire to judgment, the law of love to the love of law. The mute is more casuistically a sign of difference. A sign of the body, of presence, of sexual difference as well as of the call of the face without voice, the originary demand of justice that a space be created within which the face can be seen and the mute can be brought to communication. To attend to the mute is at least figuratively to recognize the plurality of the forms of justice, as well as the extravagance of any and all amorous demands.

A final digression. What is interesting about the contemporary debates, what motivates the Canutist desire to hold back the tide, what prompts the anxieties of lawyers as eminent even as members of the House of Lords, is the diversity or play of jurisdictions. Different genres of law get mixed. Difference appears in the secular legal realm of absolute analogy, of the law of the same. The mute erupts into the spoken. As to gays getting married, from troubadours to trans-sexuals, the anxieties that emerge are legally a product of the unsettling incursion of the spiritual into secular law. Salem is mixing with Bizance, as St. German was fond of saying. I don't want to get too technical. It doesn't matter so much in its detail, but here we are witness to a three way street. Secular law has to deal with religious (canon law) norms. The Church itself has to address the spiritual questions that inform all matters of love. Early on, 1277 in fact, the Church banned Capellanus and the *Treatise on Love*. The courts of love from then on belonged to a heretical tradition. The vast majority of heresies, from the Adamiani who went naked in public to the Venustiani who venerated the genitalia, involved significant elements of dispute over questions of love. It is hardly surprising that the diurnal passions and nocturnal emissions recommended by the laws of love gained theological disapproval. But it is a further and telling overlay to the resistance to the laws of love.

And last lines, volte face, something like this: If the distinctiveness of common law, of Anglican jurisprudence, was in significant measure a product of Henry VIII's desire to get rid of his wife, it makes sense that questions of marriage, and here gay marriage, have engendered a return to the gay science and to the laws of love. The spiritual questions of how and whom to love transpire to lie at the roots of our legal tradition, of our Anglican theology and our thoroughly mixed law. We have tended to forget that the poet preceded the jurist and that the laws of love came before the secular norm, conceptually, historically, and practically. Best then to remember as well another old legal maxim. Love first. Law second. Then both together, because love must have standing. Or, to borrow first and final words from the laws of Henry 1, in a slightly embellished translation, "amity governs agreement, and love conquers law."

Abbreviated Bibliographies: Legal and Literary

Sources and contexts of the *Lex Amatoria*

Agrippa, Heinrich Cornelius [1530] *Of the Vanity and Uncertainty of Arts and Sciences*. Northridge: California State University Press (1974).

Alighieri, Dante, *Il Convivio*. Ed. Simonelli, Bologna: Patron (1966).

Alighieri, Dante, & Forèse Donati, *La Tenson*. Ed. K. Mićević, Paris: Mićević (1999).

Anonyme d'Erfurt [c. 1290] *Tractatus de perfecto amore (Traité de l'amour parfait)*. Paris: Le Rocher (2000).

Anonymous, *Ami and Amile. A Medieval Tale of Friendship*. Trans. Samuel Rosenberg & Samuel Danon, Ann Arbor: Michigan University Press (1999).

L'Anthologie des jeux floraux. Ed. Joseph Rosès de Brousse, Paris (1924).

Arnaut Daniel, *The Poetry of Arnaut Daniel*. Ed. Wilhelm James J. New York: Garland (1978).

Arnaut Vidal de Castelnaudary [1318] *Le livre des aventures de monseigneur Guilhem de la Barra*. Paris: Champion (1977).

L'Art d'amours (The Art of Love). Trans. Lawrence Blonquist, New York: Garland (1987).

Aubignac, Abbé d', *Nouvelle histoire du temps ou la relation veritable du Royaume de la Coqueterie*. Paris: Charles Sercy (1654).

Avis au Public pour l'établissement de la Société précieuse. Ms5427 Bibliotèque de l'Arsenal. Reproduced in Ian Maclean (ed.), "Un document ambigu sur les origines de la préciosité," *Papers on French Seventeenth Century Literature* XVIII, 35 (1991) 463.

Benedictus Curtius Symphorianus [1551] *Commentariis ad utrusque juris rationem, forensiumque actionum usum quàm acutissimè accommodate*. Reprinted in Martial d'Auvergne, *Arresta amorum LII*, Amsterdam: Changuion (1731).

Bernart de Ventadorn, troubadour du XIIe siècle: Chansons d'amour. Ed. Moshe Lazar, Paris: Klincksieck (1966).

Blount, Thomas, *Fragmenta Antiquitatis*. London: Richard Atkins (1679).

Boccaccio, Giovanni [1566 ed.] *Thirteen Most Pleasant and Delectable Questions of Love*. New York: Clarkson (1974).

Breton, Nicholas, *A Poste with a Packet of Mad Letters*. London: John Marriot (1633).

Burton, Robert [1628 ed.] *The Anatomy of Melancholy*. New York: Tudor (1938).

Bussy-Rabutin, Roger de [1616–1693] *Le Pays du Tendre*. Paris: Editions de France (1928).

Callières, François, *Du Bel esprit où sont examinez les sentimens qu'on a d'ordinaire dans le monde*. Paris: Anison (1645).

———*La Logique des allans ou l'amour logicien*. Paris: Jolly (1668).

———*Nouvelles amoureuses et galantes*. Paris: Quinet (1679).

Capellanus, Andreas [1180] *Andreas Capellanus on Love*. Ed. and trans. P. G.Walsh, London: Duckworth (1982).

Carmina Burana. Ed. & trans. P. G. Walsh, Chapel Hill: University of North Carolina Press (1993).

Castiglione, Baldesar [1528] *The Book of the Courtier*. Trans. George Bull, London: Penguin Classics (1967).

Chants d'amour des femmes troubadour. Ed. Pierre Bec, Paris: Stock (1995).

Chartier, Alain [1617 ed.] *Les Oeuvres de Maistre Alain Chartier*. Paris: Pierre le Mur (reprinted 1975).

Choix des poésies originales des troubadours. Ed. M. Raynouard, Paris: Firmin Didot, (1816).

Christine de Pisan [c. 1400] *Le Livre de trois jugemens*, in *Oeuvres Poétiques de Christine de Pisan*. Ed. Maurice Roy, Paris: Firmin Didot (1891).

Le Coeur mangé. Récits érotiques et courtois XIIe et XIIIe siècles. Ed. and trans. Danielle Régnier-Bohler, Paris: Stock (1994).

Coke, Roger, *Justice Vindicated, from the False Fucus put upon it by Thomas White Gent, Mr Thomas Hobbes and Hugo Grotius*. London: Newcomb (1660).

The Comedy of Eros. Trans. Norman Shapiro, Chicago: University of Illinois University Press (2nd ed. 1997).

La Cort d'amor [c 1200] Ed. Matthew Bardell, Oxford: Legenda (2002).

[Cotin] *Oeuvres galantes de Mr Cotin*. Paris: Loyson (1665).

La Cour amoureuse dite de Charles VI. Ed. Carla Bozzolo & Hélène Loyau, Paris: Leopard d'or (1982).

The Court of Love: A Tale from Chaucer. Ed. Mainwaring, London: Jacob Tonson, (1709).

The Court of Love. In Walter Skeat ed., *The Complete Works of Geoffrey Chaucer*. Oxford: Oxford University Press (1897).

Crenne, Helisenne de, *Les Epistres familieres et invectives*. Ed. Jerry Nash, Paris: Champion (1996).

Deschamps, Eustache, *Art de dictier*. [1392] in *Oeuvres Complètes de Eustache Deschamps*. Ed. Gaston Raynaud, Paris: Frimin Didot (1841).

Drouart de la Vache, *Li Livres d'amour de Drouart de la Vache*. Ed. Robert Bossuat, Paris: Champion (1926).

Ecrivains anticonformiste du moyen âge occitan I–II. Ed. René Nelli, Paris: Phébus (1977).

Elyot, Sir Thomas [1531] *The Book Named the Governor*. London: Dutton (1962).

Emblemata amoris [1620] reprinted as *Théâtre d'amour*. Köln: Taschen (2005).

Erasmus, Desiderius, *The Adages of Erasmus*. Ed. William Barker, Toronto: University of Toronto Press (2001).

Ferrand, Jacques [1610] *A Treatise on Lovesickness*. Ed & trans. Donald Beecher & Massimo Ciavolella, Syracuse: Syracuse University Press (1990).

Ficin, Marsile, *Commentaires sur le Traité de l'amour ou le Festin de Plato (Commentarium in Convivium Platonis)*. Trad. anonyme de XVIIIe siècle, Paris: SEHA (2001).

Flamen, Albert [1653] *Devises et emblesmes d'amour moralisez*. Paris: Loysen (1652).

Folquet de Marselha, *Le Troubadour Folque de Marseille*. Ed. S. Stronski, Cracovie: Académie des Sciences (1910).

Forcadel, Etienne, *Cupido iurisperitus*. Lugduni: Ioan Tonaesium (1553).

Fortescue, John [1466] *De Natura legis naturae et de eius censura in successione regnorum suprema*. In *The Works of Sir John Fortescue, Knight*. London: Private Distribution (1869 ed.).

Godolphin, John, *Repertorium canonicum or, an abridgment of the Ecclesiastical Laws of this Realm consistent with the Temporal*. London: Atkins (1678).

Gower, John [1390] *Confessio amantis*. Ed. Russell Peck, Toronto: Toronto University Press (1980).
Guillaume de Lorris, & Jean de Meun, *The Romance of the Rose*. Ed. & trans. Frances Horgan, Oxford: Oxford University Press (1994).
Guillaume de Machaut [c. 1350] *Le Jugement du Roy de Behaigne and Remede de Fortune*. Ed. James Wimsatt and William Kibler, Athens, Ga.: Georgia University Press (1988).
Heywood, John [1534] *A Play of Love*. Oxford: Malone Society (1978).
Hoccleve, Thomas [1402] *The Letter of Cupid*. In Walter Skeat ed., *The Complete Works of Geoffrey Chaucer*. Oxford: Oxford University Press (1897).
Hotman, Antoine, *Traité de la loy Salique*. Paris: Mathieu Guilleme (1611).
Jaufré Rudel, *The Songs of Jaufré Rudel*. Ed. Rupert Pickens, Toronto: Pontfical Institute (1978).
Jonson, Ben, *The New Inn, or The Light Heart*. Ed. Michael Hattaway, Manchester: Manchester University Press (1984).
Las Flors del gay saber estier dichas las leys d'amors. 3 Vols. Ed. M. Gatien-Arnault, Toulouse: Privat (1841-43).
Las Joyas del gay saber. Ed. J-B. Noulet, Paris-Toulouse: Privat (1849).
Las Leys d'amors. Manuscrit de l'académie des jeux floraux. [c. 1341] Ed. Joseph Anglade. 4 Vols. Toulouse: Privat (1920).
Leges Henrici Primi. Ed. and trans, L. J. Downer, Oxford: Oxford University Press (1972).
Les Demandes d'amour. Ed. Margaret Felberg-Levitt, Québec: Inedita & Rara 10 (1995).
Les Droits des femmes et la loi salique. Ed. Sarah Hanley, Paris: Indigo & côté des femmes (1994).
Llull, Ramon, *The New Rhetoric* [1295] Ed. & trans. Mark Johnston, Berkeley: Hermagoras Press (1994).
[Lovedays] "A Middle English Poem on Lovedays." Ed. Thomas J. Heffenan, *Chaucer Review* 10 (1975/76) 172.
Lyrics of the Troubadours and Trouvéres. Trans. F. Goldin, New York: Anchor (1973).
Mahieu le Poirier, *Le Court d'amours et la suite de la Court d'amours*. Ed Terence Scully, Waterloo, Ontario: Wilfred Laurier University Press.
Marcabru, *Poésies complètes du troubadour Marcabu*. Ed. Dejeanne, J.-M.-L., Toulouse: Privat (1909).
Martial d'Auvergne [1460] *Les Arrêts d'amour avec l'amant rendu cordelier à l'observance d'amours*. Amsterdam: Changuion (1731).
Matfre Ermengaud, *Le Breviari d'amor*. Ed. Peter Ricketts, London: AIEO, Westfield College (1989).
Molière [1659] *Les Précieuses ridicules*. Paris: Larousse (1990).
Montpensier, Madame de [1652] *La Fronde. Le Combat du faubourg Saint Antoine*. Paris: Gautier (1896).
———*Divers Portraits*. Caen: n.p. (1659).
Munday, Anthony, *A Courtly Controversie, between Love and Learning*. London: Charlewood (1581).
Nostredame, Jehan de [1575] *Les Vies des plus célèbres et anciens des poètes provençaux*. Ed. Joseph Anglade, Genève: Slatkine (1970).
Ovid, *The Erotic Poems*. Ed. Peter Green, London: Penguin (1982).
Peirol. Troubadour of Auvergne. Ed. S. C. Aston, Cambridge: Cambridge University Press (1953).

[Philomusus] *The Academy of Complements wherein Ladyes, Gentlewomen, Schollers and strangers may accommodate their courtly practice with most curious Ceremonies Complementall, Amorous High Expressions and formes of speaking, or writing.* London: Mosley (1640).

Picus, Johan, Erle of Myrandula, *The Twelve Propertees or Condicyons of a Lover*. Ed. and trans. Sir Thomas More, Ditchling Common, Sussex: Saint Dominic's Press (1928).

Plutarch [1603 ed.] *Lives IV*. Ed. North, London: Nonesuch Press (1930).

Pure, Michel de, *La Prétieuse ou le mystère des ruelles*. Paris: Guillaume de Luyne (1656).

Puttonen, Vilho, *Etudes sur Martial d'Auvergne suivies du texte critique de quelques Arrêts d'amours*. Helsinki: Suo Malainen Tiedeakatemia (1945).

Recueil de farces Françaises inédites du Xve siècle. Ed. Gustave Cohen, Cambridge, MA: Mediaeval Soc. of America (1949).

Rotuli parliamentorum Anglie hactenus inediti. Ed. H. G. Richardson and George Sayles. CS 3rd series, 51 London, 1935.

Saint German, Christopher, *Salem and Bizance*. London: Bertheleti (1533).

Scudéry, Madeleine [1642] *Les femmes illustres*. Paris: Coté-femmes (1991).

———[1654] *Clélie, Histoire romaine*. Paris: Augustin Courbé (1660).

———[1656] *Artemene ou le Grand Cyrus*. 10 Vols. Genéve: Slatkine (1972).

Selden, John, *Jani Anglorum facies altera*. [1610] in Tracts. Ed. Redmond Westcot Gent., London: Thomas Bassett (1674).

Sommaize, Antoine Baudeau de, *Le Grand dictionnaire des prétieuses I–III*. Paris: Jean Ribov (1661).

Songs of a Friend. Love Lyrics of Medieval Portugual. Ed. & trans. Barabara Hughes Fowler, Chapel Hill: University of North Carolina Press (1996).

Sorel, Charles, *Nouveau recueil des pieces les plus agreables de ce temps. En suite des jeux de l'inconnù, & de la maison des jeux*. Paris: Nicolas de Sercy (1644).

———*Les loix de la galanterie*. Paris: Auguste Aubry (1644).

———*La description de l'isle de la portraiture et de la ville des portraits*. Paris: Sercy (1659).

Sowernam, Ester, *Ester Hath Hang'd Haman: Or An Answere to a Lewd Pamphlet*. London: N. Bourne (1617).

Tardif, Guillaume [1492] *Les Facecies de Poge*. Geneva: Droz (2003).

Tilney, Edmund [1573] *The Flower of Friendship*. Valerie Wayne, Ithaca: Cornell University Press (1992).

The Tretyse of Love [c. 1491] Ed. John Fisher, Oxford: Oxford University Press (1951).

Tronchet, Estienne du, *Lettres Amoureuses*. Lyon: Paul Frellon (1595).

Tullia d'Aragona, *Dialogue on the Infinity of Love*. Ed. & trans. Rinaldina Russell and Bruce Merry, Chicago: Chicago University Press (1997).

Urfé, Honoré de, *Les Epistres morales et amoureuses*. Paris: Gilles Robinet (1619).

———*Astrée*. Ed. Jean Lafond, Paris: Gallimard (1984).

Villedieu, Madame de (Marie-Catherine-Hortense Desjardins), *Annales galantes divisée en huit parties*. Paris: Claude Barbin (1677).

Visé, Jean Donneau de, *Nouvelles nouvelles divisées en trois parties*. Paris: Bienfaict (1663).

———*L'Amour Echapée ou diverses manières d'aymer*. 3 Vols. Paris: Thomas Jolly (1669).

———*Les Nouvelles galantes, comiques et tragiques*. Paris: Loyson (1680).

Webster, John, *The Devil's Law Case or When Women goe to Law, the Devil is full of Business*. Ed. John Russell Brown, Manchester: Manchester University Press (1996).

The Winchester Anthology: A Facsimile of British Library Additional Manuscript 60577. Intro. Edward Wilson. Cambridge: Brewer (1981).
Woman Defamed and Woman Defended. An Anthology of Medieval Texts. Ed. Alcuin Blamires, Oxford: Oxford University Press (1992).
Wotton, Henrie, *A Courtlie Controversie of Cupids Cautels, London*: Francis Caldock (1578).

Literary and critical sources

Akehurst, F. R. P. & Judith M. Davis (eds), *Handbook of the Troubadours.* Berkeley and Los Angeles: University of California Press (1995).
Assoun, Paul-Laurent, *Lc Couple Inconscient. Amour Freudien et passion postcourtoise.* Paris: Economica (1992).
Audiau, Jean, *Les troubadours et l'Angleterre.* Paris: Vrin (1927).
Barthes, Roland, *A Lover's Discourse. Fragments.* London: Faber (1979).
Becker, Karin, "La mentalité juridique dans la literature française (XIIIe-Xve siècles)" 103 *Revue d'histoire et de philologie* 309 (1997).
Bennett, Josephine Waters, "The Medieval Loveday" 33 *Speculum* 351 (1958).
Benson, Pamela J. (ed.), *The Invention of Renaissance Women.* University Park: Pennsylvania State University Press (1992).
Benveniste, Emile, *Le Vocabulaire des institutions indo-européenes 1 and 2.* Paris: Editions de Minuit (1969).
Berlant, Lauren, *The Queen of America Goes to Washington City.* Durham, NC: Duke University Press (1997).
Berlant, Lauren & Warner, Michael (eds.), *Intimacy.* 24: 2 *Critical Inquiry* (Special Issue, 1998).
Bettini, Maurizio, *The Portrait of the Lover.* Trans. Laura Gibbs, Berkeley & L. A.: University of California Press (1999).
Blamires, Alcuin, *The Case for Women in Medieval Culture.* Oxford: Oxford University Press (1997).
Bloch, Howard R., *Medieval French Literature and Law.* Berkeley and Los Angeles: University of California Press (1977).
———*Medieval Misogyny and the Invention of Western Romantic Love.* Chicago: University of Chicago Press (1991).
Bray, Bernard, *L'Art de la lettre amoureuse. Des Manuels aux romans.* Paris: Mouton (1967).
Bray, René, *La Préciosité et les Précieux de Thibaut de Champagne à Jean Giraudoux.* Paris: Albin Michel (1948).
Brook, Christopher, *The Medieval Idea of Marriage.* Oxford: Oxford University Press (1991).
Bumke, Joachim, *Courty Culture.* New York: Overlook (2000).
Burns, Jane, *Courtly Love Undressed: Reading Through Clothes in Medieval French Culture.* Philadelphia: University Pennsylvania Press (2002).
Butler, Judith, *Gender Trouble: Feminism and the Subversion of Identity.* New York: Routledge (1990).
———*The Psychic Life of Power: Theories in Subjection.* Palo Alto: Stanford University Press (1997).
Calle, Sophie, *Suite vénetienne.* Seattle: Bay Press (1988).
Casanova, Giacomo [c. 1796] *Mémoires: Histoire de ma vie.* Paris: Arléa (1993).

Chechi, Paolo, *Andreas and the Ambiguity of Courtly Love*. Toronto: University of Toronto Press (1994).
Chevalier-Wilson, Kathleen, & Elian Viennot (eds.), *Royaume de fémynie. Pouvoirs, Constraintes, espaces de liberté des femmes dela Renaissance à la Fronde*. Paris: Champion (1999).
Cheyette, Frederic, *'Suum Cuique Tribuere'* 6 *French Historical Studies* 287 (1970).
Clanchy, Michael, "Law and Love in the Middle Ages." In John Bossy (ed.), *Disputes and Settlements in the Middle Ages* (1983).
Darrigrand, Jean-Pierre, *Flamenca: L'amour courtois des troubadours à Fébus*. Orthez: Per Noste.
Dejean, Joan, *Tender Geographies. Women and the Origins of the Novel in France*. New York: Columbia University Press (1991).
———*The Invention of Style*. New York: Free Press (2004).
Denomy, A. J., *The Heresy of Courtly Love*. New York: McMullen (1947).
Dinshaw, Carolyn, *Getting Medieval*. Durham, N.C.: Duke University Press (1999).
Doniger, Wendy, *The Bedtrick. Tales of Sex and Masquerade*. Chicago: Chicago University Press (2000).
Douzinas, Costas, & Gearey, Adam, *Critical Jurisprudence: The Political Philosophy of Justice*. London: Hart Publishing (2005).
Dragonetti, Roger, *Le Gai savoir dans la rhétorique courtoise*. Paris: Seuil (1982).
———*Le Mirage des sources. L'Art du faux dans le roman medieval*. Paris: Seuil (1987).
Dronke, Peter, *Medieval Latin and the Rise of European Love-Lyric*. 2 Vols. Oxford: Oxford University Press (1966).
———*Women Writers of the Middle Ages*. Cambridge: Cambridge University Press (1994).
Duchêne, Roger, *Les Précieuses ou comment l'esprit vint aux femmes*. Paris: Fayard (2001).
Eden, Kathy, *Friends Hold All Things in Common*. New Haven: Yale University Press (2001).
Enders, Jody, *Rhetoric and the Origins of Medieval Drama*. Ithaca: Cornell University Press (1992).
Farmer, John, *Vocabula amatoria*. New York: University Books (1896).
Fish, Stanley, *Professional Correctness*. Cambridge, MA: Harvard University Press (1995).
Freud, Sigmund, "Contribution to the Psychology of Love: A Special Type of Choice of Object Made by Men," in 4 *Collected Papers*. Joan Riviere trans., London: Hogarth Press.
Gallop, Jane, *Feminist Accused of Sexual Harassment*. Durham, NC: Duke University Press (1997).
Gearey, Adam, *Law and Aesthetics*. London: Hart Publishing (2001).
Godefroy, Frédéric, *Lexique de l'ancien Français*. Paris: Champion (2000).
Goldsmith, Elizabeth & Goodman, Dena (eds.), *Going Public: Women and Publishing in Early Modern France*. Ithaca, N.Y.: Cornell University Press (1995).
Goodman, Dena, *The Republic of Letters*. Ithaca: Cornell University Press (1994).
Goodrich, Peter, *Oedipus Lex. Psychoanalysis, History, Law*. Berkeley: University of California Press (1995).
———*Law in the Courts of Love: Literature and Other Minor Jurisprudences*. London: Routledge (1996).

———"Epistolary Justice: The Love Letter as Law," 9 *Yale Journal of Law and Humanities* 245 (1997).
———"Amatory Jurisprudence and the *Querelle des Lois*," 76 *Chicago-Kent Law Review* 751 (2000).
———"Gay Science and Law," in Victoria Kahn and Lorna Hutson (eds.), *Rhetoric and Law in Early Modern Europe*. Yale: Yale University Press (2001).
Green, Richard Firth, *A Crisis of Truth: Literature and Law in Ricardian England*. Philadelphia: University of Pennsylvania Press (1999).
Groebner, Valentin, *Defaced. The Visual Culture of Violence in the Late Middle Ages*. New York: Zone Books (2004).
Harth, Erica, *Cartesian Women: Versions and Subversions of Rational Discourse in the Old Regime*. Ithaca: Cornell University Press (1992).
Harvey, Howard, *The Theatre of the Basoche. The Contribution of the Law Societies to French Medieval Comedy*. Cambridge, MA: Harvard University Press (1941).
Heinrichs, Katherine, *The Myths of Love: Classical Lovers in Medieval Literature*. State College: Pennsylvania State University Press (1990).
Huchet, Jean Charles, *L'Amour discourtois*. Toulouse: Privat (1987).
———"Les Femmes troubadours ou la voix critique," 51 *Littérature* 59 (1990).
———*Littérature médiévale et psychanalyse. Pour une clinique littéraire*. Paris: PUF (1990).
Irigaray, Luce, *I Love to you: Sketch of a Possible Felicity in History*. Trans. Alison Martin, New York: Routledge (1996).
———*The Way of Love*. Trans. Heidi Bostic & Stephen Pluhác, London: Continuum (2002).
Jaeger, Stephen, *The Origins of Courtliness. Civilizing Trends and the Formation of the Courtly Lyric 939–1210*. Philadelphia: University of Pennsylvania Press.
———*Ennobling Love. In Search of a Lost Sensibility*. Philadelphia: University of Pennsylvania Press (1999).
Jardine, Alice, *Gynesis: Configurations of Woman and Modernity*. Ithaca: Cornell University Press (1985).
Jiménez, D. & Abramovici, J.-C., *Eros volubile. Les Métamorphoses de l'amour du Moyen Age aux Lumières*. Paris: Desjonquères (2000).
Jones, Rosalind, *The Currency of Eros. Women's Love Lyric in Europe, 1540–1620*. Bloomington: Indiana University Press (1990).
Kipnis, Laura, *Against Love. A Polemic*. New York: Pantheon (2003).
Kristeva, Julia, *Tales of Love*. New York: Columbia University Press (1987).
Lacan, Jacques, *The Ethics of Psychoanalysis*. Ed. Jacques-Alain Miller, New York: Norton (1992).
Lafitte Houssat, Jacques, *Troubadours et cours d'amours*. Paris: PUF (1966).
Lathuillière, Roger, *La Préciosité. Etude historique et linguistique* I. Genève: Droz (1969).
Lazar, Moshé, *Amour courtoise et fin amors dans la littérature du XIIe siècle*. Paris: Klinckseick (1964).
Leader, Darian, *Why do Women Write More Letters than they Post?* London: Faber (1996).
———*Promises Lovers Make when it gets Late*. London: Faber (1997).
Le Doeuff, Michèle, *Le Sexe du savoir*. Paris: Aubier (1998).
Legendre, Pierre, *L'Amour du censeur*. Paris: Seuil (1976).
———*Paroles poétiques échappées du texte*. Paris: Seuil (1982).

———*Law and the Unconscious. A Legendre Reader.* Ed. Peter Goodrich, Basingstoke: Macmillan (1997).
———*Sur la question dogmatique en Occident.* Paris: Fayard (1999).
Loizidou, Elena, "Sex @ the End of the Twentieth Century: Some Re-Marks on a Minor Jurisprudence," 10 *Law and Critique* 71 (1999).
Loyson, Kathleen, *Conversation and Storytelling in Fifteenth- and Sixteenth-Century French* Nouvelles. New York: Peter Lang (2004).
Luhman, Niklas, *Love as Passion.* Cambridge: Polity Press (1986).
Lyotard, Jean-François, *Libidinal Economy.* London: Athlone (1993).
Lysyk, Stephanie, *Making a Farce out of Justice.* Stanford University PhD (1990).
———"Love of the Censor: Legendre, Censorship and the Basoche." In Peter Goodrich, Lior Barshack & Anton Schütz (eds.), *Law, Text, Terror: Essays for Pierre Legendre,* London: Glasshouse Press (2006).
Maclean, Ian, *Woman Triumphant. Feminism in French Literature 1610–1652.* Oxford: Clarendon Press (1977).
———*The Renaissance Notion of Women.* Cambridge: Cambridge University Press (1980).
———"La voix des précieuses et les detours de l'expression," in Ian Richmond & Constant Venegoen (eds.), *Présences féminines. Litérature et Societé.* Paris: Biblio (1987).
———*Interpretation and Meaning in the Renaissance. The Case of Law.* Cambridge: Cambridge University Press (1992).
Maître, Myriam, *Les Précieuses.* Paris: Champion (1999).
Markale, Jean, *L'Amour courtois ou le couple infernal.* Paris: Imago (1987).
Marol, Jean-Claude, *L'Amour libérée ou l'érotique initiale des troubadours.* Paris: Dervy (1998).
Masten, Jeffrey, *Textual Intercourse.* Cambridge: Cambridge University Press (1997).
Mills, Linda, "Killing Her Softly: Intimate Abuse and the Violence of State Interventions," 113 *Harvard Law Review* 550 (1999).
———*Insult to Injury: Rethinking our responses to intimate abuse.* Princeton: Princeton University Press (2004).
———"Intimacy and Terror," 11 *Violence Against Women* 1536 (2005).
Mukherji, Subha, *Law and Representation in Early Modern Drama.* Cambridge: Cambridge University Press (2007).
Neilson, Allan, 'The Origins and Sources of the Court of Love', VI *Studies and Notes in Philology and Literature* 1–269 (1899).
Nelli, René, *L'Erotique des troubadours.* Toulouse: Privat (1963).
Newman, F. X. (ed), *The Meaning of Courtly Love.* Albany: SUNY (1968).
Pelous, Jean-Michel, *Amour précieux amour gallant. Essai sur la representation de l'amour dans la literature et la société mondaines.* 1654–75. Paris: Klinckseick (1980).
Perella, Nicolas, *The Kiss Sacred and Profane: An Interpretative History of Kiss Symbolism and Related Religio-Erotic Themes.* Berkeley: University of California Press (1969).
Perrot, Michelle, *Les femmes ou les silences de l'histoire.* Paris: Flammarion (1998).
Pettersen, Hanne (ed.), *Love and Law in Europe.* Aldershot: Ashgate Publishing (1998).
Phillips, Adam, *On Flirtation.* London: Faber (1994).
Quilligan, Maureen, *The Allegory of Female Authority: Christine de Pizan's Cité des dames.* Ithaca: Cornell University Press (1991).

Remy, Paul, "Les 'cours d'amour': légende et réalité" 7 *Revue de l'Université de Bruxelles* 179 (1955).

Rey-Flaud, Henri, *La Névrose courtoise*. Paris: Navarin (1979).

Robertson, D. W., "The Subject of the *De Amore* of Andreas Capellanus," 50 *Mod. Philology* 145 (1953).

———*A Preface to Chaucer. Studies in Medieval Perspectives*. Princeton: Princeton University Press (1962).

Rosenthal, Margaret, *The Honest Courtesan. Veronica Franco, Citizen and Writer in Sixteenth-Century Venice*. Chicago: Chicago University Press (1993).

De Rougemont, Denis, *Love in the Western World*. Princeton: Princeton University Press (1983).

Rubin, Gretchen Craft, & Heller, Jamie G., "Restatement of Love," 104 *Yale Law Journal* 707 (1994).

Sainte-Palaie, *Histoire literéraire des troubadours*. 2 Vols. Paris: Durand (1774).

Schütz, Anton, "Legal Critique: Elements for a Genealogy," 16 *Law and Critique* 71 (2005).

———"Letter to Derrida/America," 27 *Cardozo Law Review* 301 (2005).

Stanton, Domna, "The Fiction of Préciosité and the fear of Women," 62 *Yale French Studies* 107 (1981).

Staten, Henry, *Eros in Mourning: Homer to Lacan*. Baltimore: Johns Hopkins University Press.

Stendhal, Frédéric, [1826] *De l'amour*. Leipzig: Insel-Verlag (1920).

Theweleit, Klaus, *Object-Choice (All you need is love ...). On Mating Strategies and a Fragment of a Freud Biography*, Trans. Malcolm Green, London: Verso (1994).

Thornton, Margaret, *Dissonance and Distrust. Women in the Legal Profession*. Melbourne: Oxford University Press (1996).

Tort, Michel, *Fin du dogme paternel*. Paris: Albin (2005).

Tushnet, Rebecca, "Rules of Engagement," 107 *Yale Law Journal* 2583 (1998).

Vaneigem, Raoul, *The Movement of the Free Spirit*. New York: Zone Books (1998).

White, Stephen, "'*Pactum ... Legem Vincit et Amor Iudicum*' the Settlement of Disputes by Compromise in Eleventh-Century Western France," 22 *American Journal of Legal History* 281 (1978).

Žižek, Slavoj, *The Metastases of Enjoyment: Six Essays on Women and Causality*. London: Verso (1994).

Index Amorum

Printed in the United States
79118LV00003B/15

9 780230 007185